EurographicSeminars

Tutorials and Perspectives in Computer Graphics

Edited by W.T. Hewitt, R. Gnatz, and D.A. Duce

EurographicSeminars

Tutorials and Perspectives in Computer Graphics

Eurographics Tutorials '83. Edited by P. J. W. ten Hagen.
XI, 425 pages, 164 figs., 1984

User Interface Management Systems. Edited by G. E. Pfaff.
XII, 224 pages, 65 figs., 1985

Methodology of Window Management. Edited by F. R. A. Hopgood, D. A. Duce, E. V. C. Fielding, K. Robinson, A. S. Williams.
XV, 250 pages, 41 figs., 1985

Data Structures for Raster Graphics. Edited by L. R. A. Kessener, F. J. Peters, M. L. P. van Lierop. VII, 201 pages, 80 figs., 1986

Advances in Computer Graphics I. Edited by G. Enderle, M. Grave, F. Lillehagen. XII, 512 pages, 168 figs., 1986

Advances in Computer Graphics II. Edited by F. R. A. Hopgood, R. J. Hubbold, D. A. Duce. X, 186 pages, 96 figs., 1986

Advances in Computer Graphics Hardware I. Edited by W. Straßer.
X, 147 pages, 76 figs., 1987

GKS Theory and Practice. Edited by P. R. Bono, I. Herman.
X, 316 pages, 92 figs., 1987

Intelligent CAD Systems I. Edited by P. J. W. ten Hagen, T. Tomiyama. XIV, 360 pages, 119 figs., 1987

Advances in Computer Graphics III. Edited by M. M. de Ruiter.
IX, 323 pages, 247 figs., 1988

Advances in Computer Graphics Hardware II. Edited by A. A. M. Kuijk, W. Straßer. VIII, 258 pages, 99 figs., 1988

CGM in the Real World. Edited by A. M. Mumford, M. W. Skall.
VIII, 288 pages, 23 figs., 1988

A. M. Mumford M. W. Skall (Eds.)

CGM in the Real World

With 23 Figures

Springer-Verlag
Berlin Heidelberg New York
London Paris Tokyo

EurographicSeminars

Edited by W. T. Hewitt, R. Gnatz, and D. A. Duce
for EUROGRAPHICS –
The European Association for Computer Graphics
P.O. Box 16, CH-1288 Aire-la-Ville, Switzerland

Volume Editors

Anne Mumford
University of Technology, Loughborough, GB-Leicestershire, LE11 3TU

Mark Skall
National Bureau of Standards, Institute for Computer Science and Technology,
Gaithersburg, MD 20899, USA

UNITED STATES DEPARTMENT OF COMMERCE
National Bureau of Standards
Gaithersburg, Maryland 20899

This book is a record of a Workshop which was held on September 15–17, 1987, at the National Bureau of Standards (NBS) in Gaithersburg, Maryland, USA, sponsored by Eurographics, Eurographics (UK) and NBS.

ISBN-13:978-3-642-73631-5 e-ISBN-13:978-3-642-73629-2
DOI: 10.1007/978-3-642-73629-2

2145/3140-543210 – Printed on acid-free paper

Preface

About two years ago, while attending yet another international standards meeting, a few of the meeting participants were discussing the utility and applicability of the standards we were designing. After all, if standards are not used, and used effectively, why are we spending all this time and money designing them? The ultimate test of the utility of computer standards is the number of implementations that are developed and the number of end-users that successfully use these within their own application. The number of implementations is related to the quality of a standard because vendors cannot produce correct implementations without clear, precise and unambiguous semantics within the standard. The number of users of implementations of the standards is an even greater measure of success of the standard because users will only purchase these implementations if they are useful for their applications.

"How could we determine whether or not graphics standards are useful?" we asked ourselves. " Let's ask both implementors and users about the experiences they've had with our standards. Let them tell us about the successes and the problems as well." Thus, an idea was born - the idea of a series of workshops, each one devoted to the usability of a different computer graphics standard. The only thing left to do in planning this workshop was to choose the appropriate standard to serve as the focus of the first workshop.

There were only a few viable candidates. GKS had been a standard for a while and many GKS implementations were already available in the marketplace. Users and implementors alike were discussing the pros and cons of GKS implementations. SIGGRAPH and NCGA were already providing forums for people to debate the usability of GKS as a standard. PHIGS and CGI, on the other extreme, were still being designed. Thus, implementations of these standards were at least a year or so away, making discussions of their utility premature.

The Computer Graphics Metafile (CGM), on the other hand, fit right in the middle of the two extremes. CGM had just become an international standard, but CGM implementations had not yet reached the marketplace in any great magnitude. Thus, opinions about the viability of CGM as a standard had not yet been formed. Since the workshop was being planned to take place one year later it was reasonable to assume that in this one year timeframe many implementations would reach the marketplace and would be in general use. A CGM workshop would give implementors and users a chance to assess its usability and the ways CGM could be improved in future revisions to make it more viable. All we needed now were sponsors. Eurographics, Eurographics (UK) and the National Bureau of Standards (NBS) volunteered to co-sponsor the event with NBS acting as hosts. Thus, "CGM in the Real World" was born.

Anyone who has ever planned a conference, from a small informal workshop at their place of business, to a large formal conference with refereed papers knows the time and effort that is needed to make it successful. Many people contributed to the success of this workshop.

First, we would like to thank the National Bureau of Standards (NBS) for hosting the workshop and Eurographics, Eurographics UK and NBS for co-sponsoring the workshop and providing support for some of the attendees.

Next, our thanks go to the Panel Chairmen and Discussion Chairmen who were gracious enough to volunteer their time with very short notice. They were Sharon Kemmerer, Peter Bono, Steve Carson and Lofton Henderson.

Our thanks and appreciation also to the participants who attended and who all contributed by presenting their papers and by participating in the spirited discussion.

We would like to thank Sue Quinn for taking minutes at the workshop and, especially, Dan Benigni whose help in planning, organizing and running the workshop was invaluable. Without Dan's help we could not have attained the level of success we did.

Finally, we would like to recognise the assistance given by NBS and the Computer Centre at Loughborough University, UK, in producing the final output of the workshop. Dan Benigni and Alasdair Liddell of Loughborough University helped to ensure that these papers and discussions can be shared with users and implementors of this important standard.

Anne Mumford
Mark Skall

Table of Contents

Part I: Introduction 1

Setting the Scene 3
A.M. Mumford

Integrate '88 - A Personal View 11
A.M. Mumford

Part II: Using the CGM in a Computing Service 13

After 10 Years of Metafiles Where Does the CGM Fit?................................. 15
T.N. Reed

The Use of the CGM in the U.K. University Community..............................23
A.M. Mumford

The CGM Implementation at McDonnell Douglas....................................... 29
J. Stoll

Part III: Making the CGM Pay: Commercial Needs..........................35

The Ramifications of Adopting the CGM as the Image Transfer Mechanism.........37
B. Rossin

The Implementation of the CGM as a GKS Metafile.................................... 47
C. Tucker and G. Heather

Technical and Office Protocols (TOP) CGM Application Profile.......................75
K. Hardman

The CGM Application Profile for CALS: Current Specification and Major Issues...95
L.R. Henderson

Part IV: Extending the CGM to Meet Further User Requirements ...111

Uses for CGM in Raster-to-Vector Conversion....................................... 113
P.R. Bono

Extending CGM for Publishing and Technical Drawing Exchange....................145
G.S. Carson

The CGM in the Presentation Graphics World 171
G. Silverman

Part V: Encoding Issues 175

Protocol Comparisons: CGM and Others..177
G. Davison

A Need for Character...183
S. Jepsen

Bridge that GAP (CGM at the Real Applications Interface).......................... 189
C.D. Osland

Part VI: Testing Considerations...201

Testing of the Computer Graphics Metafile.. 203
A.E.J. Pink

An Overview of ODA and ODA Conformance Testing............................... 217
R. Carr

An NBS Conformance Testing Program: Ideas and Procedures for Graphics Testing...231
S.J. Kemmerer

Part VII: Further Considerations on Using the CGM 261

Technical Barriers to Interchange Using the CGM 263

Using the CGM Within Application Profiles 267

User Requirements...271

Testing..279

Errors in the CGM Standard...283

Contact Addresses...287

Part I

Introduction

This book is concerned with the use of the Computer Graphics Metafile standard. The papers bring together contributions from experts in the field who are leading the way with CGM implementations.

This part of the book sets the scene for the papers and discussions which form the major part of this volume.

The first paper explains the nature of the CGM standard and discusses many of the concepts which are referred to in this book.

The second paper in this section describes a demonstration of the use of the CGM which happened after the workshop took place. This was the NCGA Integrate '88 event. This was an important landmark in the use of CGM in the real world. Many of the people who have papers in this volume were involved in some way in the demonstration.

Setting the Scene

A.M. Mumford

Abstract

This paper aims to introduce the reader to the Computer Graphics Metafile (CGM [1]) standard and to put it in the context of the development of standards for computer graphics. The papers presented at the workshop which are included in this volume are concerned with the use of the standard and address different aspects of the CGM as their starting point.

1 Introduction

1.1 The Need for Graphical Data Storage

Most users of graphics applications packages will be concerned with viewing their output on a graphics screen. Often, once they are satisfied with the output, some form of hard copy is required, on a plotter for example. These applications may be built on top of the functional graphics standards (GKS [2], GKS-3D [3], PHIGS [4]).

There are, however, many occasions when the output on to physical devices is not appropriate and some form of graphical storage of the picture is required. It may be necessary to:

- store a partly developed picture for later modification;
- store a picture for later viewing;
- queue the graphical image for spooled plotting;
- transfer the graphical data to another machine for display;
- include the graphical data in a document containing text and graphics.

In all these cases the picture will have to be stored in some way. The method chosen for storage must allow easy interpretation of the data so that the picture can be correctly displayed at a time in the future and/or on a different machine. The method of storage could be in the form of device dependent information which has been designed for a particular output device. This is a fairly common way of storing graphical data at individual sites but is of little value when the end device is something other than that to which the code pertains or is unknown at the time the graphical data is stored.

The file in which graphical data is saved has become known as a metafile. The term does not imply any particular structure to the storage or any method of storage. It has simply become a term in common usage in computer graphics.

1.2 The development of a standard for a computer graphics metafile

The need for a metafile has been appreciated throughout the development of standards for computer graphics. GKS recognises the need for the storage of the graphical data created in a GKS application. This is realised through the the storage of data in the GKS Metafile (GKSM). GKS has the concepts of workstations for metafile input (MI) and metafile output (MO) and supplies the functions providing access to, and interpretation of, metafiles. The GKS standard does not, however, define a metafile as part of the standard. Annex E of the standard suggests a format suitable for the storage of metafiles from the GKS environment but is not a part of the standard.

Rather than develop the proposal of the Annex to the GKS standard separate work was initiated in the area of a metafile for computer graphics. At the time this work was initiated in the standards arena it was considered that there were requirements for a standard metafile which could not be met by the proposed metafile for GKS which is now found in Annex E to GKS. It was felt that a metafile had applications outside the GKS environment and that this constituency needed to be satisfied by the production of a standard in this area. This has resulted in the ISO standard for the CGM which was published in August 1987.

The GKS concept is of an audit trail metafile where the entire process of generating a picture is stored for future replay. While a picture is being interpreted GKS anticipates that the application may or may not choose to interrupt the replay with some further graphical output or input. In contrast, a metafile to the CGM standard captures a snapshot of the graphical image. Any elements which imply dynamic change to the image are not incorporated into the CGM standard. This was an intentional philosophical decision but can cause problems for GKS applications wishing to write metafiles to the CGM standard. The relationship between the CGM and GKS is considered further by Brodlie, Henderson and Mumford [5].

It should be remembered that the CGM is only concerned with the storage of graphical data. It does not store information about the structure of the picture which it comprises. There are no possibilities in the standard for reconstructing the way that the picture was built up. The CGM does not store any other information concerning the picture such as product data. This may be stored as APPLICATION DATA but this has to be done in a non-standard way.

2 The CGM Standard

2.1 Roles of the CGM Standard

The CGM standard has two distinct roles. The first one is to define the functions which need to appear in the metafile and to lay down rules as to the structure of the metafile and the order and position of the various elements. This part of the metafile standard is defined in Part 1 of ISO 8632. The second role is to define the way that these functions are recorded in the metafile. This is known as the encoding of the elements defined in the functional part. Parts 2, 3 and 4 of the CGM standard are concerned with the encoding of the elements whose abstract functionality is described in Part 1. The CGM also contains a formal grammar in an Annex to Part 1 which describes in detail the behaviour of the elements.

2.2 The structure of a Computer Graphics Metafile

A metafile is a collection of elements. These elements may be the graphical primitives such as polyline, polygon, or attributes, such as line colour, which describe the graphical image, or may be information to the interpreter about how to interpret a particular metafile or a particular picture. The CGM standard specifies which elements are allowed to occur in which positions in a metafile. The structure of a metafile is summarised in Fig. 1 which considers the metafile as a series of levels. These levels are described below.

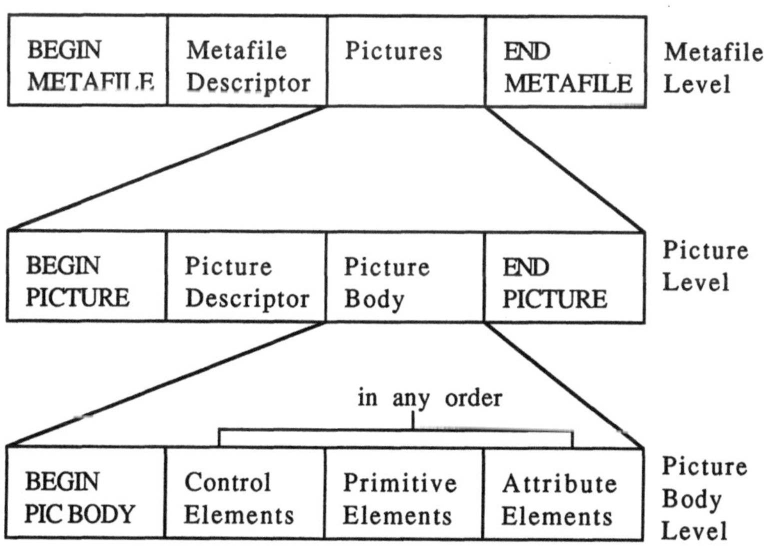

Figure 1 : The Structure of a CGM

Metafile Level: The metafile is delimited by the BEGIN METAFILE and END METAFILE elements. Within a metafile there are instructions to the interpreter contained in the metafile descriptor and these are valid for the whole metafile. The main body of the metafile contains a number of independent pictures which can be accessed individually. The content of one picture in a metafile is not dependent on the information stored in another picture.

Picture Level: A picture is bounded by the delimiters BEGIN PICTURE and END PICTURE. Within the picture there is a Picture Descriptor giving information as to the way the data is stored within the metafile which is needed by the interpreter. The rest of the information is contained in the picture body.

Picture Body Level: This primarily includes graphical primitives and attributes. Other information stored in the picture body controls the coordinate precision being used at that point and the clipping of the picture.

Escape Elements may be used in the metafile to describe device-dependent or system-dependent data in the CGM. An example would be a special hatch pattern used for a particular application. This escape would need to be known by those sites sharing the metafiles which use the pattern. There is a registration procedure which allows these escapes to be registered and thus they can be used between metafiles in a standard way.

External Elements are concerned with the storage of non-graphical data. These elements may be used to pass data between agreeing parties. The MESSAGE is intended for device-dependent information for operators when the metafile is interpreted. APPLICATION DATA allows non-graphical data to be stored. The data will have no impact on the interpretation of the picture. Such data may be user information which could be used by a spooler to identify plots in a plot queue for example.

2.3 Encodings

There are different requirements for data storage and transfer. This is not necessarily specific to the graphics community but will be addressed with reference to computer graphics here. These requirements include:

- minimal file size
- ease of transfer across networks
- the speed with which the data can be generated and interpreted;
- the readability of the stored files.

It is not possible to give equal weight to these requirements and the choice must depend on the application. For some environments it may not be necessary to transfer the stored data to other machines; in another environment it may be advantageous to be able to edit the graphical data which is stored, and thus readability is important. To address these different requirements the CGM defines 3 encodings. These three encodings being the character, binary and clear text encodings contained in Parts 2 to 4 of ISO 8632. These encodings are described briefly in this section.

The character encoding is found in Part 2 of ISO 8632. The main concerns of this encoding are to ensure that the encoding is compact and to guarantee ease of transfer across networks between machines. To achieve this second aim the character encoding is made up of only the Ascii printing characters. Each element is coded as an op-code followed by the data associated with the element.

The binary encoding is found in Part 3 of ISO 8632. The emphasis of this part of the standard is on ease of generation and interpretation of the CGM. For this reason the storage of the graphical data is in a form which is easily written and translated on most computer systems. Although compactness was not the primary consideration when this encoding was being developed the encoding should not be seen as being inefficient in its storage. In many applications it has been found that there is not a significant overhead in storage by using this encoding rather than the character encoding. The encoding does use a format which may cause difficulties when transferring the data between machines which do not adhere to the developing networking standards. To date though this has been the most popular encoding.

The clear text encoding is found in Part 4 of ISO 8632. The data which is stored in a clear text encoded CGM is human readable. This allows editing of the metafile which may be useful in environments where this is more beneficial than the minimising of the file size. A translation of a metafile in one of the other encodings into the clear text encoding may facilitate debugging of an invalid metafile.

The CGM standard specifies the abstract functions independently of the encodings. This means that a CGM can be written in a private encoding whilst adhering to the principles laid out in Part 1 of ISO 8632. This may have limited application as there may be insufficient interpreters for such an encoding.

3 Further Standards Activity

It was noted above in the general description of the CGM that the standard is concerned with the capture of static pictures. This is ideal for the majority of applications which use a metafile. There are, however, applications which require a faithful storage of a session, for example where animation is used. There are also capabilities included in the functional standards, such as GKS, which cannot be stored on the metafile conforming to the CGM standard. These include the storage of segments, which are groups of primitives and attributes which can be transformed, made visible or invisible, highlighted etc. Other features include the control of the position of the picture on the device which is controlled by the DEVICE VIEWPORT function in GKS. For these reasons, now that the basic CGM has been standardised, new work has been started within the ISO arena to address these problems. This work is known as the Computer Graphics Extended Metafile (CGEM [6]). The results will appear as an Addendum to ISO 8632 and will be strictly compatible with the CGM standard. The possibility of extending the CGM via an Addendum to support GKS-3D is also being considered within ISO and an initial draft has been prepared [7].

4 Conclusions

This paper has introduced the ideas of the CGM standard and indicated extensions which may be necessary to further support computer graphics. The papers in this volume are concerned with many issues relating to the use of this standard. These include topics which range from the use in a particular environment to the problems of one of the encodings.

Many graphics packages and CAD/CAM systems do find it useful to store files which just contain the plotting information as these can be more compact than the data file containing structure and product data. There is every reason why those software products should now turn to using the CGM. The CGM standard has been developed to provide compact and easily transferable files where these are required. Software suppliers who choose to write the CGM may find that their metafiles have a wider use for their customers. As a trade off they may find that metafiles created by other graphics systems, perhaps on other machines, can be read into their package.

The CGM is an important standard which is here to stay. There are benefits to be gained by suppliers of software and their customers if the CGM standard is used for the storage of graphical data. Customers should encourage their suppliers to move to this standard as there are clear benefits to be gained.

References

1. ISO IS 8632 Information processing systems - Computer graphics - Metafile for the storage and transfer of picture description information (CGM), 1987

2. ISO IS 7942 Information processing systems - Computer graphics - Graphical Kernel System (GKS) functional description, 1985

3. ISO DIS 8805 Information processing systems - Computer graphics - Graphical Kernel System for three dimensions (GKS-3D) functional description, 1987

4. ISO DP 9592 Information Processing Systems - Computer Graphics - Programmer's Hierarchical Interactive Graphics System (PHIGS) Part 1: Functional Description, 1987

5. K.W. Brodlie, L.R. Henderson, A.M. Mumford, "The CGM - A Metafile for GKS?", *Computer Graphics Forum*, 1987, **6(2)**

6. ISO IS 8632 Information processing systems - Computer graphics - Metafile for the storage and transfer of picture description information (CGM), Addendum 1, Proposed Draft Addendum, ISO/TC97/SC24/N19-N22

7. ISO IS 8632 Information processing systems - Computer graphics - Metafile for the storage and transfer of picture description information (CGM), Addendum 2, Initial Draft Addendum, ISO/TC97/SC24/N23

Other Reading

Arnold, D.B and Bono P.R., *CGM and CGI: Metafile and Interface Standards for Computer Graphics*, Springer-Verlag, (1988), 279pp

Henderson, L., Journey, M., and Osland, C., "The Computer Graphics Metafile", *IEEE Computer Graphics and Applications,* **6(8)**,(August 1986), pp. 24-32

Mumford, A.M., "Why Care About the Computer Graphics Metafile?", *Comput-Aided Des.*, **19(8)**, (October 1987)

Integrate '88 - A Personal View

A.M. Mumford

1 Introduction

The National Computer Graphics Association in Anaheim in March 1988 was a landmark in the use of the CGM. At this annual event the participants received their usual dose of exhibition, tutorials and papers. They also had a special exhibition to attend which was called Integrate '88.

The Integrate demonstration involved 33 vendors of graphics products. Their software was installed on a range of computer systems (such as SUN, Apollo and HP workstations) and these systems were linked together by an ethernet. A wide range of software was demonstrated in engineering, finance, graphics art and printing and publishing modules. All the software could handle CGMs written in the binary encoding using the MAP/TOP profile subset of elements.

2 Sampling a Tour

Participants at the demonstration were invited to sign up to one of 8 tours which were on offer throughout the conference. These tours involved taking part in a scenario about an imaginary company.

I went to visit the Electrowonder Company who had discovered a possible fault in an important circuit board. I saw the information regarding the fault being put together for a meeting of the management. The first information required was the detail of the circuit board which was extracted from Hewlett Packard software on one of their workstations. The resulting metafile was then sent to the graphics art department who were using Zenographics Mirage on an IBM PC/AT. Once the graphics artist was happy with the presentation then this was sent on for publishing in the report and also to the MAGICorp slide making software so that presentation material could be included.

Meanwhile back in the finance department the rest of the required information was being collated. Time and usage charts were being examined to evaluate the impact of the fault. presentation Technologies Imagemate software was used for this. The relevant charts were stored using CGM and sent to the publishing department who merged the graphics and some relevant text using Aldus Pagemaker on a Wang PC.

The final output was then sent to a Wang PostScript printer. The participants then took away a copy of the 'report'.

The demonstration was very impressive. The setting was very spacious and we were able to take time at the end of the tour to wander round and speak with the vendors. The vendors were all represented at the main exhibition and so we were able to concentrate on technical, rather than sales, issues.

There were also extended presentations on the three days by the vendors in the different modules. These allowed the suppliers to talk about their involvement in Integrate '88.

3 Further Thoughts

The event did take considerable organisation. Participants in the Integrate '88 demonstration had met on a number of occasions during the year running up to the event. The excitement generated when everything worked was quite infectious. The idea that so many people could actually work together without coming to any harm was a source of great amazement. The vendors learned that standards are not necessarily harmful to their product.

It was fun to be at Integrate '88, and that enjoyment was the result of many hours of organisation by those involved. The result was very professional. It was also a large awareness exercise for computer graphics standards in general and the CGM in particular. This was a very important outcome of an excellent demonstration of the use of the CGM in the real world.

Part II

Using the CGM in a Computing Service

The papers in this part review the problems of support in a computing service in industry, research laboratories and academic institutions. In all these cases there is invariably a wide range of hardware and software to support. The users of the service may be geographically distant from the central resource which may house high quality output devices. In industrial situations the work may be carried out by sub-contracting and then drawn together for final analysis.

All three papers recognize the role that the CGM can play in helping in the support of graphics applications on a wide range of hardware and software. To date Reed and Mumford have been involved in writing in-house software to support their users. Both look to a time when their software suppliers will provide standard graphical data storage as a part of software releases. Such software also needs to include not only efficient generators and interpreters but also tools for easy access and editing of pictures stored within metafiles.

Stoll describes the work at McDonnell Douglas Corporation in producing the toolpack of routines for generating and interpreting CGMs. This software plays an important role in their documentation process. To promote the use of the CGM the company have made the software generally available. The use of the CGM by their software suppliers is important and this is a very positive way of ensuring a wider availability of the CGM standard. This work at McDonnell Douglas has fed into the MAP/TOP Profile work which is described in Part Three of this book.

After Ten Years of Metafiles Where Does the CGM Fit?

T. N. Reed

Abstract

This paper discusses the need at Los Alamos National Laboratory for the Computer Graphics Metafile standard and supporting software. A brief history of metafile usage at Los Alamos is given. This is followed by an overview of our computing environment and a description of our computer graphics system. Issues we face in making the transition from our metafile to a system supporting the Computer Graphics Metafile (CGM) and related graphics standards is then discussed. Our present graphics software was designed to address specific needs at Los Alamos. The transition to the CGM and other related standards can take place only when these needs are met, hopefully, in the marketplace.

1 Introduction

With over 7000 users and millions of dollars invested in existing computer graphics application software, we are slowly and carefully assessing the impact of the CGM and related computer graphics standards at Los Alamos. How heavily will the CGM be used? Will the CGM become a part of vendor supported graphics packages? Will we be able to purchase software supporting the CGM in our environment instead of developing our own? These are questions we must answer before we begin the transition from our "home grown" tools and graphics packages to "standard" graphics. Although we make extensive use of metafiles, our use of the CGM has been limited to a few packages that provide it as "yet another" form of output. This paper will describe functionality in our current system that must be available in software supporting the CGM.

1.1 History of Metafile Usage at Los Alamos

The metafile we use was defined in 1976 and modified in 1977 to incorporate the SIGGRAPH Graphics Standards Planning Committee (GSPC) "Core" functionality[1]. It was this metafile that formed the basis for the metafile published in the 1979 GSPC "Core" report[2,3]. For the last 10 years, this metafile has been the primary vehicle from which our static hardcopy graphics have been generated. We currently process a gigabyte of graphics metafile information per day. Most of this metafile output is film - either microfiche, 16-mm color movies, or 35-mm slides. In addition to this, many metafiles are displayed on graphics terminals and are never processed as hardcopy output.

1.2 Los Alamos Computing Environment

Los Alamos National Laboratory is home to the world's most powerful scientific computing facility. It serves the scientific and engineering computing needs of over 7000 users who perform research and development related to national security and energy programs. About 5000 of these users work at Los Alamos, while the remainder are located at installations throughout the United States. To support these programs, the Laboratory has developed a state-of-the-art scientific computing network, the Integrated Computing Network (ICN). The various components of the ICN are shown in Fig. 1. Computer graphics plays an important role in the visualization of large scale scientific computations within the ICN.

One of the key hardware components of the ICN is the Print and Graphics Output Station (PAGES). PAGES is an ICN node to which text or graphics metafiles are sent for processing. PAGES is controlled by two DEC VAX-11/785's that drive three Xerox 9700 laser printers, four FR-80 COM recorders, a Dicomed D48 COM recorder, and a variety of paper plotters. PAGES currently processes more than 2 gigabytes of information daily, which contributes to a total output of 3 million pages of print per month, 6 million frames of microfiche per month, and about 250,000 frames of 16- and 35-mm film each month.

2 Los Alamos Integrated Graphics System

The discussion that follows describes our current graphics system and identifies key areas that are important to our user community. A successful transition to a CGM-based environment must include most of the capabilities described.

2.1 Utilities, Libraries, and Device Drivers

Most of the computer graphics generated at Los Alamos is via the Integrated Graphics System. Figure 2 illustrates the graphics software components making up this system. This software is provided on all the computing systems at Los Alamos allowing our users to choose the system best suited to their application program independent of their computer graphics needs. We would expect a CGM based environment to be available on an equally wide variety of operating systems.

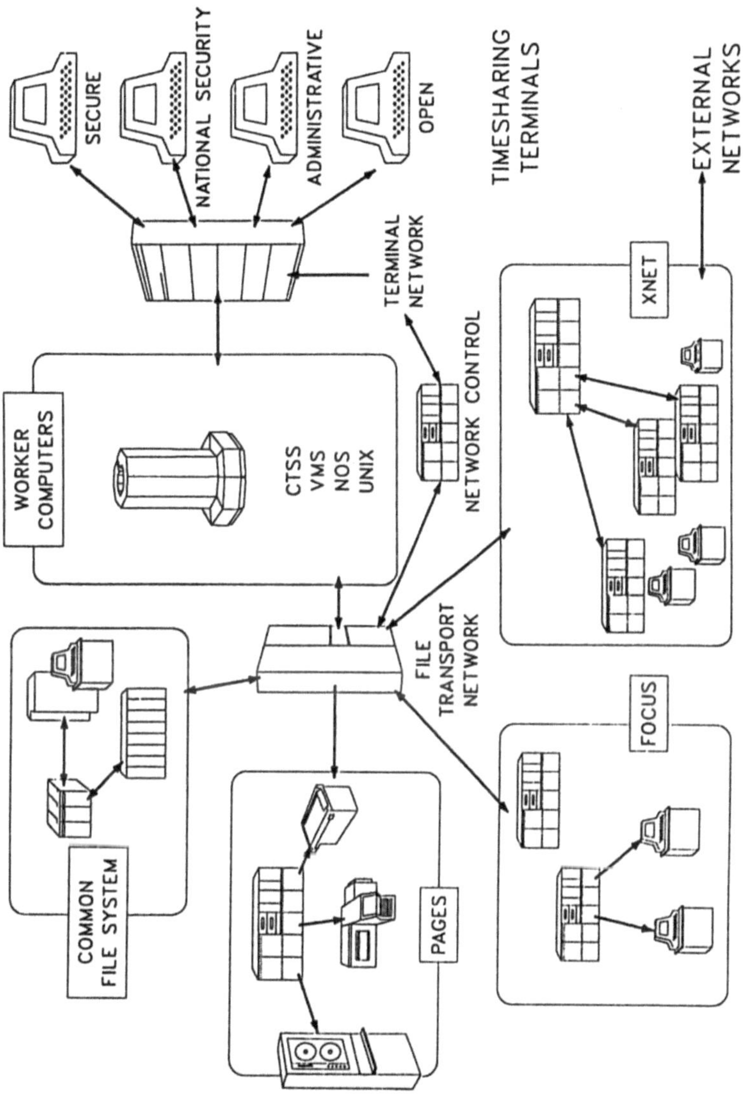

Figure 1. The Los Alamos Integrated Computing Network

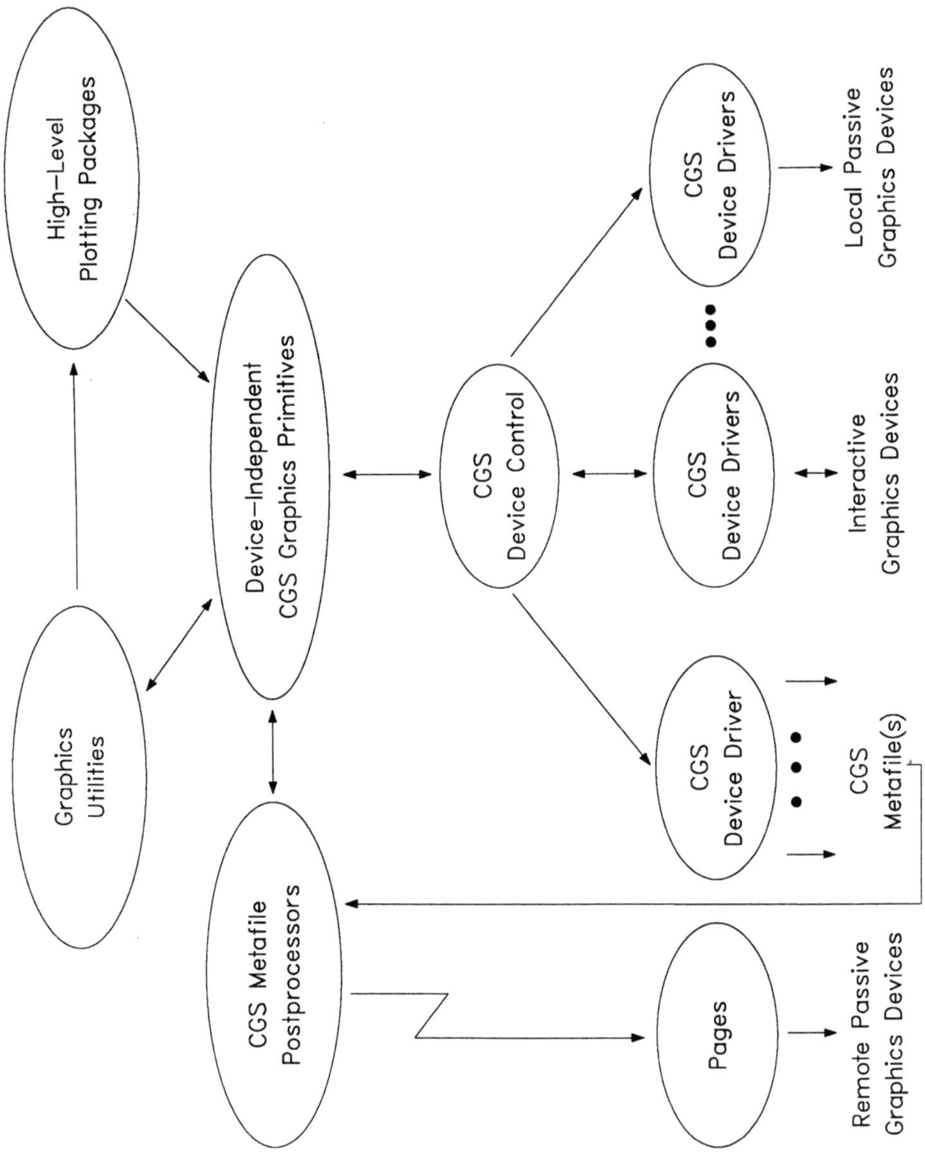

Figure 2. The Los Alamos Integrated Graphics System

The Common Graphics System (CGS) is a subroutine library containing device-independent graphics primitives, primitive attributes, and device control functions. The higher-level graphics utilities, plotting packages, and user application programs are built on this device-independent foundation. Included here are local packages providing higher-level plotting subroutines, vendor packages such as DISSPLA, and public domain software such as the NCAR graphics package and Movie.BYU.

Below the CGS foundation are various device drivers that interface to CGS and translate "virtual device" information generated by CGS into the form required by various physical graphics devices. A special device driver records this "virtual device" information as a CGS Metafile. This interface has been optimized to allow CGS Metafiles to be efficiently generated both in time and space[4]. Efficient generation of the CGM will be important to our large scientific modeling programs and will be high on our priority list when evaluating software supporting the CGM.

2.2 Metafile Movers and Translators

Once a CGS Metafile has been generated, it can be processed in two ways. The first way is to use a metafile mover. A metafile mover records information in the metafile header about how the metafile is to be processed and then sends it through the network to the PAGES system. There it is processed on the specified hardcopy device. We are evaluating the impact of translating the Computer Graphics Metafile directly on the PAGES system.

The second way is to use a metafile translator to process and display a metafile on a local device or terminal. These translators are CGS application programs that read CGS metafiles and use CGS device drivers to display the images on the user's device. This provides consistency in the displayed images independent of whether they are displayed directly as they are generated or saved as metafiles and later postprocessed to the device. We will expect similar consistency of displayed images using the CGM and supporting software.

In 1980, our metafile was extended to provide a mechanism allowing rapid random access to any individual image. We have since written metafile translators that take advantage of this capability. Our most popular and heaviest used translator allows metafile images to be viewed randomly; that is, any individual image can be immediately accessed and displayed. Additionally, selected frames can be stored in different metafiles or selected frames from several metafiles can be merged into one metafile. A limited amount of editing capability is provided to change existing images or combine several images into one.

This utility is successful because of its ability to quickly access any image of a metafile without sequentially processing preceding images. Information allowing efficient random access to individual images will have to be added to the CGM before it can replace the CGS Metafile. This information could be added to the CGM as either application data or an escape in the same way that it was added to the CGS Metafile[5].

2.3 Additional Metafile Tools

Many of our external users have expressed their need for support of their graphics devices. We support the most popular graphics devices by providing CGS device drivers. We also provide the ability for the users to write their own device drivers; however, this has not worked out in practice. As an alternative, we have provided a package that allows our users to easily write CGS metafile translators using device drivers provided in one of our vendor graphics packages. This has satisfied those users with unique devices. They don't have interactive access to the device and cannot run their programs on all our systems, but they do have a path to obtain their output. We expect vendors to provide similar capabilities using the CGM as a means of integrating various vendor products.

Another area where we have integrated new graphics capabilities has been via PostScript. PostScript files have become the Laboratory-standard format for integrated text and graphics[6]. We have written translators to convert CGS metafiles into PostScript format. We have recently updated one of our text formatting packages to convert CGS metafiles and include specified images into formatted text in PostScript format. This is becoming a heavily used product. We will write a PostScript device driver for CGS so that PostScript files can be generated directly from CGS application programs. A vendor supported tool providing this capability using the CGM would be useful.

2.4 Support Requirements for a CGM-Based Environment

To summarize, a successful transition to a CGM-based environment must include the following:

1. Vendor software supporting the CGM available on most of our operating systems.
2. Efficient generation of the CGM for our compute intensive scientific modeling programs.
3. Consistency of displayed images, whether displayed directly on the device or via metafile translation.
4. Rapid random access to individual images in a CGM.
5. CGM-based graphics editors.
6. Multiple vendor products integrated via the CGM.
7. Translators between the CGM and other graphical formats.

3 Current Use of the CGM

So far, the discussion of the CGM has been in the context of what is needed to replace our current metafile and related software. We are actively beginning to support the CGM as we provide new capabilities for our users.

3.1 CGM Subset

One shortcoming of the CGS metafile is a lack of raster capability. We are in the process of evaluating and providing raster graphics support for our user community. Several software packages exist that provide subroutines to generate raster graphic images. What they lack is a common output format. We have written a prototype system to generate a raster subset of the CGM to satisfy this need. This system will be used to evaluate the suitability of the CGM to support the raster needs of these software packages and our user community. Our hope is that we can eventually use vendor software to translate and display this subset of the CGM.

Another area where we expect to use the CGM is as a vehicle to integrate vector and raster graphics. A recent meeting of representatives of several DOE (Dept. of Energy) laboratories discussed the need to share and coordinate raster based graphics software. It was agreed to define a system based on a subset of the proposed Computer Graphics Interface (CGI) standard. This system would provide a limited set of vector and raster functions on which higher-level software could be provided. This system would drive raster graphics devices directly and would also generate a subset of the CGM containing raster and vector information. We plan to add a CGM device driver to our CGS system and are evaluating the feasibility of adding the CGI raster functions from our prototype raster system.

3.2 Networking

Perhaps the biggest payoff in actively supporting the CGM is in the rapidly growing area of workstations and networks. We have seen an explosive growth in the use of workstations in the last several years. Along with this increased use of workstations has come a variety of workstation-dependent graphics software packages. Our users want to use their workstations to generate computer graphics, but they also want to use our PAGES system and existing software in the ICN to display and manipulate these graphic images. We do not have the personnel necessary to provide translators on all these workstations to generate our CGS metafile. We are relying on vendors to provide CGM generators on their workstations as a way of integrating these diverse environments.

4 Summary

Our CGS metafile has been successful in meeting our needs and will continue to do so for some time to come. We are slowly and carefully moving in the direction of the CGM. We look forward to vendor-provided and vendor-supported software that can displace the need for our locally developed and supported software. This will require widespread adoption and support of the CGM in an integrated fashion across the industry. We are patiently waiting for this to happen.

References

1. "Status Report of the Graphics Standards Planning Committee of ACM/SIGGRAPH", *Computer Graphics*, **11(3)**, 1977.

2. Warner, J. R., "Device Independent Intermediate Display Files", *Computer Graphics*, **13(1)**, March 1979, 78-109.

3. "Status Report of the Graphics Standards Planning Committee of ACM/SIGGRAPH", *Computer Graphics*, **13(3)**, August 1979, Part IV.

4. Reed, T. N., "Experiences in the Design and Support of a Graphics Device Driver Interface", *Eurographics '81 Proceedings*, September 1981, 281-289.

5. Reed, T. N., "A Metafile for Efficient Sequential and Random Display of Graphics", *Computer Graphics*, **16(3)**, July 1982, 39-43.

6. Vigil, M. and Bouchier, S., "Text and Graphics at Los Alamos: A Systems Viewpoint", *ACM Mountain Proceedings*, April 1986, 101-107.

The Use of the CGM in the U.K. University Community

A.M. Mumford

Abstract

This paper considers the problems associated with the support of graphics software in the university community in the UK and takes the development and support of computer graphics at Loughborough University as an example. Many of the issues are not unique to graphics software and apply to the support of the very wide range of software being used in universities. The paper goes on to consider how graphics standards in general, and CGM in particular, can assist in helping universities through what is seen as being a software crisis [1].

1 Introduction

Most universities have a computer centre which has traditionally offered the major university service for both hardware and software. Large mainframes with card input and line printer output have given way in most places to networked mini computers and more distributed processing across networks. Many university departments purchase their own mini and micro computers with their own, or research, funds. Some of these may be linked to their universities central computer which exists at most sites for major software packages and larger processing requirements. The universities are also assisted in their computing by the availability of regional computer centres which cater for large resource requirements and provide expensive software and hardware for which there may not be the demand at individual university sites.

Universities and their departments are funded in the main from central government via direct funding and research council money. This has not, however, led to any obvious purchasing policies for hardware and software within or between universities. As each university has come to its turn for replacement of a major computer resource the hardware available at the time and the needs of the particular university have been the factors involved in the decision. This has resulted in a wide range of computer types and manufacturers being represented within the UK university community. Individual departments also purchase equipment and, while this may be done in conjunction with their computer centre, the decision may depend on the nature and amount of funding and whether there is a requirement for a particular type of machine. Often research councils assist projects by providing computing resources to a department as a part of the funding being made. Micro computers have been purchased by computer centres, departments and individuals. The type of purchases made have depended on the money available and the currently available hardware.

Software has similarly been purchased by individual universities and departments although some de-facto software standards have emerged for the larger machines. Most sites have a major Fortran subroutine library for computer graphics, for example. This has often been Gino-F [2] or Ghost [3] for most sites. Both offer low level graphics (initialization, line and curve drawing etc) and higher level routines for two and three dimensional data display. Most sites attempt to sit their other software on top of their chosen subroutine library as this makes driving devices much easier.

Using the base level graphics package under all other packages does have advantages for the support site as device drivers do not have to be written for the individual pieces of software. This may result in inadequate or less efficient support of the software but these factors are generally over-ridden by the easing of pressure from support staff. This is of course ideal for software on the same machine as the support package but not so for users of software on departmental machines and micros which may not be able to support many output devices.

There are also problems when software or hardware at other sites is used. Typically graphics packages at regional centres will use a popular package such as Gino-F and will output the Gino-F metafile (SAVDRA file). this can be file transferred to the home site and a program run to do the plotting. Special output devices, for example onto microfiche, are also housed at regional centres and in this case the Gino-F file can be transferred to the regional centre machine and a program run there to do the output. This is fine for users working on those machines which have access to the chosen package but not for the others.

The need for sharing experiences with software has been seen for some time. The Inter Universities Software Committee (IUSC) has organized various conferences on subject areas to assist computer centre staff to support software and to know what software is available. More recently there has been a move by this and other bodies to obtain bulk deals for popular software areas. These have included investigations of engineering software and data display software. Such deals clearly make purchasing software more economic within the universities. Expertise which is not available in every subjects in all computer centres can also help in the decision making process.

The development of standards relating to software such as programming standards and those in computer graphics have also been seen as being worth promoting within the academic community. By having a consistent underlying structure of standards for networking, programming languages, databases, computer graphics, etc. life becomes easier for the universities. They can more easily share programs and data both within and between sites to ensure the best collective use of available resources.

2 Assistance from Standards

Clearly there are problems of support for the vast range of hardware and software in Universities but there is a glimmer of hope offered by the development of international standards. This has been seen for some years within the networking community in the UK. The Joint Network Team set up within the academic community has carried out pioneering work into the way that networks can be standardized. From this effort the so called 'coloured book' software has emerged. The networking between and within Universities is now based on these standards. This has meant that the potential problems caused by the vast array of hardware selected by the academic community has been lessened. The efforts of the universities in this area have been fed into the development of the Open Systems Interconnection (OSI) standards and moves are already being made towards the use of these standards.

Computer graphics standards are also seen as having relevance in the university community in alleviating the duplication of work which often occurs. Implementation of a version of GKS (GKS-UK [4] written at the Rutherford Laboratory) is being carried out across a wide range of machine types. It is hoped that software will be developed to sit on top of this functional standard. Work has also commenced at Manchester University to extend this to support the GKS-3D standard.

The Computer Graphics Metafile (CGM) also is considered to have benefits for the University community. It is particularly pertinent at this time for a number reasons. The use of the CGM will enable sites to share software while maintaining their own output devices and to allow them to also share software. These can be achieved without committing the universities to a hardware or software supplier. This last point is important as there is a widespread requirement for graphical data storage. The use may be for sharing plot files between sites or perhaps for queuing plots for spooled output. Most sites have had to choose either a package dependent but device independent file solution, for example Gino-F SAVDRA, or have chosen a hardware specific solution for example the storage of Calcomp or Benson plotter code. Both rely on the continuing support of the supplier and long term compatibility which may not always happen. The device and package independent standard CGM offers considerable benefits.

3 A Case Study

Let us look at the way the use of computer graphics at Loughborough has emerged and the way that we started to see the role of the CGM for us and for the potential use for the academic community.

When we first obtained Gino-F it was on an ICL1900. The pictures could be displayed on our single Tektronix 4010 or output as a crude image on line printer paper or as final output via a Calcomp plotter. These devices were also made available to users via a new Prime system purchased for interactive work. Users of the Prime were offered interactive graphics via Gino-F and some in-house software written on top of Gino-F. The Calcomp output was written as Calcomp code onto a file, then written to magnetic tape as the plotter was run off line via a magnetic tape controller. Our new plotter was simply run directly by attaching it to a process on the Prime. Our facilities started to expand with more terminals being purchased for both colour and monochrome work.

Some years later next major move was to replace the ICL1900 with a Honeywell Multics computer. This caused us some problems. How were we to support both plots from the Prime and the Multics? The situation was further complicated by the purchase of more terminals and another large plotter for CAE work. Inevitably the initial solution was less than ideal. We decided to use the Gino-F SAVDRA format to transfer plotfiles from the Multics. These were processed by the Prime which serviced these by inputting them into a Gino-F program on the Prime and output occurred in the same way as before on the Prime. This was not ideal as it tied us to a particular package and it also required too many stages in the processing making turnaround slow.

The queue handling on the Multics is good so we then looked for a solution where the queuing would be done on this machine rather than the Prime. It was at this time that the CGM became a draft proposal and looked like the way forward. The solution involved changing the way we ran the Calcomp plotter from running it off line to running it on line. A Fortran subroutine library was written which generated a CGM file to the level of our requirements and to the Draft Proposal of the character encoding of the CGM. The character encoding being chosen for its compactness and ease of transfer. The routines were implemented on our Multics and Prime systems. The running of a graphics program or package at Loughborough - still based on Gino-F - caused a CGM file to be written and entered in the queue for plotting if the program was on the Multics. On the Prime the metafile was entered as a file transfer request to the Multics and then placed in the queue along with the Multics plots.

This worked well and later we added in another Prime machine in one of our departments. We are just completing implementing the software on an Apollo network. We have also been able to easily add on two other plotting devices. A major advantage is that we can leave the decision as to which output device the plot is to go to until plotting is carried out. When one of our plotters is busy or out of service for any reason we can divert the output to another device. We only use this for queued plots but there is no reason why this could not be extended to output metafiles to other devices.

4 Into the Future

Our experience of using software based on the CGM Draft Proposal was favourable. There was evidence which showed that considerable efficiencies could be obtained by using the character encoding of the CGM compared with other machine independent formats. We therefore suggested that the CGM could have benefits for other university sites. We made a proposal to the Computer Board who fund university computer centres. The Computer Board have seen the benefits of standardization of software in universities, through the implementation of GKS-UK for example. The Board have funded a two year project at Loughborough which involves the employment of a person for two years to work on the CGM software. The project aims to write a Fortran subroutine library to generate and interpret CGM character encoded metafiles. This will then be interfaced to various graphics packages. The interfacing will be at least to the GKS Fortran binding, to Gino-F and possibly to other packages where bulk purchases have been made within the University community. Deals include those with PAFEC Ltd [5] who supply CAE software and UNIRAS [6] who supply data display software. A generator for GKS-UK will be written along the lines suggested by the Annex E to the CGM standard. The interpreter code will also include a direct interface to GKS via the INTERPRET ITEM code.

The software will be freely available to the universities at the end of the project. It is hoped that its wide use will encourage other suppliers to provide CGM generators and interpreters to support the CGM. The software written by the project will also be available to software suppliers to use. Negotiations have already taken place with the CAD Centre Ltd of Cambridge who see the CGM as a means of sharing files between their various software packages (including Gino-F) and between their software and other packages.

The use of CGM for storage of output from a wide range of graphical data and the input of such metafiles into their range of graphics packages would be a considerable move. We hope that we can encourage suppliers of software to consider using the CGM as their means of graphical data storage. This may mean that in the future users of a wide range of software on a wide range of computers will be able to share graphical data and also share devices which are in scarce supply compared to the availability of computing resources of one type or another.

The CGM can thus be seen as offering the university computer centres some assistance in seeing their way out of this crisis of hardware and software support.

References

1. "The Software Crisis," IUSC Conference, Sussex University, England, July 1987.

2. Gino-F, CAD Centre Ltd, Cambridge, England.

3. GHOST 80, Culham Lab., Abingdon, England.

4. GKS-UK, PLU, Edinburgh University, Scotland.

5. GKS-3D Project, Computer Graphics Unit, Manchester University, England.

6. PAFEC Ltd, Stapleford, Nottingham, England.

7. UNIRAS, Copenhagen, Denmark.

The CGM Implementation at McDonnell Douglas

J. Stoll

Abstract

More and more, businesses are requiring the integration of technical information to increase the effectiveness of information interchange between the office and the factory. In particular, within the engineering, manufacturing, administration and product support constituencies of the aerospace industry, one of the most vital information interchange services is the ability to interchange graphics in a heterogeneous computer environment. At McDonnell Douglas, the integration of the Computer Graphics Metafile (CGM) into the Corporation is the result of a need for a single graphics file format that can meet the robust requirements of graphical interchange between internal applications, as well as external subcontractors, teaming partners and customers.

1 The Computer Graphics Metafile

Three years ago, McDonnell Douglas Corporation (MDC) initiated an effort to replace its Corporate standard private graphics plot file due to the growing obsolescence and incompatibility of the file format. The decision was made to develop the capability to generate and interpret the Computer Graphics Metafile (CGM, ISO 8632, ANSI X3.122) to eventually supplant the existing internal metafile.

The rationale to justify this decision was compelling. The CGM standard specifies an object oriented metafile that can be thought of as a device-independent plot file format. The CGM is compatible with several ANSI/ISO computer graphics standards such as the Graphical Kernel System (GKS) and its extension (GKS-3D), the Programmer's Hierarchical Interactive Graphics System (PHIGS), and the Computer Graphics Interface (CGI). The CGM is also a data format supported by the Standard Generalized Markup Language (SGML) and Open Document Architecture/Open Document Interchange format

(ODA/ODIF) for the interchange of graphics content within a document. In addition, the CGM is included in some Government and Military requirements specifications such as CALS and GOSIP, as well as in the Technical and Office Protocol (TOP) specification.

The CGM is a means to capture the graphical primitives, attributes, control, delimiter and external elements of a computer graphics picture description. The CGM includes support for such graphical primitives as: polylines, polymarkers, graphical text, polygons, polygon sets and other filled areas, ellipses and elliptical arcs, circles and circular arcs, raster cell array, and specialized drawing entities. The CGM also includes a wide variety of attributes to control the color, style, weight and orientation of the graphical primitives. The data type and precision of picture coordinate space can be altered using the control elements. The delimiter elements allow the partitioning of the metafile into multiple, independent pictures. And finally, the external elements permit storage of device- or application-dependent information. Given its inherent utility and potential for widespread use, the CGM was an obvious choice for development and integration into the Corporation.

2 The MDC CGM Toolkit

The McDonnell Douglas implementation of the CGM has come to be known as the MDC CGM Toolkit. The Toolkit consists of approximately 500 generic ANSI FORTRAN77 subroutines used to generate, retrieve and render a CGM. The Toolkit is structured to provide a straightforward interface for the integration of the CGM capability into existing and future applications. The Toolkit has currently been installed on DEC VMS, IBM MVS/TSO, IBM VM/CMS, an IBM PC running MS-DOS, DG AOS/VS, and an HP UNIX workstation. The possible environments for installation of the Toolkit are limited only by the availability of a conforming ANSI F0RTRAN77 compiler.

2.1 CGM Generation

The 500 MDC CGM Toolkit subroutines are organized into three separate service modules corresponding to the generation, retrieval and rendering of the CGM. The CGM Generator Service Module consists of approximately 150 subroutines that are responsible for the generation of the CGM. This service module is the only interface between the application process and the CGM being created. The interface is patterned after the FORTRAN77 Binding to the CGI. Of the three encodings described by the CGM standard, the Toolkit at present supports only the binary encoding. However, the planned future support for the remaining encodings will be transparent to the application process because the Generator Service Module presents an abstracted view of the data to be represented in the metafile. This data abstraction logically separates the application process and the outer layer interface subroutines from the inner layer subroutines that encode and write the data to the metafile.

2.2 CGM Retrieval

The CGM Interpreter Service Module consists of approximately 150 subroutines, also written in FORTRAN77, that are responsible for retrieving a CGM. CGM Interpreter Service Module may actually be a misnomer because the module merely parses the metafile and returns the individual CGM elements, no processing or translation of the information is performed. The CGM elements are returned in the same parameterization as if they were generated by the Generator Service Module.

2.3 CGM Display

To render the CGM, a special application process called the CGM Despooler Service Module invokes the CGM Interpreter Service Module to retrieve the metafile. The Despooler Service Module then reconstructs and translates the metafile picture into the appropriate format for the particular rendering device. The Despooler Service Module consists of approximately 200 FORTRAN77 subroutines. These subroutines are further subdivided into functional layers, called shells. The Device-Independent Shell invokes the Interpreter Service Module and receives the metafile data. The Device-Independent Shell then passes the data to one of several Device-Dependent Shells that are essentially device drivers for each supported rendering device. The Despooler Service Module included in the Toolkit currently contains Device-Dependent Shells for Tektronix 4014 devices, Calcomp plotters and QMS laser printers. Other Device-Dependent Shells will be added to future releases of the Toolkit as requirements for them are identified.

3 Toolkit Integration

Integration of the CGM Toolkit into McDonnell Douglas has not been a simple process and when completed will represent a 5 year effort. The effort has been very successful, however, given the size and complexity of the Corporation. Several key steps were taken that have proven to be instrumental in insuring the success of the project.

3.1 Corporate Commitment

First of all, the CGM Toolkit was developed under the auspices of the McDonnell Douglas Corporate Information Resource Management organization. This served to give the Toolkit integration effort a Corporate impetus, thus lessening artificial inter-departmental barriers and softening the "not invented here" nature of the project. However, integrating the CGM Toolkit into existing applications within the Corporation obviously requires the support of the organizations responsible for those applications. Enlisting the active support of these organizations within MDC has proven in some cases to be difficult. Without a direct requirement for CGM from customers or support from vendors, integration of the CGM into these applications is not given a high priority. Therefore, another key step has been taken to help promote the use of the CGM within the Corporation.

3.2 Promotion of the Standard

It was recognized early in the integration of the CGM Toolkit that one way to promote the use of the CGM within the Corporation is to promote the use of the CGM outside of the Corporation. This has been accomplished, with varying degrees of success, through three main strategies.

First, long term Corporate commitment to participate on the domestic and international standards bodies involved in the formulation of the CGM Standard has been authorized. This has given MDC the opportunity to influence the standardization process and to establish contacts with vendors in key technology areas. This has also greatly enhanced the viability and legitimacy of the MDC CGM Toolkit and established the credibility in the vendor community of MDC's commitment to the CGM Standard.

Second, through participation in the Technical and Office Protocol (TOP) organization, MDC was instrumental in getting the CGM included in the TOP specification. This in turn lead to the CGM being included in the Department of Defense Computer Aided Logistics Support (CALS) specification. Both of these specifications have added significant weight to the effort to integrate the CGM Toolkit within the Corporation.

Third, the MDC CGM Toolkit was released into the public domain and is available free of charge. Over 65 copies of the Toolkit have subsequently been distributed. Distribution of the Toolkit has contributed greatly to the wide variety and number of vendor products that now support the CGM. Having a substantial number of vendors that offer CGM import/export into their products eventually creates a demand for CGM capability in internal applications. All three of the above strategies have combined to accelerate the acceptance and integration of the CGM within MDC.

3.3 CGM "Champion"

Though seldom mentioned in most integration efforts, having a "champion" for a tool or solution to be implemented is a vital necessity. From the outset of the CGM project at MDC, there has been a core of individuals dedicated to the development, promotion and integration, i.e. "championing" of the CGM Standard within and without the Company. The existence of this group has insured the consistency, quality and continuity of the Toolkit and in some cases the CGM Standard itself, and has been vital to the success of the project. In addition, based in part on the effectiveness of the CGM "champion", a project is now underway at MDC to investigate and develop the capability to interchange digital compound documents. The experience gained from the CGM implementation effort has provided a solid knowledge base from which to attack this complex problem.

4 Summary

In order for McDonnell Douglas Corporation to remain a leader in the aerospace industry, it must integrate its information resources. A major task in this integration effort is to perfect the interchange of digital information. In 1983, MDC came to the realization that one of the first steps towards the integration of technical information resources would be to consolidate the numerous private MDC computer graphics plot file formats into a single, standard, Corporate computer graphics metafile. In 1984, the decision was made to develop the MDC CGM Toolkit and integrate CGM capability into existing applications. Steps were then taken to help expedite this process and to help insure that future vendor products and internal applications include support for the CGM. These steps include participation on national and international standard bodies, active involvement in user's groups, and the vigorous promotion of the CGM Standard inside and outside McDonnell Douglas. All of these efforts over the last three years have culminated in the emergence of the CGM as a strategic information resource.

Acknowledgement

The Author would like to gratefully acknowledge the contributions of Mr. Frank Dawson, without whose effort and determination none of this would have been necessary.

Part III

Making the CGM Pay: Commercial Needs

Standards will be of little value unless they can be used in a commercial environment in an economic way. This part contains four papers on different aspects of this theme. They all consider ways that CGM can be useful to them and their user environment. There is a concern to ensure that the CGM can be transferred easily between sites whilst also trying to guarantee that the full needs of their users are met. Such requirements include rendering information and extended hatch and line styles.

Rossin describes Wang's move from their own metafile definition (based on the CGM) to the CGM standard. While there is a corporate commitment to this move there have been problems. There is a need for page utilization and font information at interpretation. A need for predefined bundles is also identified.

The experience of Novagraphics in using the CGM as a metafile for GKS is described by Tucker and Heather. There are problems when the standards do not fit closely together to give a straightforward mapping. The problems of the CGM/GKS mapping are described in the paper. The authors recognize that some of these problems are being resolved in ISO through the extended metafile work.

A major problem of many standards is that they are very comprehensive. In a commercial environment it may not be economic to implement all the options within a standard. The problem with this is that there is a potential for particular implementations of a standard to be little better than a proprietary product. As a result of this, MAP/TOP (Manufacturing Automation Protocol and Technical Office Protocols) was born in the Open Systems Interconnection (OSI) area of standards. Specifics of the standards have been agreed upon to ensure interworking. These are known as application profiles. An application profile for the CGM has been developed by TOP and this is detailed in this section, introduced by Hardman of Boeing. This profile incorporates two ESCAPES to give compatibility with current software which uses GKS.

The concept of an application profile is considered to be useful for the US DoD in the CALS project. TOP and NBS have worked together to ensure compatibility of the two profiles where appropriate and the differences between the two are given by Henderson in his paper. Extra conformance requirements for generators and interpreters are considered necessary for the CALS environment.

Application profiles are clearly becoming important for CGM implementors and users. the CGM leaves many things implementation dependent and it is often important to have accurate and predictable results. It was agreed at the workshop that profiles must define conforming CGMs and must not compromise future standards work.

The Ramifications of Adopting the CGM as the Image Transfer Mechanism

B. Rossin

Abstract

This paper explores some of the problems Wang Laboratories has encountered in the development and introduction of graphic metafile-based products. These discussions will range from past product offerings through current developmental activities to future goals. The issues addressed here, were and are, generated by real world, market place oriented pressures. The solutions that were adopted are not necessarily correct from the standard's point of view, nor even optimal. They were, however, necessary compromises at that time.

1 Background

Wang Laboratories is a premier supplier of Word Processing and Data Processing computer systems. Since 1985, Wang has provided business graphics and integrated text and graphics processing packages to the general office automation marketplace.

The needs of the marketplace at that time were fairly simple and straightforward. Customers needed to get their financial and other data out of spreadsheet data bases, converted into business graphs, and ultimately, integrated into documents.

Wang provided two products to address these needs: VS Graphics Facility (VSGF) and VS WP PLUS. Introduced in 1984, VSGF gave the user access to a wide variety of data bases (e.g. PACE, WP documents, etc.) and produced high quality business graphs. The graphs could be printed directly by a hardcopy device or included in a document. VS WP PLUS, introduced in 1985, was the first Wang product to integrate such graphics with traditional text processing. PC based products such as Microsoft Chart and PC WP PLUS were released later. The combined use of these products was a major breakthrough for the Wang user.

2 WVDM - Past Issues

The mechanism used to transfer graphical data from VSGF to WP PLUS was the Wang Virtual Device Metafile (WVDM). WVDM was based on a 1985 snapshot of the CGM. WVDM supported most of the usual graphic drawing primitives and attributes but did not support bundles and only supported hardware text. The goal was to achieve true device independence and output consistency. However, in many ways, this goal was to prove elusive.

2.1 Shielding

The first devices supported under the WVDM were raster based displays and dot matrix printers. These devices have the common characteristic of defaulting to opaque drawing mode and, therefore, show only the last color written to overlapping areas. Color plotters on the other hand will mix the colors if different pens write to the same area. The device driver developers were a bit chagrined when their simple plotter driver did not accurately reproduce the picture on the display.

The requirement to support shielding of the picture for plotter type devices proved extremely costly in terms of development effort, memory, and performance. Totally shielding the entire picture proved prohibitively expensive in terms of time. Therefore, changes to the application were necessary to define which portions of the picture should be shielded. These changes violated the concept of device independence but were necessary at the time. The end result was delayed product introduction and reduced product functionality. This experience points out the pitfalls of not fully understanding all the implications of different device technology.

2.2 Page Utilization

Maximizing the usage of the entire output page of a business graph was a major consideration for the VSGF application. Using anisotropic mapping would guarantee complete utilization of the space on any output device. Unfortunately, it would produce oval pie charts on devices with different aspect ratios from the original device. Isotropic mapping would guarantee complete page utilization on devices with the same aspect ratio. However, the ultimate target output device might have a different aspect ratio and would not be fully utilized.

The VSGF application developers chose to adopt the concept of a target output device. The characteristics of this device would be assumed whenever the application produced intermediate output on another device. Thus, if the ultimate output device was a D sized plotter, the plotter's aspect ratio would be assumed when displaying the graph on a video terminal for editing purposes.

This approach was quite practical when Wang supported a small number of devices, when most customers used metafiles only locally and when they knew what the target devices were. Two major developments have put increasing strain on this technique. First, world wide electronic mail through Wang Office means metafiles can appear on distant systems with completely different output devices. Thus the originator can no longer assume a particular target device. Second, network gateways to foreign systems complicate the problem even more. The implementation of this feature in VSGF used actual device names and, hence, violates the concept of strict device independence. The concept of target devices, however, could be generalized to device classes which would be consistent with a broader view of device independence.

2.3 Hatch Patterns

Most high quality, cost effective output devices were (and still are) monochromatic. The number of unique, differentiable ways of drawing bars (rectangles) and pies (sectors) on monochromatic devices using standard CGM is severely limited. Only six hatch patterns are defined in the CGM standard. This limitation did not begin to use the capabilities inherent in medium to high resolution graphic printers and was not acceptable to the business graphic application developers.

Therefore, WVDM increased the number of supported hatches to 125. These predefined hatch patterns were optimized to each device. Application developers were satisfied with this solution. However there are certain ramifications. The first one is memory size. Hatch pattern tables can consume from 4 to 20 Kbytes depending upon device characteristics. This may be a relatively high overhead for a capability which is rarely used to its full extent. The second problem concerns building the hatch tables for new devices. Matching 125 predefined hatches on a new device may be extremely difficult, if not impossible, due to differences in device technology. Hatches suitable for 100 dpi displays or printers are much too small on 300 dpi laser printers. Hatches tuned for devices which paint black will be unacceptable on technology which paints white. These problems are multiplied when trying to achieve a consistent appearance across all 125 hatches.

2.4 Fonts and Text

In regards to fonts and text, only hardware text was supported in the WVDM. Therefore, applications had to insert device independent text into the metafile as a series of strokes using the polyline command. This approach suffers from several major drawbacks. Since polylines are a much less efficient mechanism for storing text than character strings, the size of the metafile was greatly increased. Also, inserting polylines into the metafile loses the essential textual nature of the data. Therefore, high quality fonts embedded in devices, such as Postscript laser printers, could not be utilized.

2.5 Color Consistency

Several color displays and hardcopy devices were supported under WVDM. Therefore color consistency from one device to another was a consideration. The general approach to this problem employed a set of predefined palettes. A fixed color device would have a single predefined palette reflecting its colors. A loadable color device such as a video display with color look up table could have multiple predefined palettes. It was left up to the user/application developer to properly choose the palette for the desired effect on a particular device. A utility was provided so that the system administrator or sophisticated user could delete, modify, or create palettes.

From the application developer's point of view, the palette approach could be seen as a predefined set of bundles limited to the color attribute. Choosing a predefined palette would be equivalent to choosing a bundle set. The palette indexes would be used the same way as bundle indexes. This approach provides some of the advantages of a full scale bundle implementation. However, since the palettes are predefined, colors cannot be modified interactively by the application. The other major limitation is encountered when trying to display a color metafile on a monochrome device. Since the color palette indexes can only be mapped into black or white, much of the distinguishability within the metafile is lost upon output to the monochromatic device.

2.6 Corporate Acceptance

During this timeframe, there was an ongoing internal debate at Wang over the merits of graphic standards. Both sides used the common arguments of performance, functionality, memory size, development time, consistency, maintainability, etc. Initially, the con side appeared to be winning. Recently, however, several factors have helped to shift the consensus in the favor of adopting graphic standards within Wang Laboratories.

The formal approval of the CGM standard by both ANSI and ISO was a major step forward. It was extremely difficult to argue for a standard which was not nailed down. This problem still plagues CGI at Wang.

The first major internal breakthrough was the delivery of a severely limited CGM interpreter (i.e., stroke text functionality for displays). The resulting standards based product had increased functionality, a ten times performance improvement and similar memory requirements, when compared to the previous non standard implementation. This delivery almost completely shattered the myths that graphic standards are poor performers and memory hogs. By providing the exact functionality that the user required, it was possible to avoid the functionality, performance, and memory size problems encountered with less flexible approaches.

The standards group's credibility and acceptability of graphic standards were further enhanced by the delivery of several increasingly broader implementations of CGM interpreters. These packages were targeted for different applications and systems which demonstrated the portability and consistency advantages of using graphic standards.

At the corporate level there was an increasing interest in graphics in general, consistency across product lines and integration of various forms of data. Graphic standards were seen as a means of achieving these diverse corporate goals. Finally, signs of customer interest in CGM were increasing. CGM capability was being referenced in major RFPs. MAP/TOP's and ODA/ODIF's acceptance of CGM was seen as a major stamp of approval of the CGM by the marketplace.

3 WCGM - Current Developments

Wang Laboratories is currently developing CGM capability on all its major product lines. This effort is being driven by the corporate goals of standardization, integration, and consistency. A series of new products and new releases of existing products are planned over the next eighteen months. The earliest products will be internally based on the Wang's implementation of the CGM called WCGM. Later releases will employ the WCGM as the graphic interchange file format.

3.1 Platform Diversity

One of the most challenging aspects of the WCGM development effort is maintaining consistency across the incredible diversity of target platforms. These range from Intel 8Ox86 and Motorola 68xxx microprocessor based systems to Wang's 32 bit VS family. Operating systems run the gamut from industry standard MS DOS, to UNIX derivatives, to sophisticated integrated window based systems with virtual memory support. Numerous existing terminals and peripherals incorporate Z8O technology, while the newest batch of intelligent peripherals are based on dedicated graphic processors like the Texas Instrument's 34010 and other even more exotic chips. Finally, Wang's joint marketing agreements with both Sun and Apollo add these platforms to the list.

There is no magic formula for handling complexity of this magnitude, just a lot of hard work and some common sense. When dealing with a problem of this size, portability is essential. Therefore, whenever possible, code is written in portable C. Performance, however, is an equally important concern and requires that certain critical routines must be written in assembler.

The core of Wang's CGM interpreter is structured into three levels: the command parser, the rendering code and the low level device driver. The command parser is entirely written in C for portability but makes use of fast table look ups to achieve high performance. Similarly, a complete implementation of the rendering or algorithm level is available in C. After porting the standard C version, certain routines may be recoded in assembler to improve performance. The amount of performance increase achieved by this method is highly dependent upon the efficiency of the C compiler's optimizer and is only undertaken after careful analysis. For obvious reasons, the low level device driver code is written in assembler.

3.2 WVDM to WCGM Transition

Backward compatiblity and smooth transitions are absolute requirements for companies with large installed bases. Product development cycles and quality assurance schedules are also facts of life. In these circumstances it is impossible to simply convert to WCGM overnight and instead, requires a transition period.

Fortunately, WVDM is almost a proper subset of WCGM. In comparing WVDM to WCGM, two commands have different functionality and about half a dozen have different class/element encodings. The two metafile formats can be differentiated by the Metafile Version command. It is relatively easy to develop an interpreter which can handle both

WVDM and WCGM. Therefore, products that function properly with current WVDM based applications and will automatically handle a WCGM based application in the future can be developed, fully tested and released.

A principal facet of managing the transition from WVDM to WCGM is to incorporate this dual mode capability into the low level device packages such as terminal emulators and printer support routines. By concentrating on providing the low level support first, the direct link of WCGM to major application development cycles is broken. Applications can upgrade to the new functionality at their own pace.

3.3 Fonts

Consistent appearance and metrics of fonts across product lines and output devices has long been a major concern at Wang. Over forty font styles (including many NBS defined fonts) are considered mandatory. Future requirements for fonts will be virtually unlimited. Since over half of Wang's business is outside of the US, international character sets are an absolute necessity. Examples range from a common Wang character set which meets the needs of Western Europe to Non-Roman character sets such as Cyrillic and Japanese.

Graphic applications require the ability to arbitrarily scale and rotate characters. Some form of scalable, strokable font is needed by these programs. Text processors are more concerned with best possible appearance, proportional spacing and kerning. Typically, tuned raster fonts are appropriate for these applications. Maintaining consistency across all the necessary fonts, formats and devices requires a monumental effort.

Wang is currently exploring a mix of internal sources and third parties to meet the font requirements. The WCGM will fully support the CGM text model and commands. In addition, the WCGM will incorporate the existing Wang printer support mechanism of searching for a best match font if an exact match is not available.

3.4 Bundles

Many Wang applications developers consider bundles as one of the most important features of the WCGM. Proper usage of bundles provides a mechanism for the application to resolve the dilemma of outputting a color graph on a monochrome device encountered with WVDM.

Bundles are a major step forward in the concept of device independence. However, certain "minor" issues remain to be resolved. Business graphic application developers want to use bundles to access their 125 hatch patterns and the various colors available on common color printers. Predefining a standard set of default bundles which handle these combinations (and any future combinations) is a formidable task. Nonetheless, defining and interpreting bundles at execution time is beyond the scope of the CGM specification.

One possible solution to this problem is to provide a utility for defining sets of bundles. The application would select a set of bundles, similar to the way palettes were selected using WVDM. This approach loses some of the device independent elegance of the "pure" bundle implementation. It does, however, address the user's requirements and does reduce the problem to a manageable size.

3.5 Colors

WCGM will fully support the color model defined by CGM. An interesting dilemma was uncovered during discussions with application developers concerning the user's expectation as colored objects were output on various devices. For instance, it is possible for an user to select a color for one graphical object in his picture and expect distinguishability when displayed on a less capable device. The problem occurs when the user chooses the same color for another object in the same picture and expects the closest approximation possible on the less capable device. The WCGM interpreters handle this situation by recommending that bundles be used in setting the attributes for the first object and the appropriate individual color attribute be used for the second. Thus, bundling is automatically invoked to achieve distinguishability for the first object, while the direct color specification is used to override the bundle default and invoke a closest approximation algorithm to display the second object. This approach to color will provide a high degree of user flexibility and device independence.

4 Future Directions

Once WCGM is fully implemented across Wang's product lines, our development focus will shift to several integration issues. Using WCGM to combine various forms of visual information including text, graphics and images is one such topic. Adapting CGM interpreters to function within window based systems is another. Finally, the low level functionality needed to optimally support emerging higher level standards like GKS 3D and PHIGs is a third such consideration.

4.1 Integration of Text, Graphics and Images

Both ODA/ODIF and MAP/TOP use CGM for graphical data interchange and other mechanisms for text and images. There is serious interest within Wang for taking a different tack. Discussions are currently underway for extending the WCGM to include additional text and imaging capabilities. This would provide the corporation with a natural mechanism for integrating text, graphics and images into one picture and would achieve a high degree of internal standardization.

These WCGM extensions would take the form of CGM Generalized Drawing Primitives (GDPs) and Escapes. Possible text extensions include structured text for compatibility reasons, buffered text to allow applications to control intercharacter spacings and diacritic text for foreign alphabets. Possible imaging extensions include Wang proprietary formats and standard formats such as CCITT Group 3 ID and Group 4 2D. Other issues include state control, inheritance of attributes, and the management of resources such as fonts, bundles, colors, etc. An utility would exist for converting the extended WCGM to a pure CGM for export to foreign systems.

4.2 Window Systems

Compatibility with MS Windows, X Windows, Presentation Services and other windowing packages will be increasingly important in the future. A WCGM interpreter could be written as a layer on top of a standard windowing system. This type of implementation is relatively simple, but the resulting performance will probably be inadequate. Significant improvements would be possible if the graphics package was allowed to interrogate the display/window manager for the necessary information and then display directly to the hardware. Unfortunately, it is highly unlikely that commercially available windowing systems will provide the required documentation.

Several other interesting issues arise when discussing CGM interpretation on window based systems. For instance, who owns the Look Up Table (LUT). If a CGM interpreter running in one window, changes the LUT, what happens to all the other windows? Another problem occurs because the CGM interpreter assumes that the default device viewport is constant. What happens if the user resizes the window, CGM is being display in. Finally, the issue of screen refresh must be addressed. Is it the responsibility of the application, the CGM interpreter or the window package? Must the CGM level include support segments in order to work in a window based system? A common solution to these problems across the various environments would be highly desirable.

4.3 GKS-3D and PHIGS

Presentation of three dimensional data and pictorial representations of hierarchical data bases are hot topics in the business graphics community. Advanced application developers are becoming very interested in the Programmer's Hierarchical Interactive Graphic System (PHIGS) and the Graphic Kernel System for 3 Dimensions (GKS-3D). By design, these higher level graphic standards could be implemented on top of a CGM interpreter. This approach would be easy to implement and would leverage the device independent advantages of CGM. In a single processor, stand alone environment, this approach should achieve near optimal performance.

Unfortunately, the simple layering approach based on CGI/CGM is unlikely to achieve maximum performance in the increasingly more common multiprocessor, coprocessor, and distributed architectures. Typically, these more complicated systems can be analyzed as pipelines. Optimal performance occurs in a pipeline when the line is balanced. Thus the performance problem becomes how to shift the various tasks from pipeline node to node to maintain overall balance. As the processors dedicated to the CGI/CGM level become more powerful, additional higher level functions should be shifted down to optimize performance.

Obvious candidates for shifting are the 3D to 2D conversion functions, further portions of the 3D pipeline and various hierarchical and segmentation functions. Detailed analysis of actual architectures is necessary to choose which functions to move. Given the diversity of Wang supported platforms, different solutions for different configurations will probably be necessary. The higher level code would adapt itself to the capabilities supported by the lower level.

5 Closing Comments

Wang Laboratories is dedicated to blending text, graphics and images into a common, user friendly, integrated system. Graphics standards, in particular CGM, play a major, strategic role in achieving this corporate goal.

The Implementation of the CGM as a GKS Metafile

C. Tucker and G. Heather

Abstract

A major goal of recent computer graphics standards development has been a high degree of compatibility among standards. Two major standards have recently been adopted which provide a test case for demonstrating this goal: the Graphical Kernel System (GKS) and the Computer Graphics Metafile (CGM). This paper discusses the relationship between GKS and CGM from the perspective of implementation of an interface to CGM from GKS. The two models of graphics metafile represented by GKSM (GKS metafile) and CGM are compared. Areas of mismatch of functionality are analyzed and solutions to the functional mismatch are presented. Experiences with integrating CGM into the GKS environment are discussed, first, in terms of the generation of a CGM by a GKS implementation, then, in terms of interpretation of a CGM (not necessarily generated by a GKS implementation). Finally, there is a brief review of current work on extensions to CGM functionality which is intended to address some of the areas of mismatch between GKS and CGM.

1 Introduction

Over the past decade, there has been very active coordinated development of national and international standards for computer graphics software and hardware systems. This work bore first fruit in 1985 with the publication of the Graphical Kernel System (GKS) both as an international and an American national standard. The Computer Graphics Metafile has since become the second in a series of specifications expected to emerge from the standards-making bodies into the "real world" of the computer graphics industry by the end of the 1980's.

One of the primary design goals for computer graphics standards is that they should comprise a family of interrelated, complementary components, each filling a particular role in the overall realm of graphics functionality. For example, it is expected that the Computer Graphics Interface (CGI) will be used to support implementations of GKS. GKS is normally seen to provide a relatively high-level applications interface with a very abstract graphics model, while CGI is intended to provide a low-level interface point, i.e. close to the graphics device, with a somewhat less abstract model of graphics functionality. Similarly, it was expected by the designers of both GKS and CGM that there would be a reasonable "fit" between the two standards, so that CGM could serve as a true GKS metafile. It is the purpose of this paper to explore this relationship in detail, pointing out where there is a good match, and where the fit is less than ideal.

The analysis is based on experience in implementing CGM as a component of NOVA*GKS, a proprietary implementation of the Graphical Kernel System. To date, NOVA*GKS supports only the binary encoding of CGM. However, most of the discussion is independent of encoding issues, and applies equally well to other possible CGM encodings.

The first section reviews the two relevant abstract models for graphics metafiles, the GKS metafile model and the CGM model. The next section covers the basic relationships among GKS, CGM and CGI. The bulk of the paper follows, with discussions of issues of CGM generation by a GKS implementation and of interpretation of a CGM by a GKS implementation. The final section contains some comments on work in progress to extend the functionality of CGM to more directly support its use within a GKS implementation.

2 The GKS Metafile Model and CGM

Support for metafile functionality is a significant part of the overall GKS specification. The concept of a graphics metafile and methods of interface to a metafile are explicit parts of the standard. The content of a metafile and the behavior of a metafile interpreter in the context of GKS is specified in Annex E of the GKS document. This annex defines a set of metafile items, consisting of well-defined "item types," logically equivalent to CGM "opcodes," each with a precisely defined (logical) record format. (Tables 1 and 2, located at the end of the paper, summarize GKSM and CGM components.) Rules of behavior are provided for the interpretation of these item types by the GKS function INTERPRET ITEM. The metafile specification in Annex E is usually referred to as GKSM, for GKS Metafile.

Annex E is non-specific about details of file organization and layout, indicating that for purposes of exchange of metafiles between different installations, "the physical structure of data sets . . . is outside the scope of [the GKS] standard." Indeed, Annex E itself is not part of the GKS standard. However, it does provide a reasonably complete specification of the form and function of a GKSM, and lacking any other specification, becomes the "de facto" specification for a GKSM.

GKS treats metafiles as special types of workstations, either of category MO, for output, or MI, for input. They may be opened, activated, deactivated, and closed just like other types of workstations. The GKS function OPEN WORKSTATION requires workstation type and workstation connection identification parameters. The connection identifier is used to define to the operating system a physical or logical connection to a workstation. The workstation type is used to specify the general class of the workstation that is being opened.

In the context of a metafile, the connection identifier can naturally be used to specify the name of the metafile in the operating system's file directory. The workstation type parameter is the only available path into GKS for specifying any specific characteristics of the metafile, such as the type of encoding being used. However, the specification of workstation type has been left unstandardized in GKS, so there is no well-defined technique for distinguishing between GKSM formatted metafiles and CGM files, or for distinguishing among the various possible encodings of either type of metafile.

GKSM is an audit trail of GKS functions at the workstation interface. It can be used to record all "transactions" of GKS functions and associated parameters to output workstations. It can be thought of in terms of a dynamic recording of GKS functions which can be used to reproduce a GKS session when "re-played" (interpreted). A GKSM is a purely sequential set of items, which must be read from start to finish for proper interpretation.

The CGM, in contrast to GKSM, is much more highly specified. Details of physical organization are specified to the bit level. Three different encodings have been developed, each with their own techniques for identification and representation of graphical information in CGM elements. CGM has more structure than GKSM: while GKSM is a simple sequential file, CGM is organized into picture bodies, each with their own identification. In this way, the CGM structure supports a limited level of direct access to pictures. The CGM organization has been syntactically specified; it is an error in structure if a CGM element occurs outside of its proper "state." There is extensive internal format control information in a CGM. For example, in a binary encoded CGM, it is possible to specify levels of precision for several different types of data, e.g. index precision, integer precision, real precision).

A CGM is intended to be used for static picture capture, rather than dynamic session capture as with GKSM. This accounts for the organization of a CGM as a set of distinct and independent picture bodies, each with their own associated control information (picture descriptions).

3 Relationships among GKS, CGM and CGI

Because of the close connection between CGM and CGI, it is useful to discuss the overall relationships among GKS, CGI and CGM.

It is tempting to assume that the relationship between CGI and CGM is analogous to that between GKS and GKSM, i. e. that CGM represents a "recording" of the data traffic passing "through" the CGI, just as GKSM can be used to "record" a GKS session. CGM is sometimes conceived of as a "near subset" of CGI functionality, and in fact, for functions (elements) common to CGI and CGM, identical encodings are defined.

This model is not valid, however, for several reasons. The CGI is a virtual device interface that specifies the behavior of a graphics device given input in the form of a properly encoded data stream. This ignores the broader question of a procedurally bound interface, but that is not really relevant to the discussion. The CGM is the specification of a static file, and does not directly address the correct behavior of an interpreter.

While it is true that the data contained in a CGM for the most part looks exactly like the data stream expected by a CGI device, a CGM file cannot be directly interpreted by a CGI device without the intervention of a higher level control program. This is unlike the relationship between GKS and GKSM: any item in a GKSM obtained via READ ITEM FROM GKSM is directly interpretable by the GKS INTERPRET ITEM function.

A CGM contains several elements that are unknown to CGI, for example delimiter elements and METAFILE DEFAULTS REPLACEMENT. In addition, certain CGM elements are constrained to occur only in a specific syntactic pattern, e. g. within a PICTURE BODY. CGI imposes no such constraints on its input.

If the CGI cannot be used to directly interpret a CGM file, then perhaps it could be used to generate a CGM? Again, the answer is "Unfortunately, no." The same non-CGI elements as before prevent this. A CGM must be organized into pictures; however CGI lacks the means of generating the proper delimiter elements. Also, at a more fundamental level, since CGI is really a device interface, it is not meaningful to speak of CGI being used to generate a CGM, which is not a graphics device at all.

Obviously, there has been a great deal of effort invested in maintaining a high level of compatibility between CGM and CGI, even to the extent that certain decisions made for CGM have directly determined similar choices for CGI as it has evolved. While the relationship between CGI and CGM is not exactly like that between GKS and GKSM, all of the pieces do fit together reasonably well. It does not require a lot of work to build a CGM interpreter given an implementation of the CGI; a small amount of overhead is required to handle file and device I/O coordination and to "filter out" non-CGI data elements. Similarly, much of the same code used to generate a CGI data stream is reusable to build a CGM generator interface callable from a client program. This has been the approach taken in NOVA*GKS. There is a common internal interface for generating data either to a CGM or to a CGI device.

4 Generation of a CGM by GKS

For purposes of generation by GKS at output level 2, a CGM is best thought of as a "dumb" output-only device such as a plotter. Since there is no support for setable bundles or for segments, these functions must be simulated by the GKS implementation's CGM "device driver" software. In particular, any action forcing a picture regeneration must be implemented by rewriting the modified picture to the output CGM. This is obviously rather expensive both in terms of the time required for regeneration from a software copy of workstation dependent segment storage as well as the file space required to store the modified picture frame. Interpretation of such a CGM reproduces the same pictures correctly, but again, there is a heavy penalty paid in redundant processing, especially if the output workstation used for the interpretation already efficiently supports GKS segment functionality. This case is especially frustrating since powerful workstation capabilities are being circumvented. This is a case where GKSM provides a much "nicer" level of functionality, since a trivial amount of data is involved in recording or processing a picture regeneration.

The following sections give a more detailed analysis of the mapping of GKS functionality to CGM elements. In several cases parameters are expected by the CGM element that are not available with the GKS function being performed. These include BEGIN METAFILE, and BEGIN PICTURE, which expect an identifying string. Arbitrarily chosen strings are written to the CGM in these cases. In other cases, the values used are stated explicitly.

4.1 Control Functions

OPEN WORKSTATION - The output file specified by the GKS connection identifier is created and initialized with the following elements (the type of encoding is determined from the workstation type):

BEGIN METAFILE (metafile name)
METAFILE VERSION (1)
METAFILE ELEMENTS LIST (DRAWING + CONTROL SET)
VDC TYPE (REAL)
BEGIN PICTURE (picture identifier)
BEGIN PICTURE BODY

CLOSE WORKSTATION - Generates the following elements and closes the metafile:

END PICTURE
END METAFILE

ACTIVATE WORKSTATION - Current attributes and clip rectangle from the GKS state list are written, to ensure that the output metafile state is up to date.

DEACTIVATE WORKSTATION - No output is generated; GKS suspends output to the CGM.

CLEAR WORKSTATION - Optionally generates the following elements, depending on the clearing control flag: if it is CONDITIONAL and the display surface empty flag is NOT EMPTY, or if the control flag is ALWAYS, then the elements are written:

END PICTURE
BEGIN PICTURE (picture identifier)
VDC EXTENT
BACKGROUND COLOR
BEGIN PICTURE BODY
current attributes
CLIP RECTANGLE

The VDC EXTENT, BACKGROUND COLOR, attribute elements and CLIP RECTANGLE must be written to override any internal CGM default values that may have been implicitly set by BEGIN PICTURE.

REDRAW ALL SEGMENTS ON WORKSTATION - See the discussion of segment functions below.

UPDATE WORKSTATION - If the update regeneration flag is POSTPONE, no action is strictly necessary, although as with other data stream-oriented device interfaces, this is a logical point to write any partially filled buffers to the output metafile, even though doing so will have no visible effect. If the update regeneration flag is PERFORM, an implicit regeneration may be triggered; this is equivalent to REDRAW ALL SEGMENTS, which is more fully described in the section below on segment functions.

SET DEFERRAL STATE - There is no equivalent CGM element; the CGM device driver software maintains the appropriate state values, and handles deferral and regeneration actions.

MESSAGE - Generates a CGM MESSAGE element, with the "action required" parameter set to NO ACTION.

ESCAPE - Generates an equivalent CGM ESCAPE element. It is necessary to perform the proper translation into CGM format of the GKS escape function parameters; until ESCAPE and GDP registration activities progress further, the exact format of CGM escape elements will be somewhat "ad hoc" and will necessarily be handled on a case-by-case basis.

4.2 Output Primitives

POLYLINE, POLYMARKER, FILL AREA - Map directly onto (CGM) POLYLINE, POLYMARKER and POLYGON, respectively.

TEXT - Maps onto CGM TEXT, with the "final" flag set to FINAL. GKS does not have the equivalent of APPEND TEXT.

CELL ARRAY - Generates a CELL ARRAY element.

GDP - Maps onto one of the standard CGM output primitives, if possible:

DISJOINT POLYLINE
RESTRICTED TEXT
POLYGON SET
RECTANGLE
CIRCLE
CIRCULAR ARC 3 POINT
CIRCULAR ARC 3 POINT CLOSE
CIRCULAR ARC CENTRE
CIRCULAR ARC CENTRE CLOSE
ELLIPSE
ELLIPTICAL ARC
ELLIPTICAL ARC CLOSE

If a GDP cannot be handled by one of the above cases, then it is mapped onto the CGM GDP element. The same comments as for ESCAPE apply equally here.

4.3 Output Attributes

The following list shows the GKS functions and CGM elements where there is direct support of GKS functionality:

GKS Function	CGM Element
SET POLYLINE INDEX	LINE BUNDLE INDEX
SET LINETYPE	LINE TYPE
SET LINEWIDTH SCALE FACTOR	LINE WIDTH
SET POLYLINE COLOR INDEX	LINE COLOR
SET POLYMARKER INDEX	MARKER BUNDLE INDEX
SET MARKER TYPE	MARKER TYPE
SET MARKER SIZE SCALE FACTOR	MARKER SIZE
SET POLYMARKER COLOR INDEX	MARKER COLOR
SET TEXT INDEX	TEXT BUNDLE INDEX
SET CHARACTER EXPAN FACTOR	CHARACTER EXPANSION
SET CHARACTER SPACING	CHARACTER SPACING
SET TEXT COLOR INDEX	TEXT COLOR
SET CHARACTER HEIGHT	CHARACTER HEIGHT
SET TEXT PATH	TEXT PATH
SET TEXT ALIGNMENT	TEXT ALIGNMENT
SET FILL AREA INDEX	FILL BUNDLE INDEX
SET FILL AREA INTERIOR STYLE	INTERIOR STYLE
SET FILL AREA COLOR INDEX	FILL COLOR
SET PATTERN SIZE	PATTERN SIZE
SET PATTERN REFERENCE POINT	FILL REFERENCE POINT
SET ASPECT SOURCE FLAGS	ASPECT SOURCE FLAGS

The following GKS functions require special consideration:

SET PICK IDENTIFIER - This function is not directly supported by CGM; this is a case where the GKS "audit trail" model is difficult to implement via CGM.

SET TEXT FONT AND PRECISION - Generates TEXT FONT INDEX and TEXT PRECISION elements.

SET CHARACTER UP VECTOR - Generates a CHARACTER ORIENTATION element, incorporating, as with a regular GKSM, both character up and base vectors.

SET FILL AREA STYLE INDEX - GKS uses a single interior style index for both patterns and hatch fill; depending on the value of the fill area interior style that is eventually bound, either a HATCH INDEX or a PATTERN INDEX element is written to the metafile. See the discussion in the next section on setting bundle representations.

Certain elements are generated under the assumption of default CGM mode settings. In particular, LINE WIDTH and MARKER SIZE elements require that the default settings of LINE WIDTH SPECIFICATION MODE and MARKER SIZE SPECIFICATION MODE (abstract) are in effect. Also, all of the color setting functions, e. g. SET POLYLINE COLOR INDEX, assume the default setting of COLOR SELECTION MODE (indexed).

4.4 Workstation Attributes

SET POLYLINE REPRESENTATION, SET POLYMARKER REPRESENTATION, SET TEXT REPRESENTATION, SET FILL AREA REPRESENTATION - These functions are not directly supported by CGM. As with segments, it is necessary for the GKS implementation to simulate this functionality at the device driver level. This can be accomplished by maintaining bundle tables in software and deferring attribute binding until an output primitive is to be generated to the metafile. All attributes are treated as if they are bound from individually set attributes in the GKS state list.

As a concrete example, assume the following sequence of GKS calls:

SET POLYLINE REPRESENTATION
SET POLYLINE INDEX (with the same index value)
SET LINETYPE ASPECT SOURCE FLAG (to BUNDLED)
POLYLINE

Nothing is written to the metafile until the POLYLINE call. The polyline bundle and aspect source flags are maintained in data structures in the device driver. When the POLYLINE call is received, the current polyline attributes are bound from the GKS state list, if the ASF is INDIVIDUAL, or from the bundle table entry pointed to by the polyline index value. In this case, the line type value is retrieved from the bundle table entry and a LINE TYPE element is written with that value. After elements for all polyline attributes have been written, a POLYLINE element is written to the metafile.

The implication of this technique is that no element of the form <xxx> INDEX is ever written to the CGM; nor do any ASPECT SOURCE FLAG elements ever get written, since there is no way to control the contents of setable bundles at interpretation time. Note also that the default setting for aspect source flags in a CGM is INDIVIDUAL.

SET PATTERN REPRESENTATION - Generates a PATTERN TABLE entry with one pattern table entry.

SET COLOR REPRESENTATION - Generates a COLOR TABLE element with one color value.

4.5 Transformation Functions

SET WINDOW, SET VIEWPORT, SELECT NORMALIZATION TRANSFORMATION - These functions cause elements affected by changes in the current normalization transformation to be written to the metafile, as with GKSM. These elements include CHARACTER HEIGHT, CHARACTER ORIENTATION, PATTERN SIZE and FILL REFERENCE POINT. SET VIEWPORT and SELECT NORMALIZATION TRANSFORMATION also generate a new CLIP RECTANGLE element, since these functions (may) change the current GKS clip rectangle definition.

SET CLIPPING INDICATOR - Generates a CLIP RECTANGLE element depending on the new value of the GKS clipping indicator. If it is NOCLIP, then a clip rectangle of (0,0,1,1) is written; if it is CLIP, the current GKS clip rectangle (current normalization transformation viewport) is written.

SET WORKSTATION WINDOW - Generates the same sequence of elements as CLEAR WORKSTATION, but for a slightly different reason. The only way to achieve the effect of a change to the workstation window is to write a VDC EXTENT element. However, this element may only occur as part of a CGM picture description (BEGIN PICTURE ... BEGIN PICTURE BODY sequence), so it is necessary to end the current picture and start a new one with the adjusted VDC extent.

SET WORKSTATION VIEWPORT - There is really no way to achieve the proper behavior of this GKS function in a CGM; the same sequence as with SET WORKSTATION WINDOW can be used to effect the desired change of scale, but since CGM does not have any facility for recording device coordinates, there is no way to achieve the proper placement of the workstation viewport on a display device at interpretation time. This GKS function can therefore only be partially implemented.

4.6 Segment Functions

CGM has no direct support for any segment functions. All segment manipulation and attribute setting must therefore be handled in device driver software. The workstation dependent segment storage (WDSS) is maintained by the driver. Whenever a picture regeneration is required, segments are "redrawn" to the CGM by a sequence of:

END PICTURE
BEGIN PICTURE
VDC EXTENT
BACKGROUND COLOR
BEGIN PICTURE BODY
reset attributes
CLIP RECTANGLE
output primitives and attributes from WDSS,
after segment attributes have been applied

4.7 Input Functions

These are not applicable to CGM output.

4.8 Metafile Functions

WRITE ITEM TO GKSM - generates an equivalent APPLICATION DATA element.

4.9 Inquiry Functions

These are not applicable to CGM output.

4.10 Error Handling

These are not applicable to CGM output.

5 Interpretation of a CGM by GKS

The interpretation of a CGM by NOVA*GKS follows the GKS Annex E rules of behavior, modified as necessary to fit the exigencies of CGM. That is, a CGM file is interpreted as if it were a GKSM. There are no constraints on the source of the CGM to be interpreted; subject to the conditions noted below, NOVA*GKS can interpret any properly encoded and structured CGM, even if it was not generated by NOVA*GKS.

The rest of this section describes the modifications to "normal" GKSM behavior necessary to interpret a CGM.

5.1 The visibility of a GKSM to a GKS application program

The interface to GKSM can be thought of as a "black box"; the GKS application program has no detailed information about the internal structure of individual metafile item data records. The contents are described by the GKS specification only in terms of logical content, not in terms of physical layout. The functions GET ITEM TYPE FROM GKSM, READ ITEM FROM GKSM and INTERPRET ITEM are assumed to share enough information about internal physical structure to be able to correctly interpret a GKSM, at least within the same implementation - transferring GKSMs among different GKS implementations is more difficult, and for the same reason.

Here is an example of a simple GKSM interpreter program fragment:

```
repeat
{

        GET ITEM TYPE FROM GKSM;

        if item_type = 0 then exit_loop;
        READ ITEM FROM GKSM;

        INTERPRET ITEM;

};
```

This program requires minimal information about what is being interpreted or even the nature of the metafile. The only control information it uses is the fact that an item type of zero indicates end of file. This type of program is useful for displaying the contents of a metafile, in toto.

Still, the application does maintain overall control, and may elect not to interpret certain items, or may interpret items from several different input metafiles to a single output workstation. In such cases, the application exerts processing control based at least on the item type, as shown in the next example:

```
repeat
{
        GET ITEM TYPE FROM GKSM;
        switch on item_type:
        {
        case POLYLINE:
                /* override current attributes */
                SET POLYLINE INDEX;
                .
                .
                .
        case TEXT:
                .
                .
                .
        }
        READ ITEM FROM GKSM;
        INTERPRET ITEM;
};
```

Finally, a more sophisticated program could actually modify the **content** of a metafile item prior to interpretation:

```
repeat
{
        GET ITEM TYPE FROM GKSM;
        READ ITEM FROM GKSM;
        switch on item_type:
        {
        case SET POLYLINE TYPE:
                (modify line style according to type of output device)
                .
                .
                .
        case SET TEXT FONT AND PRECISION:
                .
                .
                .
        }
        INTERPRET ITEM;
};
```

These examples illustrate a range of possibilities in using metafiles. The first two examples, which are easily implemented using GKSM, require little knowledge about the contents of the metafile. The last example would be difficult to implement using a standard GKS metafile interface. However, the CGM specification does provide the detailed level of information about metafile element content required to make this type of application. A very simple example of such a modifiable metafile system is to use a text editor to modify the contents of a cleartext encoded CGM.

5.2 Mapping of CGM element opcodes to GKSM item types

There is no direct correspondence between CGM element identifiers and GKSM item types. In order for GKS to properly interpret a CGM element, there must be a well-defined mapping from CGM element identifiers (opcodes) to GKS item types. This mapping applies only to the functions GET ITEM TYPE FROM GKSM and INTERPRET ITEM, for which the item type is a parameter. It must be assumed that the application program is smart enough to know, based on the workstation type used in OPEN WORKSTATION and the workstation identifier used in GET ITEM TYPE, which type of metafile is being interpreted, i. e. whether it is a "pure" GKSM or a CGM, and to allow for this mapping of item types. For example, an item type corresponding to a POLYLINE item in a GKSM will not have the same value as an equivalent one from a CGM.

The mapping from CGM opcodes to GKS item types is defined by the following relationship:

GKS_item = - (128 * CGM_element_class + CGM_element_id),

where the element class and identifier values are taken from the binary encoding for CGM. The mapping is independent of any particular CGM encoding, being based only on the abstract element class/identifier values for CGM elements. The binary encoding opcodes are used simply as a "normal form" for defining this mapping.

This mapping forces all CGM-derived item types to be negative (in the range [-1000..-1]), thus avoiding any confusion with "normal" GKSM item types, which are non-negative, or GKSM user data items, which are required to be greater than 100. Note that this mapping is particular to NOVA*GKS; other GKS implementations may choose a different scheme. In that sense a small degree of non-portability of GKS applications is being introduced, but for lack of any other standardized way of doing this, it is unavoidable.

5.3 Syntactic Error Checking

The structure of a CGM must conform to a well-defined syntactic specification, in the sense that it is possible to treat a sequence of CGM elements as a "string" in a language that can be generated by a certain context-free grammar (see Annex A of Part 1 of the CGM specification for more specific details on the CGM abstract grammar). A GKSM is simply a sequence of metafile items, with minimal structural constraints. There is a required metafile header followed by zero or more item records, followed by an end item. The question arises as to how much a GKS implementation should "worry about" checking for the syntactic integrity of an input CGM. Obviously, a GKS implementation should be able to generate a correctly formed CGM file. On interpretation, if NOVA*GKS detects a CGM element out of place, it logs an appropriate error to the GKS error log and attempts to continue processing the remainder of the file.

The exact behavior of NOVA*GKS as it interprets each CGM element is described next. Those elements that cannot be interpreted cause no change in the state of GKS or of any open workstation, and an error is logged to the GKS error logging file, where appropriate.

5.4 Delimiter Elements

BEGIN METAFILE - This must be the first metafile element. It is read as part of OPEN WORKSTATION processing. At the same time, all elements up to, but not including, BEGIN PICTURE are also processed by OPEN WORKSTATION, not by INTERPRET ITEM. The metafile identifier is ignored.

END METAFILE - This is equivalent to GKSM item 0 (end of metafile), and is assumed to be the last element in the file.

BEGIN PICTURE - All CGM default values are reset in the GKS state list, and in the state lists of all active workstations, as appropriate.

An interesting problem arises here if several input metafiles are being interpreted simultaneously. The CGM default values to be reset are maintained internally in a metafile description table structure (see the discussion below on metafile descriptor elements). However, the resetting of defaults must be controlled by INTERPRET ITEM, which has no knowledge of which CGM was the source of the element, since there is no workstation identifier parameter passed to this function. One alternative might be for GET ITEM FOR GKSM or READ ITEM FROM GKSM to update the GKS and workstations states, but this would be an undesirable hidden side effect, and would not allow the possibility to the application of not interpreting this element. The attributes would be reset whether or not the application invoked INTERPRET ITEM.

Another alternative is to "secretly" maintain the workstation identifier as part of the data structure returned from READ ITEM FROM GKSM. This would provide INTERPRET ITEM with the information it needs to select the proper default attribute settings.

The picture identifier read from this element is ignored. GKS provides no mechanism for direct access to individual picture frames within a CGM. A CGM being interpreted by GKS is treated as a sequential file. A useful GKS escape function could be implemented to provide access to the picture identifier, thus allowing at least at least a primitive type of metafile "scanning" capability.

BEGIN PICTURE BODY - Interpretation of this element causes a CLEAR WORKSTATION on all active workstations.

END PICTURE - Interpretation of this element causes is equivalent to UPDATE WORKSTATION on all active workstations with the update regeneration flag set to POSTPONE. This is not strictly necessary; however, it seems to be a natural action to take at the end of a picture. Note that only deferred output is displayed; a pending regeneration is not forced.

5.5 Metafile Descriptor Elements

These elements are processed by OPEN WORKSTATION; some identification data is ignored. VDC TYPE and precision setting elements control decoding of subsequent metafile elements only; data from these elements is used to initialize an internal "metafile description table" structure (MFDT) for each input metafile.

The metafile description table structure is not the same as the normal GKS workstation description table for the metafile workstation type. Each open CGM has its own separately maintained MFDT, used only for storing default values needed for decoding and interpretation of the CGM and for resetting defaults after each END PICTURE element.

The implication of this approach is that none of the CGM metafile description information can be made available to the application. Similarly, CGM elements which are used purely for control of data representation, e. g. INTEGER PRECISION, have no effect on the state of GKS or any output workstations. In effect, they are "invisible" to the application. The one exception to this would be the case where GKS is interpreting a CGM to a CGI output device which can accept all of the detailed control information available in a CGM. The problem lies in making the internal connection between the CGM and the CGI; the structural requirement inherent in the GKSM model is that all data read from the metafile "passes through" the application program and then through INTERPRET ITEM. A more direct connection is clearly desirable if a CGI is to be used as an output workstation receiving its data from a CGM.

METAFILE VERSION - This is a required element. The version number is checked. Only version 1 is supported; any other value causes a failure of OPEN WORKSTATION.

METAFILE DESCRIPTION - The metafile description text is ignored.

VDC TYPE - The MFDT is updated. The VDC type and other control parameters are used when reading and decoding the metafile elements. For simplicity of internal data communication, all data read from the CGM is "normalized" into a set of standard representations which are independent of the type of encoding and current control parameters. For example, all VDC coordinates are represented as floating point values. If the VDC type is INTEGER, coordinates are converted to floating point as they are read.

INTEGER PRECISION, REAL PRECISION, INDEX PRECISION, COLOR PRECISION, COLOR INDEX PRECISION - The MFDT is updated. As before, these elements are used purely for decoding the metafile. They have no effect on interpretation.

MAXIMUM COLOR INDEX, COLOR VALUE EXTENT - These elements are used to define a mapping from CGM direct color values to GKS color representations. The color value extent defines minimum and maximum direct color value components; these are mapped onto the range [0..1] in the GKS color representations.

METAFILE ELEMENT LIST - This element is ignored. Any element in the metafile that is not supported by NOVA*GKS is reported in the GKS error logging file as it is read.

METAFILE DEFAULTS REPLACEMENT - This is actually a set of other metafile elements, used to reset default values for the remainder of the metafile. The MFDT is updated accordingly.

FONT LIST - CGM uses font names, while GKS uses font numbers. A mapping from names to GKS font indices must therefore be established. The list of font names read from the CGM is matched against a table of available fonts for NOVA*GKS; a new table is built that can be used to map CGM font indices, corresponding to the list of font names read from the CGM, to GKS font numbers.

For example, suppose the CGM font list consists of the following font names (the name format is based on the TOP/MAP Application Profile):

NBS HERSHEY:TRIPLEX_ROMAN
NBS HERSHEY:COMPLEX_GREEK
NBS HERSHEY:TRIPLEX_ITALIC

A font index is implicitly assigned to each of these names, starting with index 1.

This is the list of available NOVA*GKS (Hershey stroke) fonts:

Font No.	Font Name
-1	HERSHEY:SIMPLEX_ROMAN
-2	HERSHEY:DUPLEX_ROMAN
-3	HERSHEY:TRIPLEX_ROMAN
-4	HERSHEY:SIMPLEX_SCRIPT
-5	HERSHEY:GOTHIC_ENGLISH
-6	HERSHEY:COMPLEX_ROMAN
-7	HERSHEY:COMPLEX_ITALIC
-8	HERSHEY:TRIPLEX_ITALIC
-9	HERSHEY:COMPLEX_SCRIPT
-10	HERSHEY:SIMPLEX_GREEK
-11	HERSHEY:COMPLEX_GREEK
-12	HERSHEY:GOTHIC_GERMAN
-13	HERSHEY:GOTHIC_ITALIAN
-14	HERSHEY:CYRILLIC

By matching the names in the two lists, a table is generated as part of the MFDT, mapping CGM font indices to GKS font numbers, to be used in processing subsequent TEXT-related output:

CGM index	GKS font number
1	-3
2	-11
3	-8

CHARACTER SET LIST, CHARACTER CODING ANNOUNCER - These elements are ignored. Only the standard printable ASCII character set is supported.

5.6 Picture Descriptor Elements

Certain of these elements are used to update an internal "metafile state list" (MFSL) structure, which contains modal parameters used in decoding subsequent metafile elements. The values of the modal parameters may be reset to their defaults by interpreting BEGIN PICTURE, from values stored in the metafile description table. The metafile state list structure is not the same as the normal GKS workstation state list that is maintained for the metafile workstation.

The relationship between the metafile description table and the metafile state list is analogous to that in GKS between the workstation description table and the workstation state list: the MFDT contains static, invariant control information, while the MFSL can be dynamically changed with each new picture in the metafile. Unlike the GKS workstation state list, however, the MFSL is reset to its default state at the end of each picture, using information contained in the MFDT. The GKS workstation state list is initialized only at OPEN WORKSTATION.

SCALING MODE - The MFSL is updated.

COLOR SELECTION MODE - The MFSL is updated. GKS does not support direct color specification. Any use of this specification mode (with, for example, LINE COLOR) is ignored, and an error logged by GKS. If the COLOR SPECIFICATION MODE value is DIRECT, an error is logged. However, it is necessary to retain the proper setting of the color selection mode in the MFSL, since the physical format of subsequent elements may be determined by its setting.

There are techniques available that would allow GKS to support this functionality. For example, the color representation that "most nearly" matches the direct color specification can be found by using a simple 3-dimensional Euclidean distance function. NOVA*GKS does not attempt to solve this problem; only indexed color representations are supported.

LINE WIDTH SPECIFICATION MODE, MARKER SIZE SPECIFICATION MODE, EDGE WIDTH SPECIFICATION MODE - The MFSL is updated.

VDC EXTENT - VDC coordinate space is logically equivalent to NDC coordinate space in GKS. However, NDC coordinates are constrained to the range [0..1] in both x and y, while VDC coordinates may have any range of values as determined by VDC INTEGER PRECISION or VDC REAL PRECISION. If the VDC extent is a subset of the unit square, then VDC coordinates can be used directly by GKS. Otherwise, an implicit transformation will be defined to map the VDC extent into the NDC unit square, such that the lower left corner of the VDC extent rectangle maps onto (0,0) in NDC space. All VDC coordinates will then be subject to this transformation as they are read from the metafile.

The (possibly transformed) VDC extent rectangle is used to define the current workstation window on all active workstations. Note that this may cause an implicit regeneration on all workstations.

BACKGROUND COLOR - Interpretation of this element is equivalent to SET COLOR REPRESENTATION for color index 0 on all active workstations.

5.7 Control Elements

Data from these elements are used to update the MFSL; they may occur within a picture body. The VDC precision setting functions are used only for decoding subsequent metafile elements containing VDC coordinate data.

VDC INTEGER PRECISION, VDC REAL PRECISION - The MFSL is updated.

AUXILIARY COLOR, TRANSPARENCY - These elements are ignored.

CLIP RECTANGLE - If the current value of the GKS clipping indicator is CLIP, the clip rectangle read from the CGM (as transformed into NDC space - see VDC EXTENT) is used to define the workstation window on all active workstations. The possibly transformed clip rectangle is used to update the current "clip rectangle" entry in the GKS state list.

CLIP INDICATOR - Equivalent to SET CLIPPING INDICATOR.

5.8 Graphical Primitive Elements

GKSM points are assumed to be in normalized device coordinates (NDC). They are therefore not subject to a normalization transformation. In general, any CGM element that is not directly supported by GKS is interpreted as a GKS GDP. See also the discussion above on generation of CGM escape and GDP elements.

POLYLINE - Interpretation of this element is equivalent to (GKS) POLYLINE.

DISJOINT POLYLINE - This element is interpreted as a GKS GDP.

POLYMARKER - Interpretation of this element is equivalent to (GKS) POLYMARKER.

TEXT, APPEND TEXT - There are two choices for interpreting these related elements. The first is to treat CGM TEXT like GKS TEXT by ignoring the final flag parameter. "Ignore" is not quite the right word; if a value of NOT FINAL is detected, the initial text string will be processed by GKS, with a warning message logged to the GKS error log indicating that subsequent APPEND TEXT elements will be ignored. The other approach is to implement both TEXT and APPEND TEXT as GKS GDP's, fully supporting the intended CGM interpreter behavior. At the present, NOVA*GKS takes the first approach, although future versions will probably support the second option.

RESTRICTED TEXT - This element is interpreted as a GKS GDP.

POLYGON, POLYGON SET - The situation here is similar to that with TEXT. Since CGM has functionality that is not directly available in GKS, one is faced with a choice of implementation alternatives. Either POLYGON can be treated like GKS FILL AREA by "ignoring" unsupported interior style options (EMPTY) and edge attribute elements, i. e. edges must always be invisible; or CGM functionality can be supported by a combination of GKS GDP and ESCAPE functions which can be used to properly implement the expected CGM interpreter behavior. As with TEXT, we have initially taken the "conservative" approach of implementing only the GKS subset behavior, with releases in the near future supporting full CGM functionality.

CELL ARRAY - If the CGM cell array is a rectangle with sides parallel to the x and y coordinate axes, the interpretation of this element is equivalent to (GKS) CELL ARRAY. If the cell array is non rectangular (a parallelogram) or not aligned with the axes, then the element cannot be interpreted by GKS. However, it can be broken down into a series of FILL AREAs, at some cost in performance.

GENERALIZED DRAWING PRIMITIVE - This is equivalent to (GKS) GDP.

RECTANGLE, CIRCLE, CIRCULAR ARC 3 POINT, CIRCULAR ARC 3 POINT CLOSE, CIRCULAR ARC CENTRE, CIRCULAR ARC CENTRE CLOSE, ELLIPSE, ELLIPTICAL ARC, ELLIPTICAL ARC CLOSE - These elements are interpreted as GKS GDP's.

5.9 Attribute Elements

The following list shows the GKS functions and CGM elements where there is more or less equivalent functionality:

CGM Element	GKS Function
LINE BUNDLE INDEX	SET POLYLINE INDEX
LINE TYPE	SET LINETYPE
LINE WIDTH	SET LINEWIDTH SCALE FACTOR
LINE COLOR	SET POLYLINE COLOR INDEX
MARKER BUNDLE INDEX	SET POLYMARKER INDEX
MARKER TYPE	SET MARKER TYPE
MARKER SIZE	SET MARKER SIZE SCALE FACTOR
MARKER COLOR	SET POLYMARKER COLOR INDEX
TEXT BUNDLE INDEX	SET TEXT INDEX
CHARACTER EXPAN FACTOR	SET CHARACTER EXPAN FACTOR
CHARACTER SPACING	SET CHARACTER SPACING
TEXT COLOR	SET TEXT COLOR INDEX
CHARACTER HEIGHT	SET CHARACTER HEIGHT
TEXT PATH	SET TEXT PATH
TEXT ALIGNMENT	SET TEXT ALIGNMENT
FILL BUNDLE INDEX	SET FILL AREA INDEX
INTERIOR STYLE	SET FILL AREA INTERIOR STYLE
FILL COLOR	SET FILL AREA COLOR INDEX
HATCH INDEX	SET FILL AREA STYLE INDEX
PATTERN INDEX	SET FILL AREA STYLE INDEX
FILL REFERENCE POINT	SET PATTERN REFERENCE POINT
PATTERN TABLE	SET PATTERN REPRESENTATION
PATTERN SIZE	SET PATTERN SIZE
COLOR TABLE	SET COLOR REPRESENTATION
ASPECT SOURCE FLAGS	SET ASPECT SOURCE FLAGS

Deviations from "equivalence" will now be noted:

LINE WIDTH, MARKER SIZE - GKS does not support absolute size specification, as does CGM. Only abstract scaling is implemented in NOVA*GKS.

LINE COLOR, MARKER COLOR, TEXT COLOR, FILL COLOR - only indexed colors are allowed; if the current color specification mode is DIRECT, an error is logged to the GKS error file and these elements are ignored.

TEXT FONT INDEX, TEXT PRECISION - Interpretation of these elements is equivalent to SET TEXT FONT AND PRECISION, using the current value of "text precision" from the GKS state list. The current GKS text font and precision is inquired, and one of the two parameters is modified, leaving the other unchanged.

CHARACTER ORIENTATION - As with GKSM, interpretation of this element causes the current character up and base vectors in the GKS state list to be updated.

TEXT ALIGNMENT - Interpretation of this element is equivalent to SET TEXT ALIGNMENT, unless "continuous" alignment is indicated, either horizontally or vertically. In that case, the function is not supported, and an error is logged to the GKS error logging file.

CHARACTER SET INDEX, ALTERNATE CHARACTER SET INDEX - These elements are ignored. Only the standard ASCII printable character set is supported. (See also CHARACTER SET LIST and CHARACTER CODING ANNOUNCER SET.)

INTERIOR STYLE - Interpretation of this element is equivalent to SET FILL AREA INTERIOR STYLE, except that interior style EMPTY is not supported.

EDGE BUNDLE INDEX, EDGE TYPE, EDGE WIDTH, EDGE COLOR, EDGE VISIBILITY - These elements are not presently interpreted by NOVA*GKS. GKS has no equivalent functions. In future releases of NOVA*GKS, these will be supported using GKS escape functions, in conjunction with POLYGON/POLYGON SET GDPs.

PATTERN TABLE - Interpretation of this element is equivalent to repeated instances of SET PATTERN REPRESENTATION.

COLOR TABLE - Interpretation of this element is equivalent to repeated instances of SET COLOR REPRESENTATION.

ASPECT SOURCE FLAGS - Interpretation of this element is equivalent to SET ASPECT SOURCE FLAGS, insofar as ASF's directly supported by GKS are concerned. For all others, the MFSL is updated. "All others" means edge attribute ASF's and separated hatch/pattern and text font/precision ASF's.

5.10 Escape Element

ESCAPE - Interpretation of this element is equivalent to GKS ESCAPE. See the comments under generation of escape elements.

5.11 External Elements

MESSAGE - Interpretation of this element is equivalent to GKS MESSAGE; the "attention required flag" is ignored.

APPLICATION DATA - This element is treated as a GKSM user item, and as such it cannot be interpreted by GKS.

6 Notes on the CGEM Work in Progress

In this final section, the "problem areas" that have been identified in integrating CGM into the GKS environment will be briefly reviewed, with comments relative to current efforts to extend CGM to support GKS requirements.

Clearly the main problem areas are the lack of setable bundle representations and segment handling capabilities. The addition of suitable CGM elements to support these functions would greatly simplify the GKS interface, and improve the performance of GKS-based interpreters. These elements should obviously be based on the current CGI model, which is certainly sufficient for the requirements of GKS. The other significant problem noted was the lack of a technique for implementing SET WORKSTATION VIEWPORT. Again, CGI has an equivalent function (DEVICE VIEWPORT) which should serve as the basis for extending CGM. The only element that does not seem to have been taken into account in current CGEM work is support for SET PICK IDENTIFIER. The current pick identifier is maintained in the GKS state list, and GKS expects GKSM to be able to record all current attributes.

Problems of interpretation are by and large due to insufficiencies in GKS, rather than missing features in CGM, where CGM/CGI have functionality beyond that supported by GKS. Rather than extending CGM, it is more a matter of determining how to extend GKS on its next update. Areas for alignment might include the addition of POLYGON/POLYGON SET and edge attributes, TEXT/APPEND TEXT functions, as well as a generalized COLOR TABLE function along the lines of CGI/CGM.

Appendix - Tables of GKSM and CGM Components

In Table 1, GKSM item types are indicated, where applicable; letters in parenthesis refer to notes immediately following the table.

In Table 2, opcodes from the binary encoding for CGM are indicated; these are used to derive GKSM item type values for interpretation by NOVA*GKS.

Table 1: GKS Functions Relevant to GKSM

Control Functions

Item Type	CGM Element
(a)	OPEN WORKSTATION
0	CLOSE WORKSTATION
(b)	ACTIVATE WORKSTATION
n/a	DEACTIVATE WORKSTATION
1	CLEAR WORKSTATION
2	REDRAW ALL SEGMENTS ON WORKSTATION
3	UPDATE WORKSTATION
4	SET DEFERRAL STATE
5	MESSAGE
6	ESCAPE

Output Primitives

11	POLYLINE
12	POLYMARKER
13	TEXT
14	FILL AREA
15	CELL ARRAY
16	GENERALIZED DRAWING PRIMITIVE

Output Attributes

21	SET POLYLINE INDEX
22	SET LINETYPE
23	SET LINEWIDTH SCALE FACTOR
24	SET POLYLINE COLOR INDEX
25	SET POLYMARKER INDEX
26	SET MARKER TYPE
27	SET MARKER SIZE SCALE FACTOR
28	SET POLYMARKER COLOR INDEX

Table 1 continued

Item Type	CGM Element
29	SET TEXT INDEX
30	SET TEXT FONT AND PRECISION
31	SET CHARACTER EXPANSION FACTOR
32	SET CHARACTER SPACING
33	SET TEXT COLOR INDEX
34(c)	SET CHARACTER HEIGHT
34(c)	SET CHARACTER UP VECTOR
35	SET TEXT PATH
36	SET TEXT ALIGNMENT
37	SET FILL AREA INDEX
38	SET FILL AREA INTERIOR STYLE
39	SET FILL AREA STYLE INDEX
40	SET FILL AREA COLOR INDEX
41	SET PATTERN SIZE
42	SET PATTERN REFERENCE POINT
43	SET ASPECT SOURCE FLAGS
44	SET PICK IDENTIFIER
Workstation Attributes	
51	SET POLYLINE REPRESENTATION
52	SET POLYMARKER REPRESENTATION
53	SET TEXT REPRESENTATION
54	SET FILL AREA REPRESENTATION
55	SET PATTERN REPRESENTATION
56	SET COLOR REPRESENTATION
Transformation Functions	
(d)	SET WINDOW
(d,e)	SET VIEWPORT
(d,e)	SELECT NORMALIZATION TRANSFORMATION
61(e)	SET CLIPPING INDICATOR
71	SET WORKSTATION WINDOW
72	SET WORKSTATION VIEWPORT
Segment Functions	
81	CREATE SEGMENT
82	CLOSE SEGMENT
83	RENAME SEGMENT
84	DELETE SEGMENT

Table 1 continued

Item Type	CGM Element
85	DELETE SEGMENT FROM WORKSTATION
(f,g)	ASSOCIATE SEGMENT WITH WORKSTATION
(g)	COPY SEGMENT TO WORKSTATION
(g)	INSERT SEGMENT
Segment Attributes	
91	SET SEGMENT TRANSFORMATION
92	SET VISIBILITY
93	SET HIGHLIGHTING
94	SET SEGMENT PRIORITY
95	SET DETECTABILITY
Metafile Functions	
>100	WRITE ITEM TO GKSM
n/a	GET, READ and INTERPRET ITEM TYPE FROM GKSM
Inquiry Functions	
n/a	(workstation state list inquiry functions)

Notes on Table 1:

a For an output metafile, the metafile header is written, followed by item 1 (CLEAR WORKSTATION) with a clearing control flag of CONDITIONAL. For an input metafile, the metafile header is read.

b For an output metafile, items 61 and 21-44 are written to the metafile to ensure that the metafile reflects the current state of GKS transformations and attributes.

c Character height and up vector are combined into a single metafile item.

d On output, items affected by changes to the current normalization transformation are written; these include items 34 (character height/up vector), 41 and 42 (pattern specification).

e A single item (61) is used to encode clipping information (clipping indicator and clip rectangle). On output, this item is written whenever there is a change to the current normalization transformation viewport or to the clipping indicator. Interpretation of this item sets the GKS clipping rectangle and sets the GKS clipping indicator to CLIP.

f ASSOCIATE SEGMENT WITH (metafile) WORKSTATION is achieved by writing item 81, followed by items generated according to note (g), followed by item 82.

g Items are written to the metafile that correspond to the graphical primitives and their attributes contained in the segment in workstation independent segment storage (WISS).

Table 2: CGM Elements

Opcodes from the CGM binary encoding (element class and element identifier) are listed with each element.

Delimiter Elements

Opcodes	CGM Element
0/1	BEGIN METAFILE
0/2	END METAFILE
0/3	BEGIN PICTURE
0/4	BEGIN PICTURE BODY
0/5	END PICTURE

Metafile Descriptor Elements

1/1	METAFILE VERSION
1/2	METAFILE DESCRIPTION
1/3	VDC TYPE
1/4	INTEGER PRECISION
1/5	REAL PRECISION
1/6	INDEX PRECISION
1/7	COLOR PRECISION
1/8	COLOR INDEX PRECISION
1/9	MAXIMUM COLOR INDEX
1/10	COLOR VALUE EXTENT
1/11	METAFILE ELEMENT LIST
1/12	METAFILE DEFAULTS REPLACEMENT
1/13	FONT LIST
1/14	CHARACTER SET LIST
1/15	CHARACTER CODING ANNOUNCER

Picture Descriptor Elements

2/1	SCALING MODE
2/2	COLOR SELECTION MODE

Table 2 continued

Opcodes	CGM Element
2/3	LINE WIDTH SPECIFICATION MODE
2/4	MARKER SIZE SPECIFICATION MODE
2/5	EDGE WIDTH SPECIFICATION MODE
2/6	VDC EXTENT
2/7	BACKGROUND COLOR
Control Elements	
3/1	VDC INTEGER PRECISION
3/2	VDC REAL PRECISION
3/3	AUXILIARY COLOR
3/4	TRANSPARENCY
3/5	CLIP RECTANGLE
3/6	CLIP INDICATOR
Graphical Primitive Elements	
4/1	POLYLINE
4/2	DISJOINT POLYLINE
4/3	POLYMARKER
4/4	TEXT
4/5	RESTRICTED TEXT
4/6	APPEND TEXT
4/7	POLYGON
4/8	POLYGON SET
4/9	CELL ARRAY
4/10	GENERALIZED DRAWING PRIMITIVE
4/11	RECTANGLE
4/12	CIRCLE
4/13	CIRCULAR ARC 3 POINT
4/14	CIRCULAR ARC 3 POINT CLOSE
4/15	CIRCULAR ARC CENTRE
4/16	CIRCULAR ARC CENTRE CLOSE
4/17	ELLIPSE
4/18	ELLIPTICAL ARC
4/19	ELLIPTICAL ARC CLOSE
Attribute Elements	
5/1	LINE BUNDLE INDEX
5/2	LINE TYPE
5/3	LINE WIDTH

Table 2 continued

Opcodes	CGM Element
5/4	LINE COLOR
5/5	MARKER BUNDLE INDEX
5/6	MARKER TYPE
5/7	MARKER SIZE
5/8	MARKER COLOR
5/9	TEXT BUNDLE INDEX
5/10	TEXT FONT INDEX
5/11	TEXT PRECISION
5/12	CHARACTER EXPANSION FACTOR
5/13	CHARACTER SPACING
5/14	TEXT COLOR
5/15	CHARACTER HEIGHT
5/16	CHARACTER ORIENTATION
5/17	TEXT PATH
5/18	TEXT ALIGNMENT
5/19	CHARACTER SET INDEX
5/20	ALTERNATE CHARACTER SET INDEX
5/21	FILL BUNDLE INDEX
5/22	INTERIOR STYLE
5/23	FILL COLOR
5/24	HATCH INDEX
5/25	PATTERN INDEX
5/26	EDGE BUNDLE INDEX
5/27	EDGE TYPE
5/28	EDGE WIDTH
5/29	EDGE COLOR
5/30	EDGE VISIBILITY
5/31	FILL REFERENCE POINT
5/32	PATTERN TABLE
5/33	PATTERN SIZE
5/34	COLOR TABLE
5/35	ASPECT SOURCE FLAGS

Escape Element

6/1	ESCAPE

External Elements

7/1	MESSAGE
7/2	APPLICATION DATA

Technical and Office Protocols (TOP) CGM Application Profile

K.Hardman

Abstract

The TOP CGM application profile was developed by the TOP Graphics Subcommittee, under the auspices of the MAP/TOP Users Group. The purpose of this profile is to promote interoperability between different implementations of the CGM. The TOP CGM Application Profile is the culmination of work done by the TOP Graphics Subcommittee, and comments received from a public review period which ended in March 1987.

1 Introduction

TOP defines interoperability in an OSI (Open Systems Interconnection) environment. To interchange files the use of MHS (Message Handling System) or FTAM (File Transfer and Access Mechanism) is specified. OSI defines how information is exchanged between two systems, but not the format of the information. That is where standards such as CGM, ODA (Office Document Architecture), IGES (Interactive Graphics Exchange Specification), etc., come into play. These data formats are needed to exchange meaningful information.

The purpose of the application profile is to define implementation constraints and conformance characteristics. CGM implementations adhering to the application profile will be able to be integrated into other application processes, such as compound document interchange.

The TOP Version 3.0 Specification will be finalized in June 1988, concurrent with the Enterprise Networking Event '88 International (ENE '88i). ENE '88i will be held in Baltimore, Maryland, USA, June 6-8, 1988, and will demonstrate MAP/TOP implementations.

A goal of the TOP Graphics Subcommittee is to make the TOP CGM application profile compatible with other CGM application profiles, such as CALS (Computer-aided Acquisition and Logistic Support), for the purpose of interoperability. Comments and suggestions are gladly welcomed.

The TOP CGM Application Profile which follows, is a copy of the TOP Graphics Subcommittee's working document which has been edited after an errata change period and is scheduled to be in the finalized TOP Version 3.0 Specifications.

To obtain a complete copy of the TOP Version 3.0 Specifications contact the following:

TOP 3.0 Specification
Society for Manufacturing Engineers
One SME Drive
P.O. Box 930
Dearborn, MI 48121
USA

The TOP Application Profile

Extracted from TOP V3.0 IR (extract - edited)

6.2 Computer Graphics Metafile

This section defines the TOP CGM Application Profile (AP) for the Computer Graphics Metafile Interchange Format Building Block. The functional description and binding rules for this building block are found in Chapter 2, Section 2.4.10.

6.2.1 CGM Introduction

The TOP CGM AP defines the conformance characteristics or permissible combinations for all possible data streams that are specified in the profile. In addition, the TOP CGM AP defines additional requirements for transmitting, receiving, interpreting and handling valid CGM data streams. The definition of such implementation constraints is usually outside the scope of an ISO standard. However, such APs are required and necessary to insure uniform implementation of such standards, especially where interchange in an open system environment is concerned.

6.2.2 CGM Scope

The TOP CGM AP defines the CGM implementation that is required for computer graphics picture information interchange. CGM implementations that conform to this AP will be able to be integrated into other application processes such as compound document interchange. This AP can, in the future, be supplemented by additional CGM APs.

6.2.3 Definitions

APPLICATION PROFILE - A specification that defines the use of an International Standard, with a definition of all possible data streams that conform to that profile. An AP insures interoperability of implementations of an International Standard.

BASIC VALUE - The subset of permissible values for parameters of a CGM element that are mandatory for conformance to this AP.

CGM MI - A CGM metafile input workstation.

CGM MO - A CGM metafile output workstation.

COMPOUND DOCUMENT - A digital analog of a document containing more than one component objects (such as character, computer graphics, image or facsimile data).

COMPOUND DOCUMENT INTERCHANGE FORMAT - The specification for a mechanism for storing and transferring a compound document. Refer to ISO 8613.

COMPUTER GRAPHICS INTERFACE (CGI) - The specification for interface techniques with graphical devices.

COMPUTER GRAPHICS METAFILE (CGM) - The specification for a mechanism for storing and transferring picture description information. Refer to ISO 8632.

DATA INTERFACE - The communication boundary (i.e., interface) between software modules or devices comprising one or more operation codes and data (as contrasted with a subroutine call interface).

DEFAULT VALUE - The implicit value for a parameter of a CGM element. For example, default Metafile Name in Begin Metafile element is a null string.

DEVICE DRIVER - The device-dependent portion of a graphics system which supports a physical device. The device driver generates device class specific output.

GRAPHICAL KERNAL SYSTEM - A standardized application programmer's interface to graphics systems. Refer to ISO 7942.

METAFILE - Synonymous with CGM. A representation for the storage and transfer of graphical data and control information. This information contains a device-independent description of one or more pictures.

METAFILE GENERATOR - Synonymous with CGM Generator. The software or hardware that creates a picture or conveys information in the CGM representation.

METAFILE INTERPRETER - Synonymous with CGM Interpreter. The software or hardware that reads the CGM and interprets the contents.

PERMISSIBLE VALUES - The range of valid values for a parameter of a CGM element as specified in ISO 8632.

VIRTUAL DEVICE - An idealized computer graphics device that presents a set of graphics capabilities to graphics software of systems via the CGI.

NOTE: Refer to ISO 8632, clause 3 and ISO 7942, clause 3, for further definitions of computer graphics terms.

6.2.4 CGM Architectural Concepts

The CGM is designed to be usable and useful to a wide range of applications, graphics systems, and devices or workstations. The CGM is graphics system independent, as well as device independent. The CGM is created by a CGM Generator. The CGM Generator resides at the level of the device driver and is invoked by the application callable layer. The CGM Generator can be used to record device-independent picture descriptions, conceptually in parallel with the presentation of images on actual devices. Figure 6.2-1 illustrates the TOP Graphics Reference Model for creation of the CGM.

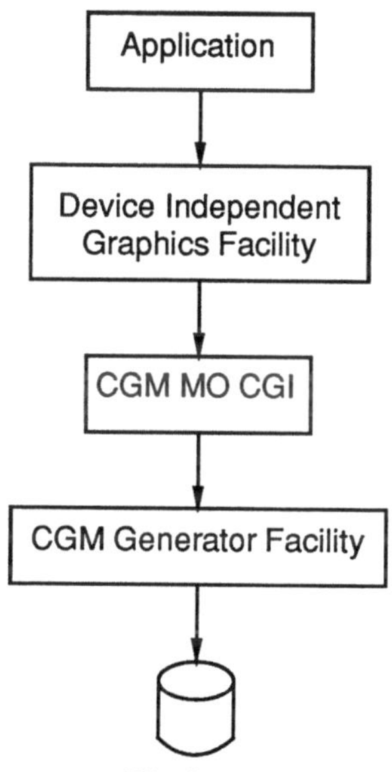

Figure 6.2-1: CGM Generator Reference Model

The CGM is designed to be interpreted in one of two ways. First, the CGM can be interpreted by a special application program, that in turn invokes a device-independent graphics system to render the CGM. Second, a device-independent graphics system may have functions that can be invoked by an application to get, read, and interpret metafile elements using the facilities of a CGM metafile input workstation. Figure 6.2-2 illustrates a CGM Generator (primary) Reference Model. Figure 6.2-3 illustrates the CGM Interpreter (alternate) Reference Model.

The GKS may be the device independent graphics system that is used in figures 6.2-2 and 6.2-3. GKS (ISO 7942), however, does not specifically refer to the CGM any more than it does to another specific class of graphics device.

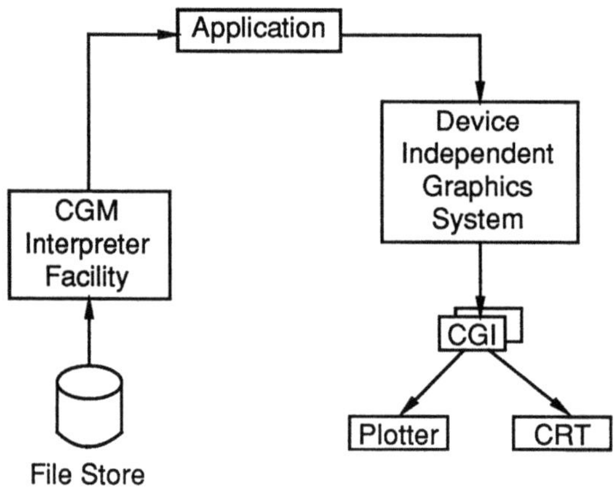

Figure 6.2-2: CGM Interpreter Reference Model

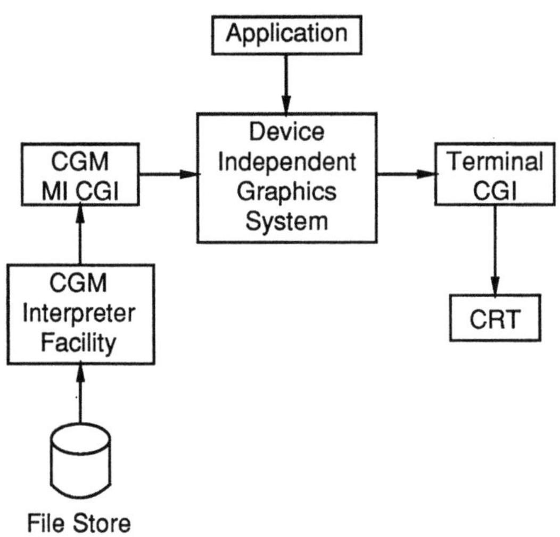

Figure 6.2-3: Alternate CGM Interpreter Reference Model

6.2.5 CGM Conformance

The TOP CGM AP specifies conformance in terms of "permissible and "basic" values. Permissible values are the range of values of CGM elements as specified in ISO 8632. Basic values are a subset of the permissible values that constitute the "basic set". For example, permissible values of LINE TYPE include all non-zero integers, while basic values include the standardized enumerated values 1 to 5.

TOP defines a conforming "basic metafile" to be one that contains no elements or parameter values outside of the basic set. TOP defines a conforming "basic interpreter" to be one that correctly interprets any conforming basic metafile and may have more capability as well. TOP defines a conforming "basic generator" as one that produces only conforming basic metafiles, or can reliably be directed to function in a mode of producing basic metafiles.

In addition, any TOP basic interpreter should correctly parse and pass over any elements that it does not support and any parameter values that it does not support.

CGM (ISO 8632) defines the form (syntax) and the functional behavior (semantics) of the ordered set of metafile elements. There are three different encodings of the CGM that have been standardized. These include Clear Text Encoding, Character Encoding, and Binary Encoding. This AP specifies the CGM Binary Encoding, ISO 8632/3. Future application profiles may be developed for the other encodings.

For interchange of CGM files on a TOP network the binary encoding is required.

6.2.6 Metafile Constraints

The basic set is defined by the limitations on permissible values below. Where an element is not mentioned, it is implied that the basic set includes all values permitted in the CGM.

6.2.6.1 Delimiter Elements

Element	Basic Value
NO-OP	An arbitrary sequence of n octets, n=0,1,2,...,32767

Table 6.2-1: Delimiter Element Constraints

6.2.6.2 Metafile Descriptor Elements

Element	Basic Value
Metafile Description	(Note 1)
Integer Precision	16
Real Precision	0,9,23 (floating point) ; 1,16,16 (fixed point)
Index Precision	16
Color Precision	8,16
Color Index Precision	8,16
Maximum Color Index	255
Font List	(Note 4)
Character Set List	0,4/2 (Note 2) ; 1,4/1 (Note 3)
Character Coding Announcer	0,1

Note 1: Implementors are encouraged to use the Metafile Description element's string to include a brief identification of their company or product, so that interpreters can account for known idiosyncrasies of generators. The string "TOP/BASIC-1" shall be included within the Metafile Description string to label the metafile as conforming to this profile.

Note 2: The character set is ANS X3.4, 7-bit American National Standard Code for Information Interchange (7-bit ASCII).

Note 3: The character set is ANS X3.134/2, 8-bit American National Standards Standard Code for Information Interchange (8-bit ASCII). This is equivalent to ISO 8859/1, Right-Hand Part of Latin Alphabet Part 1.

Note 4: Four simultaneous fonts are supported. The font names are selected from the basic font names in Table 6.2-8.

Table 6.2-2: Metafile Descriptor Element Constraints

6.2.6.3 Picture Descriptor Elements

Element	Basic Value
Scaling Mode	(Note 1)

Note 1: Implementors should use care in specifying the value of the metric scaling factor to ensure that it has sufficient significant resolution to specify the intended accuracy.

Table 6.2-3: Picture Descriptor Element Constraints

6.2.6.4 Control Elements

Element	Basic Value
VDC Integer Precision	16,32
VDC Real Precision	0,9,23 (floating point)
	1,16,16 (fixed point)

Table 6.2-4: Control Element Constraints

6.2.6.5 Graphics Primitive Elements

To ensure portability and predictable results, TOP conforming basic metafiles may not contain any Generalized Drawing Primitive (GDP) elements.

6.2.6.6 Attribute Elements

Element	Basic Value
Line Bundle Index	1-5
Line Type	1-5
Marker Bundle Index	1-5
Marker Type	1-5
Text Bundle Index	1-2
Text Font Index	1-4
Character Set Index	1-2
Alternate Character Set Index	1-2
Fill Bundle Index	1-5
Hatch Index	1-6
Pattern Index	1-8
Edge Bundle Index	1-5
Edge Type	1-5
Pattern Table	Pattern Table Index, 1-8
	nx, 1-16
	ny, 1-16
Color Table	Starting Color Index, 0-255

Table 6.2-5: Attribute Element Constraints

6.2.6.7 Escape Elements

To ensure portability and predictable results, TOP conforming basic metafiles may contain only those ESCAPE elements that are defined in Section 6.2.8.2 of this AP.

6.2.6.8 External Elements

Element	**Basic Value**
Message	Action Required Flag, 0

Table 6.2-6: External Element Constraints

6.2.7 CGM Defaults

The CGM specifies a complete set of defaults. In a few cases, these defaults are not appropriate for TOP requirements. However, any TOP metafile must be a legal CGM. This includes implicit defaults specified in ISO 8632/1, clause 6, and ISO 8632/3, clause 8. Therefore, each deviation from the implicit defaults requires that the affected element either:

1. Appear in the Metafile Defaults Replacement element, or
2. Be explicitly specified for its value to be applicable.

Each TOP conforming basic metafile shall contain in the Metafile Descriptor a Metafile Defaults Replacement element that includes at a minimum:

1. Text Precision element, where precision is set to 2 (stroke).

Each TOP conforming basic metafile shall also contain in the Metafile Descriptor, the following elements:

1. Maximum Color Index element, where the maximum color index is set to 255.
2. Character Set List element, where the first two character set indices are set to (0,4/2) and (1,4/1).

It is not apparent in the CGM standard what the default value for the precision of the floating point real parameter of Scaling Mode should be. TOP conforming generators and interpreters shall assume that the real precision for this parameter is (0,9,23).

Color table defaults for color indices 0 and 1 are explicitly defined in the CGM standard as corresponding to the nominal background and nominal foreground colors, respectively.

TOP conforming CGM interpreters will initialize their color table with the starting color table index set to 2, and the list of direct color values for the remaining 254 entries a repetition of the following eight values:

Index	Values	Meaning
2	(255, 0, 0)	Red
3	(0, 255, 0)	Green
4	(0, 0, 255)	Blue
5	(255, 255, 0)	Yellow
6	(255, 0, 255)	Magenta
7	(0, 255, 255)	Cyan
8	(0, 0, 0)	Black
9	(255, 255, 255)	White

Table 6.2-7: Default Color Table

6.2.8 CGM Related Private Use of Elements

6.2.8.1 Fonts

The fonts in Table 6.2-8 are public domain fonts, available from the U.S. National Bureau of Standards (NBS) [CGMRef5]. All of these fonts are considered to be basic capabilities of a TOP conforming basic metafile. Any of these fonts may appear in the Font List element in a CGM that conforms to this AP. The font names are specified in a manner compatible with ISO 9541, Font and Character Information Interchange [CGMRef11]. The font name (Font Identifier for Base Font) is a concatenated string of the Universal Font Name and a User Readable Font Name. The Universal Font Name for these fonts is assumed to be "NBS", pending the registration of the National Bureau of Standards with an Organization Name. The User Readable Font Name is the concatenated string "HERSHEY:", to designate one of the Hershey fonts, and "name string", to designate the particular typeface.

NOTE: The Hershey "fonts" are really combined specifications of font and character set, in the terminology of standards. So support of the Hershey "fonts" really implies support of a number of fonts and character sets.

1. NBS HERSHEY:CARTOGRAPHIC_ROMAN
2. NBS HERSHEY:CARTOGRAPHIC_GREEK
3. NBS HERSHEY:SIMPLEX_ROMAN
4. NBS HERSHEY:SIMPLEX_GREEK
5. NBS HERSHEY:SIMPLEX_SCRIPT
6. NBS HERSHEY:COMPLEX_ROMAN
7. NBS HERSHEY:COMPLEX_GREEK
8. NBS HERSHEY:COMPLEX_SCRIPT
9. NBS HERSHEY:COMPLEX_ITALIC
10. NBS HERSHEY:COMPLEX_CYRILLIC
11. NBS HERSHEY:DUPLEX_ROMAN
12. NBS HERSHEY:TRIPLEX_ROMAN
13. NBS HERSHEY:TRIPLEX_ITALIC
14. NBS HERSHEY:GOTHIC_GERMAN
15. NBS HERSHEY:GOTHIC_ENGLISH
16. NBS HERSHEY:GOTHIC_ITALIAN

Table 6.2-8: Basic Font Names

6.2.8.2 CGM Escape Elements

The following Escape elements are required to be supported in all TOP basic conforming CGM implementations.

6.2.8.2.1 Disable Clearing of View Surface

The normal interpretation of a CGM is such that the view surface of a device will be cleared on each Begin Picture Body element. This Escape element will disable the clearing of the view surface for all of the pictures in a metafile. The effect of this Escape element is to permit multiple metafile pictures to be imaged on the same view surface in a temporal manner (i.e., last picture overlays previous picture) with a mapping as described in the CGM standard. Pictures in the metafile may have different VDC Extents. Each picture will be mapped into the current Device Viewport for the picture. This Escape element must appear in the metafile description (i.e., between the Begin Metafile element and the first Begin Picture element). The Device Viewport is defined by the Device Viewport Escape element. The default Device Viewport is the available view surface.

This Escape element will have no effect on the resetting of the metafile defaults on each Begin Picture element. This Escape element is a basic capability of this application profile.

Escape Identifier: -301
Escape Data Record: N/A

6.2.8.2.2 Device Viewport

The default Device Viewport for interpreting a picture in the CGM is the available view surface of the interpreting device. This Escape element will redefine the Device Viewport for the picture to some portion of the available view surface. This Escape element must appear in the Picture Descriptor (i.e., between the Begin Picture element and the Begin Picture Body element). The specification units for the Device Viewport definition is a real fraction, in the range [0.0, 1.0], of the default Device Viewport. The default Device Viewport is the maximum rectangle with the same aspect ratio as the default VDC Extent (i.e., the maximum square). This Escape element is a basic capability of this AP. If this Escape element is specified when the Scaling Mode has been set to metric units, then the Device Viewport Escape will take precedence and Scaling Mode will be ignored. The VDC Extent is mapped into the specified Device Viewport such that the origin of the VDC Extent coincides with the origin of the specified Device Viewport.

Escape Identifier: -302

Escape Data Record: A single string of text. This string is the specification of the Device Viewport. Parameters in the string are separated by at least one blank character and/or a single comma character. The decimal point of the real fraction is required. Leading zeroes of the real fraction are optional. There are four parameters. Invalid parameters will result in this Escape element being ignored.

P1: First corner x-coordinate. Real fraction of the default Device Viewport, in the range [0.0, 1.0].

P2: First corner y-coordinate. Real fraction of the default Device Viewport, in the range [0.0, 1.0].

P3: Second corner x-coordinate. Real fraction of the default Device Viewport, in the range [0.0, 1.0].

P4: Second corner y-coordinate. Real fraction of the default Device Viewport, in the range [0.0, 1.0].

For example, a Device Viewport equal to the upper right quarter of the default Device Viewport would be coded with the following Escape element:

Escape Identifier: -302
Escape Data Record: ".5,.5,1.,1."

OR

Escape Identifier: -302
Escape Data Record: "0.50 0.50 1.0 1.0"

A Device Viewport equal in width to the left one tenth of the default Device Viewport and equal in height to the default Device Viewport would be coded with the following Escape element:

Escape Identifier: -302
Escape Data Record: "0., 0., .1, 1."

6.2.9 CGM Implementation Dependencies

This section describes the implementation dependencies and environmental constraints for this AP. Specifying the nominal values for such implementation practices, defaults, and options will facilitate uniform generation and interpretation of the CGM.

6.2.9.1 General Guidelines for CGM Elements

Unless otherwise noted in this AP, all of the guidelines of ISO 8632, Annex D, shall be adhered to by TOP CGM generators and interpreters. In particular, the interpreter minimum capabilities of ISO 8632, Annex D.5, plus the interpreter functions defined in Section 6.2.6, should be the minimum supported capabilities.

Name: Metafile Defaults Replacement

Description: The Metafile Defaults Replacement element shall not be partitioned. In addition, no part of the element will be partitioned.

Note: Multiple occurrences of the Metafile Defaults Replacement element are allowed by the CGM standard and this AP.

Name: Restricted Text

Description: Minimal capability of a basic conforming TOP interpreter shall render the complete restricted text string (i.e., Append Text elements permitted), scaled isotropically (i.e., specified aspect ratio for the text is not distorted), such that the text string fits into the Text Extent parallelogram.

Name: Color Table

Description: The Color Table element has an unspecified effect when it appears in a picture, subsequent to any graphical primitive elements. The Color Table element should appear prior to any graphical primitive elements to insure that interpreting systems without dynamic color update capabilities can render the intended effect.

6.2.9.2 Implementation Guidelines for Generators and Interpreters

This section is meant to augment ISO 8632/1, Annex D.5 and ISO 8632/3, clause 8.

6.2.9.2.1 Minimum Data Structure Support

Name: Maximum Color Array Dimension

Description: The basic value for the number of color values that can appear in a color array or color list parameter. CELL ARRAY has a color list parameter. PATTERN TABLE has a color array parameter. COLOR TABLE has a color list parameter.

Basic Value: 1048576 for CELL ARRAY (i.e., one 1024 x 1024 image),

2048 for PATTERN TABLE (i.e., eight 16 x 16 patterns),

256 for COLOR TABLE (i.e., entries 0-255)

Name: Maximum Point Array Length

Description: The basic value for the number of points that can appear in parameters for metafile elements.

Basic Value: 1024

Name: Maximum String Length

Description: The basic value for the length of an individual string of characters.

Basic Value: 256 for all string parameters except data records, 32767 for data records

Name: Bundle Table

Description: The bundle representations are not settable in the current version of the CGM. This implementation dependency detracts from the open interchange of the CGM. The following default bundle table values will permit a picture to be uniformly rendered by all conforming basic TOP interpreters.

Basic Value: Refer to Table 6.2-9

Bundle Type	**Bundle Index**				
Bundle Representation	1	2	3	4	5
Line Bundle					
Line Type	Solid	Dash	Dot	Dash-dot	Dash-dot-dot
Line Width	1	1	1	1	1
Line Color	1	1	1	1	1
Marker Bundle					
Marker Type	Dot	Plus	Asterisk	Circle	Cross
Marker Size	1	1	1	1	1
Marker Color	1	1	1	1	1
Text Bundle					
Font Index	1	1			
Text Precision	Stroke	Stroke			
Character Expansion Factor	1	0.5			
Character Spacing	0	0			
Text Color	1	1			
Fill Area Bundle					
Interior Style	Hatch	Hatch	Hatch	Hatch	Hatch
Fill Color	1	1	1	1	1
Hatch Index	1	2	3	4	5
Pattern Index	1	1	1	1	1
Edge Bundle					
Edge Type	Solid	Dash	Dot	Dash-dot	Dash-dot-dot
Edge Width	1	1	1	1	1
Edge Color	1	1	1	1	1

Table 6.2-9: Basic Bundle Table

6.2.9.2.2 CGM Transfer Format

Operating system dependencies for file formats can often be more of a burden on interoperability than differences in interchange formats. To ensure CGM interoperability, some conventions for file formats are required.

The file containing the CGM should be formatted into fixed length 80 octet records. If the record length is optionally less than 80 octets, even octet records are required.

NOTE: When the files are being transferred on magnetic tape, 80 octet records should be formatted into blocks of 800 octets.

6.2.10 CGM Error Processing

A TOP conforming interpreter should gracefully recover from any exception condition. If there is something which is not processable by the interpreter, processing of the metafile should continue with the metafile element following that which caused the exception, if possible. Exact details for exception handling are outside the scope of this recommendation.

6.2.11 CGM Conformance Testing

Conformance testing recommendations for the conforming TOP basic metafile will be addressed by subsequent releases of this recommendation.

6.2.12 CGM References

These references relate to documents applicable to this specification.

CGMRef1 ANS X3.4 - 1986, 7-bit American National Standard Code for Information Interchange

CGMRef2 ANS X3.41 - 1974, American National Standard Code Extension Techniques for Use With the 7-bit Coded Character Set of American National Standard Code for Information Interchange

CGMRef3 ANS X3.134/1, American National Standard Code for 8-bit ASCII Structure

CGMRef4 ANS X3.134/2, American National Standard Code for 7-bit and 8-bit ASCII Supplemental Multilingual Graphic Character Set

CGMRef5 NBS Special Publication 424 - April 1976, Hershey Fonts

CGMRef6 ISO 8613, Information Processing - Text and Office Systems - Office Document Architecture and Interchange Format (ODA/ODIF)

CGMRef7 ISO 8632/1, Information Processing Systems - Computer Graphics Metafile (CGM) for the Storage and Transfer of Picture Description Information - Part 1; Functional Specification

CGMRef8 ISO 8632/2, Information Processing Systems - Computer Graphics Metafile (CGM) for the Storage and Transfer of Picture Description Information - Part 2; Character Encoding

CGMRef9 ISO 8632/3, Information Processing Systems - Computer Graphics Metafile (CGM) for the Storage and Transfer of Picture Description Information - Part 3; Binary Encoding

CGMRef10 ISO 8632/4, Information Processing Systems - Computer Graphics Metafile (CGM) for the Storage and Transfer of Picture Description Information - Part 4; Clear Text Encoding

CGMRef11 ISO 9541, Information Processing Systems - Font and Character Information Interchange

CGMRef12 ISO DIS 8859/1, Information Processing - 8-bit Single Byte Coded Graphical Character Sets - Part 1; Latin Alphabet Part 1

CGMRef13 ISO 7942, Information Processing Systems - Computer Graphics - Graphical Kernal System (GKS) Functional Description

CGMRef14 ISO DIS 8805, Information Processing Systems - Computer Graphics - Graphical Kernal System for Three Dimensions (GKS-3D) Functional Description

CGMRef15 ISO DP 9592, Information Processing Systems - Computer Graphics - Programmers Hierarchical Interactive Graphics System (PHIGS)

CGMRef16 ISO TC97/SC21 N1179, Information Processing Systems - Computer Graphics - Interfacing Techniques for Dialogues with Graphical Devices (CGI)

6.2.13 The Use of OSI Data Transfer Services

To transfer a CGM file between two TOP End Systems, the services provided either by FTAM or by MHS can be used. Remote access to part of a CGM file is not addressed at this time.

Using FTAM to transfer CGM files:

One should specify the CGM file Document Type entry number as FTAM-3, Document-Type-Name as '{ISO standard 8571 document-type (5) unstructured-binary (3)}' for Contents-Type-Attribute or Contents-Type-List. The contents of the CGM file should be mapped onto a sequence of octet strings. The boundary of the octet strings has no significant meaning.

NOTE: As there is no standard defined document type at this time for a CGM type file, the presentation layer facilities can not be fully used and it is left up to the user or application programs that remotely access files using FTAM to know that a given file contains CGM formatted information.

Using MHS to transfer CGM files:

One should specify the Body as USABodyParts BodyPartNumber '1', and the contents of the CGM file is mapped in the body of an IMP as a sequence of octet strings. The boundary of the octet strings has no particular semantics.

The CGM Application Profile for CALS: Current Specification and Major Issues

L. R. Henderson

Abstract

The Computer Automated Logistics Support (CALS) is a DoD initiative to establish a near paperless logistic technical information system. The CGM has been designated as a standard interchange mechanism for 2D vector graphics. The necessity of a CGM Application Profile (AP) has been identified and an initial draft has been produced. As the profile has not yet been published, significant portions of it are presented here, along with discussion of major issues (resolved and still pending) in its formulation. A high degree of compatibility with the TOP Application Profile has been achieved. There is need to go further with functional extensions to meet CALS user requirements. Work is in progress on some functional extensions, which should be adopted into the profile when they are mature and stable enough.

1 Background

The Computer Aided Logistics Support (CALS) program is an initiative within the Department of Defense to solve the problems arising from its current paper-intensive logistics processes. The solutions involve automation of those processes, with the goal of producing a near paperless logistic technical information system. Integration of the many efforts already underway independently in various agencies is a primary requirement. The integrated solutions will have to deal with large investments of existing technology (e.g., CAD/CAM systems) and must make use of large existing databases (e.g., CAE and CAD design data for insertion into technical manuals).

CALS, through the National Bureau of Standards (NBS), has made a major effort to identify and incorporate national and international standards for data and application interfaces within CALS application environments. Graphics standards are one such category of interface standard, and CGM in particular has been singled out as having an key role to play. It's major uses are anticipated to be for recording and interchanging technical illustrations, project planning charts, raster-to-vector converted scanned images, etc. for later review and incorporation into technical documentation, maintenance manuals, and management and administrative documents of all kinds.

2 Overview of the Profile

A high priority of the CALS profile was avoidance of proliferation of incompatible specifications. This meant in particular avoiding incompatibility with the TOP AP for CGM. This was accomplished in large part by collaborative effort between the experts of the two projects.

The TOP profile forms the basis for the CALS profile. The CALS profile corrects some problems (editorial errors, etc.) that still exist in the TOP profile. In addition, it adds some conformance requirements for generators and interpreters that do not exist in the TOP profile. In particular, two levels of conformance for interpreters are specified:

- preview-quality conformance - the fallback actions of Annex D may be used, monochrome may be substituted for color, etc.

- publication-quality conformance - the semantics of the Basic conformance set of the profile must be exactly rendered.

The TOP profile, and the initial version of the CALS profile as well, are still functionally lean when measured against the requirements to efficiently support the CALS constituency. As part of another CALS/NBS project (see the paper by Carson, "Extending CGM for CALS," in these proceedings), functional extensions to CGM have been recommended in a number of areas. The mechanism for achieving these is the Graphical Registration of ESCAPE and GDP elements. A number of proposals have already been submitted.

The initial Application Profile for CALS recommends that the profile should be amended or extended to include such functionality as soon as it is stable enough in the standards processing pipeline. Similarly, it is recommended that CALS begin adopting Extended Metafile (ISO Addendum 1 to CGM) functionality as it stabilizes (i.e., those functions, such as symbol library facility, that are important for CALS constituents).

The most serious functional deficiency of CGM, in an environment of automated publishing and technical illustration, is the lack of text fonts of decent quality. The draft CALS profile does not solve this directly (it basically follows TOP here, with some conformance guidelines); but it recommends following the work of ISO draft standard 9541 on font and character set specification as it stabilizes. In particular, the profile recommends: future work for CALS should focus on a method of specifying an adequate and useful set of fonts; and this should be done in a way which relieves conformers to the profile of financial obligations to font copyright holders.

3 Introduction

The following sections, defining application profiles and stating the need for same, are largely repeated from the CALS draft profile.

3.1 Overview of CGM

The Computer Graphics Metafile (CGM) standard, ANSI X3.122-1986 and ISO 8632/1-4, specifies the syntax and semantics of a standard file format for storing and communicating computer graphics pictures. By intentional choice of scope, it limits the specification to the syntax and semantics of a set of CGM "elements" for the device-independent description of computer graphics pictures.

In the year that it has been an ANSI standard CGM's use and its incorporation into other standard interface and exchange specifications has been increasing. There are over two dozen implementations existing or known to be in progress in the US alone (there are more internationally). It has, of course, been specified as the 2D vector graphics exchange mechanism for CALS. It has been designated as a Federal Information Processing Standard (FIPS). It has been incorporated as the graphical metafile of the MAP/TOP V3.0 specification. It is designated as the Geometric Graphic Content Architecture of the ISO compound document standard (ISO 8613, currently in DIS stage), known as "ODA/ODIF". It has been specified for vector graphics interchange by MIL-STD-1840.

3.2 The Need for CGM Application Profiles

Even though it is achieving widespread acceptance as a graphical standard there are still problems using CGM in some environments. The syntactic specification in the CGM standard is complete and unambiguous. It is, as well, redundant in the sense that there are three distinct encodings of the same functionality - binary, character, and clear text (according to CGM, each encoding is tailored and optimized to certain computing environments and applications area).

The semantic specification is less complete. The expected overall results of using the geometric primitive elements are well enough specified. However some of the finer details, such as the precise appearance of joints and endpoints in lines, are unspecified. This underspecification of semantics was intentional on the part of the designers the CGM - it allows a wider range of existing systems to be accommodated and makes the standard more adaptable. CGM was written for the needs and philosophies of a diverse clientele.

On the other hand, the semantic ambiguity does mean that there will be no single correct interpretation of a given CGM, and hence it will be difficult to unambiguously describe an intended picture using CGM. This is a distinct drawback in certain applications environments. The CGM application areas of Technical Illustration and Technical Publishing, which are central to the CALS effort, represent such environments where unambiguous semantics are critical.

There are further sources of uncertainty in using CGM in an application environment. The CGM standard specifically excludes standardization of the behavior of metafile generators and metafile interpreters. In doing so, a certain unpredictability of results is introduced into the graphics system viewed as a whole - for example, CGM generators serving GKS (Graphical Kernel System, ANSI X3.124-1985) clients in the product lines of two different vendors might map out-of-range attributes differently.

The CGM is a basically suitable protocol for application areas such as technical publishing and illustration (ISO 8613, ODA/ODIF adopted it for example). But these two sources of ambiguity in using CGM - incomplete semantics and non-specification of the behavior of generators and interpreters - do mean that some further specification (beyond that in the published standard) is required in order for the use of CGM to be effective, efficient, and unambiguous.

Such a specification is precisely what an Application Profile (AP) consists of.

In the case of CGM, an AP can:

1. specify complete semantics;
2. specify the behavior of CGM generators and CGM interpreters;
3. extend the functionality by ESCAPE or GDP elements.

An AP at least specifies minimal and maximal requirements for generators and interpreters, and ties down all implementation dependencies of the CGM. As the name suggests, an AP is a set of specifications appropriate to a given application environment.

One such CGM AP has already been targeted and printed - the CGM Application Profile of TOP (Technical Office Protocol) that is being endorsed by a number of major industrial constituents and has been incorporated into the MAP/TOP V3.0 specification.

For CGM to be used effectively in the CALS Technical Publishing, Administrative Publishing, and Technical Drawing applications, an AP has been designated for CALS as well.

4 Issues and Objectives in Formulating the Profile

4.1 Conceptual Issues in Specifying the CALS Application Profile

There are two categories of specification that were considered in specifying the CALS Application Profile of CGM:

1. resolution of ambiguities in the metafile and in the behavior of generators and interpreters;
2. extension of the CGM functionality to handle perceived functional deficiencies in the standard.

There are two ways to accomplish the second task: firstly, by definition of ESCAPE and GDP elements, which are then submitted for Graphical Registration; secondly, by revision of the CGM itself via normal processes (e.g., ISO Addendum 1, CGEM).

Any Application Profile must accomplish the first task. The second task is important for CALS constituents as well. The CGM is functionally lean when measured against the requirements of automated publishing and technical illustration. Almost any picture from these application areas can be represented. For example lines and areas can be used to represent in the CGM many of the "higher-level" entities of IGES. But the consequence of simulating the entities with very primitive geometric elements is a loss of efficiency and data compaction in the CGM.

In order to be an efficient picture mechanism in the CALS environment, extension of the functional capabilities of CGM is required. Such extension is taking place formally now within ISO (the Extended Metafile - Addendum 1 to CGM). Unfortunately, even the "fast-track" ISO addendum process is a slow process.

The CALS project has completed a study (see Carson's paper) to:

1. identify needed extensions to CGM, and;

2. prepare and submit Graphical Registration proposals for same.

Adopting such proposals into a profile at this time presents a dilemma. Doing so would surely result in their immediate use. While they are needed functionality, the proposals will be examined and likely modified by graphics standards bodies before they have official standing in the Standards arena. Implementations which use the proposals too early in the registration process will likely be non-standard when the proposals eventually complete standards processing.

The initial Application Profile for CALS therefore does not include any extended functionality, with a minor exception: the published TOP profile contains two specified ESCAPES, one of which is an encoding of a function that is stable in ISO CGI and in the CGEM. These have been adopted by CALS as well.

The TOP committee, working with CALS and ASC X3H3, removed from its report (among other things) two user-definable attributes, line and hatch style; this was done allow graphics experts to formulate the proposals and allow opportunity for adequate review. These are not included in the current CALS profile, but two specific proposals are attached to the draft for insertion into the Graphical Registration process.

In summary, the CALS CGM Application profile:

1. specifies semantics and syntax that are ambiguous or unspecified in CGM;

2. does not, except as noted above, specify extended functionality for CGM.

With regard to point number 2: the problem at this time is the immaturity of the proposals and the immediate need for an initial AP for the CALS community. The CALS AP recommends that extended functionalities should be included in a "Version 2" upgrade of the CALS AP in the near future - as soon as the work of the ISO and Graphical Registration committees has progressed far enough.

4.2 Relationship to the TOP Profile

Proliferation of "dialects" of CGM is clearly undesirable and contrary to the interests of the graphics industry and users. Accordingly, one principle priority in formulating the CALS profile was to realize an AP that is either identical to, or is backwardly compatible with, the TOP AP. In other words, where the APs overlap they should be identical, but CALS may be somewhat richer or may go further in specifying constraints.

Fortunately there is significant common interest and shared requirements between the sectors of industry represented on the MAP/TOP committees and the clientele of the CALS initiative, particularly in the areas of technical illustration and compound document exchange. This made collaboration and convergence of the profiles achievable.

4.3 Specific Goals of the Application Profile

Other specific objectives in the specification of the CALS CGM AP included:

1. A CALS metafile must be a legal CGM - CALS syntax must be a subset of CGM syntax and CALS semantics must be legal CGM semantics. This means, for example, that the CALS environment cannot assume or specify implicit element defaults that differ from the CGM standard.

2. The picture specified by a CALS metafile must be unambiguous. This means, for example, that private values of attributes (such as private linetypes) cannot be allowed, and private elements (escapes and GDPs, for example) must be prohibited.

3. The behavior of generators in producing a CALS metafile should be specified so that identical sequences of activity at the application level result in identical metafile contents (intermediate layers in a graphics environment may complicate this).

4. The behavior of interpreters in parsing and rendering CALS metafile should be as unambiguous as possible. This means that such things as fallback actions when the interpreter lacks capability, or fallback actions in the face of geometric degeneracies, should be specified.

5. The format ambiguities of the CGM, such as the "record size" of the binary encoding (unspecified in CGM) should be specified.

6. The CALS CGM AP should be rich enough to accomplish useful things economically.

7. The AP should be formulated with awareness of the evolution of graphics standards. In particular, the content of the Extended Metafile (ISO 8632 Addendum 1 - the first set of extensions to CGM, currently near DP stage) should be carefully followed. No specifications should be made in the CALS AP which compromise compatibility with these standard activities.

8. Similarly the activities of the Graphical Registration process should be tracked. Future compatibility must again be protected.

9. A CALS metafile should be self-identifying as such.

In some cases, these criteria are mutually contradictory - it is not necessarily possible to satisfy all of them at once.

5 Definition of the Profile

5.1 Basic Definition

The MAP/TOP V3.0 specification (references below are to the version most current on 1 August 1987) is the basis of the CALS Application Profile for CGM.

The CALS Application Profile for CGM comprises:

1. all of the specifications of the MAP/TOP V3.0 Application Profile for CGM with only modifications as specified in the next section;

2. extensions and additions as specified in subsequent sections.

5.2 CALS Modifications to the TOP AP

This section details those modifications to the baseline MAP/TOP V3.0 CGM AP that were required for CALS. Most of these are believed to be errors in the TOP profile, and are being submitted to TOP for erratum processing.

1. The restrictions of section 6.2.5 - command headers and text strings must use long form - are removed. (TOP experts indicate agreement with removing the restriction from the TOP profile as well.)

2. In section 6.2.6.2, Note 1, replace last sentence with; "If the metafile is a CALS Basic metafile, the substring CALS/BASIC-1 shall appear in the METAFILE DESCRIPTION element."

3. Section 6.2.6.2, table 6.2-2 - the CALS profile allows both floating point and the simpler fixed point reals in the Basic values of REAL PRECISION; the omission of fixed point from the TOP profile is believed to be a mistake.

4. Section 6.2.6.2, table 6.2-2 - typing error, "Font Index" should read "Font List".

5. Section 6.2.6.4, table 6.2-4 - the CALS profile allows both floating point and the simpler fixed point reals in the Basic values of VDC REAL PRECISION; the omission of fixed point from the TOP profile is believed to be a mistake.

6. Section 6.2.8.2 - the sentence should be replaced by: "The following Escape elements are required to be supported by all TOP Basic conforming CGM implementations." Clearly it is not intended, as literally stated, that all occurrences of metafiles contain the elements.

7. Section 6.2.8.2.1 - the last sentence should be replaced by: "The implicit default viewport is the largest area of the available view surface that has the same aspect ratio as the implicit default VDC EXTENT. The latter is square, so the implicit default viewport is the largest square area of the available view surface". ANSI/ISO CGI and CGEM, from which this element is taken, must be followed here. In those specifications the default window/viewport mapping is isotropic.

8. Section 6.2.10 - the second sentence appears to be an error, and in any case is an inappropriate sort of specification. Replace it with "If there is an element which the interpreter cannot understand or render, then processing should continue if possible with the next element following the problem element."

9. Section 6.2.9.2.1 - the specification of the data structure support for COLOR TABLE is incorrect and contradicts table 6.2-5, which is correct. The COLOR TABLE line should be replaced by "256 for COLOR TABLE (i.e., entries 0-255)."

10. Section 6.2.8.1 - as specified in the TOP profile, the only fonts available for predictable interchange are the Hershey fonts. These are of poor quality for modern illustration and publishing needs, particularly when the characters become large. The CALS profile considers any rendering of a requested font conforming if the rendering is "metrically identical" to the font metrics of the requested font. This means that the placement and alignment of the string and the placement, size, and shape of individual characters (i.e., the drawn portions of the character cells) are measurable identical. This would allow a good quality filled font to be substituted for a stroked Hershey font, for example.

5.3 CALS Extensions to CGM that are in the TOP Profile

TOP AP contains the following two extensions to CGM functionality:

1. DISABLE CLEARING OF VIEW SURFACE, section 6.2.8.2.1: this element gives control over an aspect of CGM that is unspecified - whether or not the view surface should be cleared upon the occurrence of BEGIN PICTURE BODY;

2. DEVICE VIEWPORT, section 6.2.8.2.2: this element gives control over placement of the virtual image on the view surface, and together with 6.2.8.2.1 allows production of composite images (several CGM pictures); its formulation is taken from the stable elements of the ISO CGI and CGEM work.

These elements are included in the CALS profile. This is contrary to the general policy of the CALS profile not to extend CGM functionality, but it is done because the extension has already been made in TOP.

A number of functional extensions were removed from early drafts of the TOP profile. Some were inappropriate or not of broad enough interest. Some were useful but needed to be studied by a wider audience and reformulated. Two were considered particularly useful. These are user-defined linetype and user-defined hatch style. User-defined linetype has been recommended for registration by CALS (see Carson report).

The initial CALS profile recommends that these two items not be included in the profile now, but be submitted to the Graphical Registration process along with other functional extensions. The reasoning is the same as for the larger number of functional extensions and registration proposals referred to above. For reference, the proposals are presented in the last section of this paper.

5.4 Encoding and File Format

The CALS AP raises the question of whether conforming interchange should be limited, as in the TOP AP, to the binary encoding. The CGM claims that the attributes of the three encodings are sufficiently unique that all three are justified. Implementation of all three encodings is considerably more of an effort than just the binary (which is the simplest in any case). Such a requirement could be a deterrent to acceptance of the CGM and the AP. There has not yet been a quantitative measurement of the differences between the encodings. The CALS AP recommends that such be done to justify or reject the specification of additional encodings in the next revision of the profile.

With regard to the physical format of the Binary metafiles - for the CALS profile, the weakly stated requirements of TOP AP section 6.2.9.2.2 are strengthened: the logical records shall be 80 octets in record-oriented environments; on magnetic tape, the records shall be blocked 10 at a time, forming 800 octet physical tape records.

In addition, the bit/octet/word order of section 4.3 of Part 3 of CGM (ANSI x3.122-1986) is the correct order for interchange between conforming CALS implementations.

5.5 Additional Requirements for Generators

In Section 6.2.6.6 of the TOP AP, restricted ranges are given for the values of primitive attributes. Implementation experience has showed that there is an ambiguity in connecting a "TOP Basic" CGM generator to an Application Programmer Interface (API) graphics system such as GKS. If the API layer passes attributes out of the Basic range, what should the generator do?

This CALS AP specifies that the values of attributes in 6.2.6.6, when passed to the generator outside of the Basic range, be handled as follows:

- If the index is selecting an attribute (e.g., linetype), then the CGM generator should map it by MODULO onto the Basic range;
- If the index is defining an attribute (e.g., color table), then it should be ignored if outside the Basic range.

These choices for the generator are consistent with Annex D of CGM, and with the reference to Annex D in clause 6.2.9 of the TOP AP.

In addition, it should be noted that the minimum data structure support of TOP AP section 6.2.9.1 are maximal limits for generators. CALS Basic CGM generators should not generate elements longer than those listed, because conforming CALS Basic interpreters are not required to accept longer primitives.

5.6 Additional Requirements for Interpreters

The TOP AP points to the specifications of Annex D of CGM for interpreters that do not have sufficient capability to accurately render the contents of a metafile. One of the goals of the CALS AP is to make the use of CGM completely unambiguous. This is not always required; for example, for preview of pictures black-and-white will often suffice where color has been specified. But at the time that a picture is to be incorporated into a document, the results must be completely predictable. An interpreter of such fidelity is going to be relatively expensive to produce and run, and is not needed all of the time.

Therefore the CALS AP determines that two conformance levels are needed for certifying interpreters:

1. preview-quality conformance - the fallback actions of Annex D of CGM may be used in some cases.
2. publication-quality conformance - the rendered picture must exactly correspond with the specification contained in the CGM - fonts must be correct, colors correct, ...

5.7 Specification of Semantic Ambiguities

The CGM leaves the semantics of a number of graphical details unspecified or "implementation dependent". This compromises predictable interchange. Although there will continue to be applications where it doesn't really matter, there are also those where it matters very much (technical illustrations for high-quality publications). These graphical details need to be addressed soon by additional functions, ESCAPES and GDPs. Some of these are already being specified and submitted for registration, as mentioned previously.

The CALS AP considered specifying the default behavior of these additional controls and attributes - items such as line join, cap, etc. Once again, doing so risks the possibility of being in conflict with standardized or registered elements. Specification of these details was thus deferred.

Clipping. Clipping shall be done to the intersection of the viewport and the device view surface limits when the clipping indicator is 'off'. Clipping shall be done to the intersection of the clip rectangle, the viewport and the device view surface limits when the clipping indicator is 'on'.

Linetype Continuation. Linetype shall be maintained (continued) across the interior vertices of a polyline.

Edge Type Continuation. Edge type shall be maintained (continued) across the vertices of a filled area boundary.

Line Cap. Deferred pending results of Graphical Registration.

Line Join. Deferred pending results of Graphical Registration.

6 Significant Issues Remaining for the CALS AP

The current specification of the CGM Application Profile for CALS has met most of its primary objectives. In particular, the profile is immediately usable, is a superset of the TOP profile, and reasonably implementable. The profile is viewed as an initial specification and is expected to grow and evolve to meet more advanced user requirements. There are several major issues that should be addressed before the next revision. They should be revisited and resolved in a year or less.

6.1 Exact Set of Functional Extensions

The paper by Carson presents a substantial list of extensions to CGM needed by CALS. This paper presents a couple more. The list of proposed extensions now includes:

1. a symbol library facility (under development in CGEM);
2. user defined linetype (2 different proposals);
3. user defined hatch style;
4. approximately 10 registered linetypes;
5. approximately 20 registered hatch styles;

6. several types of spline curves;

7. conics and conic arcs;

8. closed figure primitive;

9. arbitrary clipping boundary;

10. a number of registered fonts;

11. a completely new text model, via ESCAPEs and GDPs;

12. raster "input" and associated attributes for image processing;

13. additional line attributes, e.g., line cap, line join ...

More proposals may be forthcoming. Some of the collected proposals are likely to be controversial. It will be a significant task to sort through the proposals and registered items and adjust the profile.

6.2 Fonts

There are some more serious problems with the current state of the TOP and CALS APs - particularly the question of the Hershey fonts - than noted above. First, the Hershey fonts are not really fonts but are font/character set combinations. The motivation for their inclusion is that they are public domain, and some specification of fonts was desirable. The "CGM Extensions" study has pointed to a number of more useful and higher quality fonts. These should be considered for inclusion in an early revision of this profile.

Meanwhile, the Hershey fonts really require of the interpreter a certain number of typefaces and a certain number of character sets. The CALS profile states that the requirements of the CALS profile are served, and compatibility with the TOP profile is maintained, by requiring that the necessary character sets be supported in part, and the necessary typefaces be supported in part, so that the combinations required to render the listed 16 Hershey "fonts" are supported in full. Furthermore, "recognizably similar and of at least as high quality" is the criterion applied to font conformance. The exact (stroked) Hershey fonts then just become one way to realize this support.

The most serious problem in the area of fonts is that the Hershey fonts do not meet the needs of high quality illustration and publishing. Specification of a rich, useful and mandatory set of fonts for CALS is be a high priority future work item. The fonts of IGES are considered as starting point. However, the list in the "Needed CGM Extensions" report (of Carson) contains some proprietary names. It is undesirable to obligate conformers to the profile to have to pay commercial license fees. It may be possible to specify a useful set of fonts in terms of reference to font metrics, rather than reference to copyrighted names. This is a topic which CALS should pursue in the near future, before the next revision of the profile.

6.3 Encodings

There are suggestions that 2 or all 3 encodings should be conforming interchange - all 3 have distinct and valuable use. On the other hand, this would definitely increase the implementation burden for those adhering to the CALS profile. This question should be studied quantitatively, and experience with the binary profile accumulated, over the next year. It should then be determined if other encodings should be included in the next version of the profile.

6.4 3D CGM

The needs of the CALS constituency for 3D have not been much studied yet. IGES provides some 3D capability for product data, but is not a graphical metafile in the sense of CGM. Work is underway for CGM Addendum 2 (3D extensions) but will be a long time until completion. It is unclear whether CALS has immediate need for a 3D metafile, and whether whatever needs it might have are being addressed by the ISO 3D extension work. A clear reference model for CALS would help resolve the issue of the need for 3D.

7 Registration Proposals Developed as Part of the CALS AP Specification

The following two items were removed from the TOP AP draft. They were subsequently reformulated and are considered valuable functionality for the CALS community. It is recommended in the CALS AP that they be submitted for registration.

7.1 User Defined Linetype

This element defines a linetype and associates it with an index for future reference:

Parameters:

linetype (IX) - index of linetype being defined;
number of dash elements (I) - number of elements in the defined line pattern;
list of dash elements (nI) - I>=0, n>=1
  n=1 means a solid line;
  I=0 interpreted as a dot;
  First element is a dash, second a space, etc;

Additional parameters (or ESCAPE attributes):

duty cycle unit selector = {VDC, mm, native device units,abstract} the value of 'abstract' indicates that the implementation may normalize and map the sum of the dash pattern elements at its discretion.

duty cycle (repeat length in units of '..selector')
These two controls define the length of the dash pattern.

adaptive flag = {no, yes} - an "adaptive" linetype is one where every vertex falls on an inked portion of the line. This is accomplished in plotters by temporarily modifying the duty cycle for each line segment (ceiling function) such that there is always an integral number of repeats (and all predefined linetypes have their gaps_array defined such that they begin and end with inked or "pen down" portions). Default is "no" or non-adaptive, so that the duty cycle is always the same regardless of line segment length, unless the user requests otherwise.

7.2 User Defined Hatch Style

This element defines a linetype and associates it with an index for future reference:

Parameters:

hatch index (IX) - index of hatch style being defined;
style indicator (E) - {parallel, crosshatch};
number of hatch elements (I) - number of elements in
the defined hatch style;
list of hatch elements (nI) - I>=0, n>=2
the array gives alternating (line width, gap width) - a direct analogy to the linetype array. Center of the first hatch line is matched up with PATTERN REFERENCE POINT, if implemented. 0 interpreted as thinnest line width available. Error if sum of hatch elements is 0.

Additional parameters (or ESCAPE attributes):

units indicator = {VDC, mm, device units, abstract}

specifies the units in which 'angle' and 'duty cycle length' are specified. Also controls the manner of transformation of the hatching: If VDC, then the hatching transforms with segment transform and anisotropic transforms (as if you had done POLYLINES); otherwise, the hatching is like "wallpaper" that shows through the polygon-shaped hole - you've mapped all that's necessary into device units and are doing hatching in device space. The value of 'abstract' indicates that the implementation may normalize and map the sum of the dash pattern elements at its discretion.

angle (dx, dy)* - default is horizontal;

duty cycle (repeat length)
Specifies the distance measured perpendicular to the hatch line. The sum of hatch elements in the hatch element list is normalized to this distance before presentation of the hatch on the view surface.

Part IV

Extending the CGM to Meet Further User Requirements

This part of the book considers extensions to the CGM which are required to meet present user requirements.

Bono addresses an unusual and exciting application for the CGM. It is often desirable to incorporate existing hardcopy documents into an information system by scanning them to create digitized raster data representing the document's content. Since many computer graphics systems are vector oriented, the requirement arises for raster-to-vector conversion. Bono considers these requirements. He looks at the current technology for scanning and storing images and the need to extract and store entities contained in the images. Bono suggests that the CGM can be used as a vehicle for transferring such images. He defines extensions via registration and/or revisions to the standard necessary for this purpose.

In Part 3 of this book the use of CGM in the US DoD was considered by Henderson. In this group of papers, Carson looks to the future to consider the requirements of CALS for extensions to the CGM via the registration procedure and, possibly, future revisions of the standard. Carson shows how the CGM can be used in the engineering and office environments for final form drawing, exchange and storage. Carson defines those extensions to the CGM which are necessary to meet user requirements in these areas and shows how these extensions can be implemented quickly through established registration mechanisms. He also sees the need for the inclusion of references to externally defined objects - such as fonts - in the metafile. Carson also establishes the need for further raster support.

Silverman describes the use of the CGM in MAGICorp's slide making service. He describes the conversion work necessary to make a good slide from a metafile conforming to the CGM standard. Again, like Carson and other presenters at the workshop, he identifies problems associated with CGM text definition. More information must be available to CGM interpreters to allow the production of the high quality text required for presentation graphics applications. This requirement, from Silverman's viewpoint, applies particularly to kerning and to required font characteristics.

Uses for CGM in Raster-to-Vector Conversion

P. R. Bono

Abstract

This study of the state-of-the-art in raster-to-vector conversion shows that the CGM is generally suitable as a storage and exchange mechanism for the vector entity files that result from the conversion process. However, the CGM would be much more valuable if additional features such as global segments (symbols), font metric information, and support for arrows, splines, and closed figures were available as CGM elements.

1 Background

The US National Bureau of Standards, in support of the US Department of Defense Computer-aided Acquisition and Logistics Support Program (CALS), commissioned a study of the state-of-the-art in raster-to-vector conversion reflecting the technology commercially available in late 1986.

The overall objective of the CALS Program is to integrate the design, manufacturing, and logistics functions through the efficient application of computer technology. Achievement of this objective requires the development of compatible system architectures that can be rapidly implemented by government and industry without incurring excessive costs. These system architectures must be built around an initial "core" of CALS functional and interface standards and procedures that provide a kernel for specifying CALS requirements in contracts with industry.

2 Objectives

The purposes of this study were to assess the state-of-the-art in raster-to-vector conversion technology, analyze the process for the applicability of picture interchange standards, and develop recommendations for CALS.

The assessment covers:

- a comprehensive list of suppliers of this type of technology;
- what types of output formats they produce;
- a comparison of output types with those of IGES and CGM;
- a forecast of the time frame for such systems capable of performing in the CALS environment; and
- both short term and long term recommendations.

3 Requirements

In 1986, the NBS contracted for a study comparing the capabilities of IGES and CGM [1]. NBS also commissioned a study to review and analyze the requirements of CALS-related projects for graphics standards. This report surveyed a selection of Army, Navy, and Air Force projects that fell into the following three broad application areas: printing and publishing systems, paperless presentation and maintenance aids, and automated engineering data repositories and product definition data. The salient results of that study documented in an SDC report [2] are summarized in the following text. Those conclusions bearing on raster-to-vector conversion are shown in bold text.

> In the technical manuals area, there is an urgent need to define a common DOD approach to SGML, including the use of CGM files to import graphics pictures. IGES is needed for the transport of product data between CAD systems, CGM for transport of pictures between publishing systems, and **a raster standard-perhaps a subset of CGM to store the print-on-demand images, which have already been laid out on the page and formatted.** Strong, reliable validation procedures are required to build user confidence in the standard products available from the commercial marketplace.
>
> **There is a general need for a raster-to-vector conversion capability, but product definition data need not be carried along. The users want a family of standards, with increasing capabilities available at an increase in complexity and cost. They want text and graphics capabilities in a single standard.**
>
> In the engineering data repositories area, there is an expressed need for textual data standards and for data base standards. There are some instances where IGES

is used to maintain pictures; CGM could be used instead, with a savings in storage, processing time, and complexity.

In all areas, there is a tremendous backlog of data that must be accessed, manipulated, and outputted, currently in raster format. Much of this data is archived on aperture cards that would have to be digitally scanned. Data in this format will be part of the CALS database for a very long time.

In general, there is a broad, short range need for saving images in raster format. However, in the long term, all users indicate that they'd like to convert to an all-vector format. This would permit them to modify the picture, transform it, and exchange it with otherwise incompatible systems. Whatever format is chosen-facsimile-based, CGM-based, or something entirely new, a strong validation program for file generators and interpreters is required.

In a subsequent report [3], architectures for four CALS applications areas-engineering design, publishing, procurement support, and interactive delivery systems-were proposed. Use of raster, CGM vector, and CAD databases are shown. These architectures are useful in understanding where the raster-to-vector conversion process fits into CALS programs.

4 Relevant Standards

4.1 CCITT Facsimile Standards

Two CCITT facsimile standards, known informally as Group 3 and Group 4 facsimile, cover the encoding and transmission of raster data. Both formats deal with black-and-white images only; gray-scale and full color images are not presently covered by these standards.

Group 3 facsimile provides for two options: (a) a one-dimensional Huffman coding compression method and (b) a two-dimensional compression method based on differences between scan lines. Group 4 facsimile specifies exactly the same coding method as Group 3 option b, but the protocol is designed for packet switched networks, so the Group 4 protocol assumes error-free transmission.

The encodings support only a restricted number of resolutions. For Group 3 facsimile, horizontal resolution is stated as 1728 dots over 215 mm; vertical resolution is either 3.85 lines per mm or 7.70 lines per mm. For standard A4 paper, this is equivalent to about 200 dots per inch in both X and Y for the fine resolution mode. Group 4 facsimile supports higher resolutions of 240, 300, and 400 dpi square, in addition to the 200 dpi square mode of Group 3 facsimile.

4.2 The Computer Graphics Metafile

The CGM provides a file format suitable for the storage and retrieval of picture description information. The file format consists of an ordered set of elements that can be used to describe pictures in a completely device-independent way. One or more pictures can be stored in a single metafile, and the metafile is defined in such a way that, in addition to sequential access to the whole metafile, random access to individual pictures is well defined. That is, the pictures are completely independent, one from another: their appearance does not depend upon the order in which they are accessed or displayed.

In addition to a functional specification, the CGM standard documents three standard encodings of the metafile semantics. The Character encoding requires minimum metafile size and is suitable for transmission across networks of heterogenous systems but is expensive to encode and decode. The Binary encoding requires minimum effort to generate and interpret but is not well-suited for exchange between computers of different arithmetic data types. It is nearly as efficiently coded as the Character encoding. The Clear-text encoding provides maximum readability and editability for ease of use by humans (e.g., for debugging purposes) but, generally, pays a heavy penalty in size and performance. The size is much larger because English and other natural languages contain a lot of redundancy. The performance is worse because parsing and recognizing text strings and converting text strings to internal numbers for use by a graphics subsystem is expensive in its use of CPU cycles.

In the absence of any facsimile standard capable of handling multicolor images (i.e., those with more than one bit per pixel), a CGM employing only the CELL ARRAY primitive could be used. Images expressed with either indexed and direct color specifications can be represented. In the Character-Coded and Binary encodings, run-length encoding may be used to reduce the size of the resulting CGM files.

The CGM was approved as ANSI/X3.122-1986, ISO 8632-1987, and US Federal Information Processing Standard 128.

4.3 The Initial Graphics Exchange Specification

The Initial Graphics Exchange Specification (IGES) is a mature standard, first published in 1981, for the digital exchange of database information among present-day CAD systems. Now in its third version, engineering drawings, 3D wireframe and surfaced part models, printed wiring product descriptions, finite element mesh descriptions, and process instrumentation diagrams are application usages addressed by IGES.

IGES information, including drawings and 3D wireframe product models, is intended for human interpretation at the receiving site. However, IGES is often used to attempt interchange between CAD databases and to feed external geometric data into a CAD system, where the data are expected to be processed automatically by computer as well as being worked on by human operators. Consequently, when used for this kind of interchange-a purpose it was not originally designed for, IGES files are often restricted in the kinds of entities used.

5 Approach

The 6 phases listed below were adopted for this work:

1 **Survey the Literature.** The recent computer graphics literature was surveyed to find articles describing raster-to-vector conversion methods, techniques, and uses. The articles located are included in the bibliography.

2 **Locate and Contact Vendors.** From a variety of sources, twelve companies were identified and contacted. These companies are listed in Table 1. Seven companies (ANA Tech, Audre, Autodesk, Optigraphics, Scan-Graphics, Skantek, and SysScan) were sent a special letter requesting their cooperation and assistance. In particular, they were asked to send technical information documenting their proprietary vector output files and to describe what elements of IGES are being used when IGES output is selected. Four of these companies (ANA Tech, Autodesk, Optigraphics, and Scan-Graphics) supplied the requested technical documentation.

Table 1: Vendors Contacted

Vendor Name	Tech Doc	Sales Lit.
Ana Tech Corp *	+	+
Audre, Inc. *		+
Autodesk, Inc. *	+	+
Metagraphics		+
Optigraphics *	+	+
QC Data		+
Scan-Graphics *	+	+
Scitex		+
Skantek Corp		
SysScan, Inc. *		+
Versatec		+
Vidar		+

* A special letter was sent to these vendors

3 **Learn the Process.** After reading all the vendor literature, technical documentation, and articles, we worked out a complete picture of the overall raster-to-vector conversion process. These results are documented in the next section.

4 **Analyze the Process.** Each stage in the raster-to-vector conversion process was analyzed with respect to some or all of the following characteristics: speed; accuracy and consistency; system cost; conversion cost and time; and data interchange requirements and opportunities. The Analysis section contains the results.

5 **Analyze the Vector and CAD Entity File.** For the four vendors who supplied technical documentation, we determined the global structure and the specific entities used to represent the scanned-in picture or drawing. We then compared these entities with the representational power of CGM. Finally, we looked at which IGES entities are actually used to transfer the picture to a CAD database using IGES. The Entity File Contents section reports these results.

6 **Draw Conclusions and Make Recommendations.** Based on the analyses, conclusions about the current usability of off-the-shelf, commercial raster-to-vector systems to meet some or all of the CALS requirements are drawn. The final sections document these conclusions and make recommendations, addressing both short term and long term issues.

6 The Process

Figure 1 represents a synthesis of all the processes conventionally included in the phrase "raster-to-vector conversion." Not all vendors provide products that accomplish all these processes; in fact, most vendors do not! However, all the stages must be progressed through when converting a representation of a drawing or image of a geometric object to a form whereby it can be incorporated into a design and subjected to engineering analysis and modification. Less ambitious objectives permit some of these stages to be skipped. The rest of this section defines and discusses the current state-of-the-art of each step in the process. We identify the inputs and outputs of each step and explore the possible uses of each output in its native form (as directly produced by the process) and in some modified form (as transformed by some auxiliary conversion process).

6.1 Step 1: Scanning and Storing the Document

The first step is the physical scanning process in which the paper sketch or drawing, aperture card, or photograph is raster-scanned. Millions of discrete samples are taken at closely spaced intervals across the entire surface of the document. Each sample is converted to a digital value that indicates the tone (black-and-white, gray-scale, or color value) of the drawing at a given point. This process results in producing a so-called raster database.

Such a database simply represents an image by storing, for each horizontal and vertical picture element (pixel), the code for the color representing that pixel. Even when compressed, these raster files vary greatly in size, but they typically are very large, easily 10 to 20 times the size of geometrically defined CAD files for the same picture. When uncompressed, they can be another order of magnitude larger.

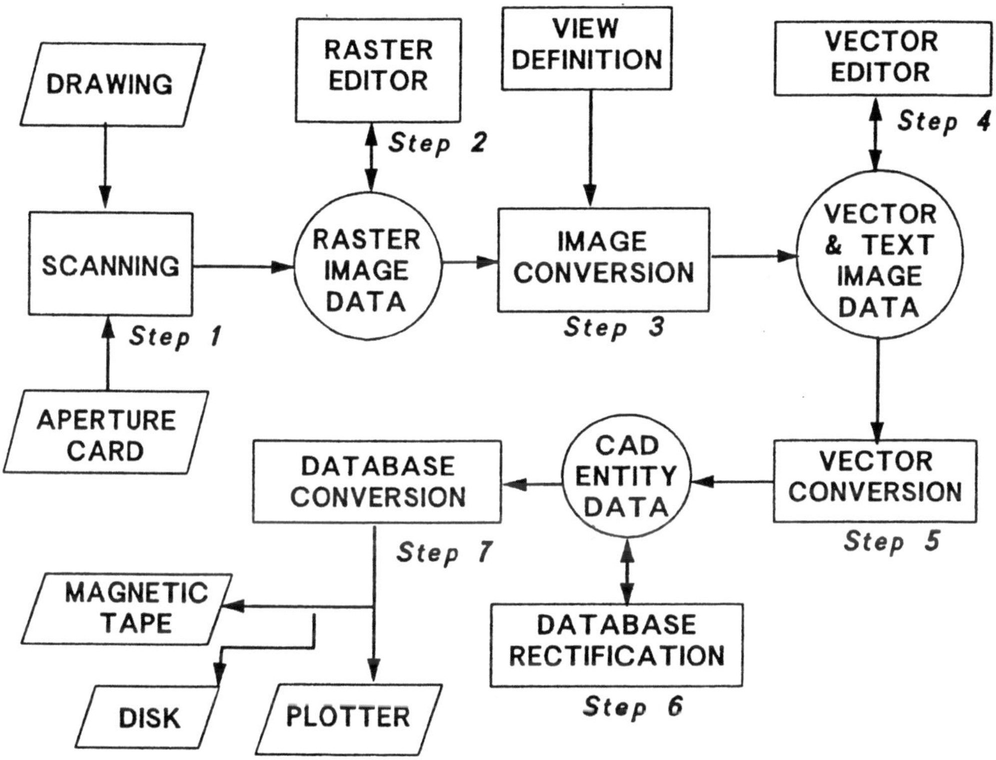

Figure 1: The Raster-to-Vector Conversion Process

For example, a simple uncompressed black-and-white (1 bit per pixel), PC resolution (640 by 480) picture occupies at least 640x480x1 bits or 38,400 bytes not counting any control and structural information required by the file format. A more typical black-and-white E-size drawing scanned at 200 dots per inch will occupy (36x200)x(48x200)x1 bits or 8,640,000 bytes, 225 times larger than the simple PC image.

When color or gray-scale images are involved, the numbers grow even more impressively. A 16-level (4 bits per pixel) gray scale or color picture of that E-size drawing would occupy over 34 million bytes of storage, while a more typical A-size photograph at the same resolution and color depth would still occupy 7.48 million bytes. For publishing purposes, one must often store 24 bits of color or more. This blows up our A-size color photographic image to more than 22 million bytes.

Raster file compression techniques, such as those specified by the CCITT Group 3 and Group 4 Facsimile standards, can be applied to reduce the amount of space required, but they are costly in computing time and, depending upon the nature of the image, may not achieve more than a 5-15% reduction in size.

These compression techniques were designed originally for and are most effective on documents that evidence a lot of visual uniformity, such as is found in office memos and reports with standard typewriter fonts and in simple engineering drawings. Long runs of all white or all black areas are replaced by counts of the number of all white or all black areas. Compression ratios of 10:1 to 20:1 are common.

However, many maps, satellite images, and photographs do not contain such visual coherence. Furthermore, these standards do not address the coding and compression of gray-scale and full color images. Consequently, compression of less than 20% is often seen for these more complex and life-like images.

There is practically no intelligence in a raster database. It neither represents nor differentiates between line, arcs, and text. This raster type of data can be stored, edited, retrieved, and distributed, but it cannot be sent directly to a CAD/CAM system. A raster storage system is seen either as a replacement for a microfilming system (with appropriate data management and distribution capabilities), a picture reproduction system, or as the first step in the drawing conversion process.

If the image to be captured and vectorized is already in raster format-such as would be delivered by video capture boards or satellite imaging systems, this first step can be bypassed.

6.2 Step 2: Editing the Raster Image

Before attempting to apply pattern recognition techniques to find the geometric entities, it is often productive to use a **raster editor** to modify the raster data by adding, deleting, or altering pixel information. Non-zero pixel values caused by specks of dirt, smudges, and creases in the paper may be removed. Lines of uneven width may be "airbrushed" to a more uniform consistency. Broken lines caused by a faulty pen or pencil in the drawing may be joined.

A raster image that is edited is typically held in working image memory, thus permitting rapid access to the data. With mouse control, the system operator can continuously pan and zoom over the entire image to select an area of interest. For large drawings and images, this requires megabytes of memory.

6.3 Step 3: Recognizing the Geometric Entities

This principal step in the raster-to-vector conversion process, sometime called **image conversion** converts raster data to CAD compatible vector data, that is a **geometry definition file** or **vector file**. In the more sophisticated systems, text information is extracted from the raster data and converted to ASCII character strings by automatic and user interactive processes. Graphic information is extracted from the raster data and automatically converted to geometric entities like lines, polylines, circles, arcs, arrowheads, and solid areas.

Among competing raster-to-vector systems there is great diversity in the nature of the contents of the vector file. The less capable systems produce a file of short line segments combined to represent text, polylines, arcs, circles, etc. Depending on the quality of the vectorization software, real CAD lines may be made up of 10 or 15 short vectors and arcs and circles may be made up of hundreds of line segments. Like raster data, short vector data can be stored, retrieved, edited, and distributed. Additionally, this type of data may be used as input into a CAD/CAM system.

The problem with this type of data is its limited usefulness for most CAD applications. For engineering drawings, the file size may be as large or larger than the corresponding raster image file. Consider the following example.

A black-and-white "D" size drawing scanned at 200 dots per inch requires 4.32 Mbytes in pixel storage. Compressed at a conservatively estimated 10:1 ratio, this drawing would require about 432 Kbytes in its raster form. A sample view in this "D" size drawing could require 50,000 short vectors, especially if there is a lot of annotation or a lot of curved objects in the drawing. Assuming that each short vector occupies 9 bytes (1 byte for the line opcode plus 4 x 2 bytes for each 16-bit coordinate), this same drawing in vector form could occupy 450 Kbytes. Furthermore, many CAD systems-especially the PC-based ones-cannot accept even this much data in a single drawing file.

Because the data are not differentiated as CAD entities (e.g., lines, arcs, text, splines, and dimensions), editing it on a CAD system is nearly impossible. For example, to change the radius of what appears to be a circle on a CAD system, the operator must redefine the group of short vectors as a circle. That is, all the line segments comprising the circle would have to be erased and a new circular element, specified by the CAD system, would have to be defined, before the element could be manipulated directly as a circle. An even more painful example is text. Correcting a simple typographic error or updating a date is nearly impossible if the text characters are known to the system only as short vectors.

Despite their obvious problems, short vector databases have a place in CAD. They can be used to produce backgrounds that won't change and therefore don't have to be edited. A prime example of this application is providing street, sewer, and railroad background for utility mapping. In these cases, vectors do not have to be geometric entities at all. The advantage of short vectors over raster images in this application is that the image is represented in a device-independent form: the picture can be scaled and rotated at will to fit the needs of the application. This has particular value in publishing and procurement applications.

In most of those systems that provide more that just short vectors as a result of the image conversion process, the extracted geometric, textual, and symbolic elements are placed into separate layers. These layers help the operator during the next step-editing the vector file. The layers help sort the mass of information generated during this stage into manageable and more uniform collections of objects.

In some systems, in addition to the geometry definition file, the conversion process will also build a condition or constraint file, as the expert system within the software automatically assigns changeable constraints to the geometry (such as tangents, symmetry, and collinearity).

6.4 Step 4: Editing the Vector File

The vector editor allows the system user to examine the quality of data being produced by the image conversion process and make modifications. The editor typically includes provisions for adding, modifying, or deleting geometric primitives in the vector image. The operator may also reorganize the layered data and standardize any of the following information:

- the width of various sets of lines
- the line type-e.g., dashed or dotted-of various lines
- the line join and end characteristics
- the heights of characters
- the fonts of character strings
- the grouping of similar items into symbols of a uniform size and orientation
- the solid or hatched patterns used to fill areas.

6.5 Step 5: Converting to a CAD Entity File

In the more expensive and sophisticated systems, steps 3 and 4 may be combined with step 5. That is, the output of the image conversion process is a set of CAD elements that can be accepted directly into a CAD data base. However, more frequently, there is a human-assisted, semi-automatic process required to convert the standardized vector file into higher level CAD entities.

Often referred to as "geometric elements," the highest level of database intelligence is referred to as CAD entities. To create this intelligence level, the drawing conversion system must pass to a CAD system neither pixels nor short vectors, but rather the same entities that are used and stored in the target CAD system database-lines, arcs, splines, polygons, ASCII text, notes, dimensions, labels, and the like.

Even the few drawing conversion systems that can produce this type of data automatically vary vastly in the level of usefulness and intelligence within the database. To evaluate the level of database intelligence, it is helpful to ask a series of questions:

- Is there connectivity between the different elements of geometry? Is a given line, for example, connected to a given arc that it appears to be connected to?

- Can I move a geometric entity like a template simply by touching a point and executing the move command? Will I move the simple entity (the given line) I touch or will I move the entire entity consisting of its sub-entities?

- When data is passed to the CAD system, are physical conditions such as crucial tangencies, true perpendicularity, true parallelism and collinearity maintained? All the above elements of intelligence are assumed by the appearance of the drawing until the user tries to use the data he obtains from the drawing conversion system and finds it imprecisely or incompletely defined.

6.6 Step 6: Checking the File for Consistency and Accuracy

To be fully useful, a CAD database must not only be intelligent in its maintenance of geometry, connectivity, ancestral relationships, and physical relationships, but also the database must be accurate and checked for consistency.

When we say a database is accurate, we mean that the geometry sent to the CAD system is absolutely accurate to the corresponding dimensions present in the drawing at the specified scale of the drawing. This means that, if the dimension of a line is 9.876 mm, that value is the mathematical norm (i.e., length) of the vector whose coordinates are passed to the CAD system as the geometric representation of that line.

A few raster-to-vector conversion systems can pass accurate geometry that is driven by dimensions and is stored with an accuracy of up to 14 significant figures. Drawing conversion systems based primarily on hardware actually may introduce inaccuracy into the database. This is true if you consider that generally the starting point for these systems (the drawing that was prepared with a pencil) is generally not accurate even to the width of a line (about one-hundredth of an inch). In addition, the accuracy provided by the scanner alone is, at best, equal to its resolution (e.g., about 8 pixels per mm). Furthermore, unless the original mylar (if it exists) is used for the scan, the drawing will not normally be even as accurate as it was drawn.

The only way to guarantee true database accuracy is to attack the problem from a software standpoint. This means taking the scanned data with its dimensions and reproducing a new set of geometry based on the exact dimensions, definitions and physical properties of the geometry. Consequently, to get an accurate database, the system-perhaps with varying amounts of operator assistance-must build a numeric dimension and tolerance file prior to image conversion. To do this, the system must recognize, convert, and store the pixel dimension and associated tolerances.

To build up a 3-D CAD entity file from a drawing consisting of 2-D orthographic or perspective projections, the system needs to be more intelligent than is required for processing 2-D drawings. Furthermore, the operator must participate and specify view information by indicating on the drawing view windows, names of views, the view scale, and a point that is coincident in all views. During the conversion to CAD entities, a "cross-view" linking process builds a 2 1/2-D model based on this information.

An accurate file is not necessarily checked for consistency; that is, the file is not necessarily:

- free of conflicts in dimensions (e.g., an overall dimension adds up to several subdimensions) even when considering multi-view drawings;
- free of ambiguities, such as geometry with no dimensions or geometry that has the potential to be confusing to a designer or to a CAD system with regard to tangency points, parallelism, perpendicularity, collinearity, etc.; and
- free of errors in basic design logic.

6.7 Step 7: Interchanging the File with Other Systems

The output of step 5 (and step 6, when performed) is an entity file in each vendor's proprietary format. A entity file is not a CAD database. In order to be accepted by any CAD system, it is necessary to translate the vendor-specific CAD entity file into a format that is recognized by the target CAD system. Two approaches are used: one based on standards and one not.

The standards-based approach converts the CAD entity geometry file to an IGES file. The data then can be acquired by any CAD system that can read IGES files. The non-standards-based approach simply provides translators to the more widespread CAD database formats: Autotrol, AutoCAD, CADAM, Computervision, and Intergraph are among the most popular.

The advantages of the first approach are obvious: only one translator is needed. The principal disadvantage is that the various CAD systems don't all accept all the IGES elements specified in the IGES standard. Consequently, a "lowest common denominator" for IGES is often followed. In a later section, we report on exactly which IGES entities are actually produced by some of the raster-to-vector conversion systems.

7 Analysis

7.1 Overview

It is impossible to compare systems on the basis of vendor literature and documentation alone. Not only do each of the systems have different architectures, prices, and mixes of hardware and software, but also they are positioned to serve different niche markets. Consequently, one system may be optimized for engineering drawings, another for well logs, and still another for mapping applications. When asking the question, "Which system is best?," the only answer is It all depends . . . :

- It all depends on what you want to do with the picture after it is scanned. Is the drawing only to be included in a technical manual or is the conversion process simply the first step in a redesign of the part shown in the drawing?
- It all depends on how much throughput you need. How many drawings must be converted over what period of time? Is conversion needed for one project only, for a limited time? Or is this going to be a continuing process?
- It all depends on how much you are willing to pay!

To further complicate the analysis, the performance of each system is directly related to the nature of the drawing being scanned. The density of the lines, the number of symbols, line weights, and text fonts, the amount of text, the extent of and variation in filled areas, the amount of crossing and touching lines-all contribute to the measure of complexity.

In order to make speed comparisons across competitive systems, benchmarks on the identical drawings would have to be performed. But speed is directly related to the price you pay and is not the only consideration. Accuracy, consistency, and richness of the resulting CAD entity file may also be important for many applications.

7.2 Speed

The ANA Tech VANA system, with its hardware vectorizer, can automatically convert an E-size drawing to vectors in 5-7 minutes. Up to an additional hour is typically required to transform the dumb vector file into CAD entities. The other high-end systems also take in the 30 minutes to 2 hour range. At the low end, Autodesk's CAD/Camera will take from 5 to 7 hours on a PC/AT for a drawing of similar complexity.

The scanning process, producing only a raster database, takes from 90 seconds to about 4 minutes at 200 lines per inch. Not unexpectedly, the more expensive systems have greater throughput or scan at greater resolution.

7.3 Accuracy and Consistency

Minimum detectable line width ranges from .002 to .005 inches. This is a function of the resolution of the scanner. However, as explained above, the accuracy of the resulting vector file depends heavily upon the quality of the original document, unless human-assisted methods are used to correlate the vector geometry as scanned in with the intended absolute dimensions as represented by dimension lines and other annotations on the drawing.

Only by performing the functions from Step 6 can a CAD-accurate database be produced. As yet, no system can perform this step without human intervention.

7.4 System Cost

Prices for automatic scanner systems range from $100,000 to almost $300,000, depending upon speed, sophistication, editing capabilities, and hardware capacity. Where editing is supported, an Apollo, Digital microVAX, or Sun class workstation with stand-alone computing power is provided.

Scanners without workstations are priced in the $40K to $125K range, depending on speed, accuracy, intelligence, and resolution. The highest priced offering-the ANA Tech Eagle 800 for $125K-includes on-the-fly vectorizing of the drawing. The other systems create only a raster database, which is later processed by software to create the vector and CAD databases.

Software-only solutions that run on the IBM PC/AT like Autodesk's CAD/Camera and Professional CAD/CAM's ProCAD+V/R are much less expensive ($3K to $10K), but are also much less capable and very much slower.

Service bureaus are available if the lease or purchase of dedicated in-house systems cannot be justified. They charge from $150 to $300 for each E-size drawing converted.

7.5 Conversion Cost and Time

No formal studies have been published concerning the time and cost of converting drawings. Consequently, one must depend upon anecdotal information and marketing claims. However, there is generally good agreement on the numbers.

Optigraphics claims that the payback for a scanning and conversion system can be achieved by processing about 1000 drawings (about one year's work for most engineering departments).

Audre estimates that conversion of a complex E-size drawing costs about $110 and takes four hours, compared with $1,350 and 30 hours using a standard CAD digitizing approach.

Anderson Reports estimates $225-$550 for the automated path (taking 5-9 hours) and $450-$1000 for manual digitizing (taking 16-40 hours). A reported side benefit of the automatic path is better quality: one experiment reported 30% fewer errors. Anderson also estimates that the tradeoff point between using a service bureau and buying your own system is about 800 drawings.

For consistent and accurate drawings (the highest level of CAD database), Metagraphics claims that their system is 4 times faster than digitizing via a conventional CAD/CAM system. They also claim a 3:1 cost advantage.

7.6 Data Interchange

Most of the commercial systems studied can accept already digitized raster databases at the front-end (that is, after Step 1). CCITT Group 3 and 4 facsimile formats are generally the only standards supported at this interface. As mentioned in Relevant Standards Section above, these formats apply only to black-and-white (one bit per pixel) images. At present, this is not a limiting factor because none of the commercial raster-to-vector systems can handle multiple bit-per-pixel (color or gray scale) images. However, this could become a concern in the future.

No formal standardized format for the CAD-compatible or CAD-accurate vector databases has been adopted across the commercial systems. As described in the next section, each product has a proprietary vector file format and structure, but none are compatible with any of their competitors. Autodesk's CAD/Camera product does produce an AutoCAD DXB file-a format that has become a de facto industry standard on PC-based CAD systems.

To export these databases, the suppliers offer translators. As explained previously, translators to IGES as well as to the proprietary formats of the major CAD/CAM systems are available. In the next section, we will see that, in general, only a few IGES entities are used. Consequently, some of the semantic content of the CAD-compatible database may be lost when using IGES to transfer the data into a CAD/CAM system.

Also in the next section, we see that the Computer Graphics Metafile standard could serve as a common representation of CAD entity databases, especially if enhanced with a few features as recommended in the final section.

8 Entity File Contents

Four vendors-ANA Tech, Autodesk, Optigraphics, and Scan-Graphics-provided sufficient technical information to permit a detailed examination of the vector and CAD entity file elements generated by their systems. All of these systems perform some automatic recognition of CAD entities. In the following sections, the results of the analysis are presented and are summarized in Table 2.

Table 2: Entity File Contents

	ANA	AutoD	Opti.	Scan-G
Solid Lines	+	+	+	+
Line Width	+	+	+	
Line Type				
Arrows		+	+	
Circle/Arc	+	+	+	+
Ellipse/Arc	+		+	
B-splines			+	
Outlined Areas	+	+	+	+
Solid Areas	+	+	+	
Areas w/holes	+		+	
Rectangles			+	
Pattern/hatch				
Text	+		+	+
Hgt/orient/spacing	+		+	+
Char exp factor			+	+
Text fonts	+			+
Text alignment				+
Color				
Points	+	+	+	+
Symbols	+	lim	+	+
Symbol rot/scale			plan.	+

8.1 Entities Used

Line Entities. All four systems support solid lines; only Scan-Graphics appears not to store line width information in the entity file. None appear to have a line type attribute (e.g., dashed, chained); rather, broken lines seem to be represented by a series of short vectors.

Curved Entities. All systems can recognize circles and circular arcs. ANA Tech and Optigraphics also can detect ellipses and elliptical arcs. Optigraphics can also represent curved entities as B-splines.

Area Entities. All systems can recognize outlined or "hollow" filled areas without holes. Only Scan-Graphics cannot detect solid areas. Both ANA Tech and Optigraphics can also detect and represent filled areas with holes. Optigraphics can also detect the special case of a solid filled or hollow rectangle. Autodesk (CAD/Camera) and Optigraphics provide special support for an arrow entity.

Fill Styles. Only outlined ("hollow") and solid fills are supported by some systems. None support patterned or hatch filled regions.

Text. Only Autodesk has no automatic recognition of text entities. From the remaining three systems, support for the various text attributes is uneven. All support character height, orientation, and spacing. Only ANA Tech and Scan-Graphics support recognition of several text fonts, while only Optigraphics and Scan-Graphics support character expansion factor. Only Scan-Graphics stores text alignment information.

Color. None of the systems support the storage and representation of color or gray-scale information.

Symbols. ANA Tech supports only "points" or "dots." Autodesk supports both "points" and a limited concept of symbols or "blocks." Both Optigraphics and Scan-Graphics support a general symbol recognition and symbol representation facility. Symbol rotation and scale can be detected and represented in the Scan-Graphics system, while this feature is planned for but not yet supported on the Optigraphics system.

8.2 Structure

ANA Tech. The output of the image conversion process is structured into layers. As mentioned earlier, layers are used to sort out the mass of information generated during raster-to-vector conversion into more manageable and more uniform collections of objects. For example, all text may be placed in one layer, all geometric elements in another, and all symbols in a third layer. For the ANA Tech system, it is unclear from the documentation what criteria are used to decide which elements are placed in which layer. ANA Tech's vector file is called Standard Output Format (SOF). Entities can be grouped and connectivity relationships expressed.

Autodesk. All vectors produced by the image conversion system are stored in an Autodesk DXB file that is readable by Autodesk's widely-used AutoCAD program. The vectors are placed on layer "LINES" in the vector database, and solids are placed on layer "SOLIDS." The raster scan lines comprising any text strings or symbols that were identified are placed on layer "SYMBOLS," with borders drawn around them on layer "OUTLINES." Text and symbols are not automatically processed or recognized by the system. Instead, human intervention using the AutoCAD product is required.

Optigraphics. Optigraphics Database Format (ODF) is a more highly structured file format than ANA Tech SOF or Autodesk DXB. Three sections comprise the file: a header section containing global attributes, a symbol library section containing the definitions of various symbols discovered in the drawing, and the geometry entity section containing the representation of the drawing itself. Within the geometry entity section, layers and groups of primitives may be identified.

Scan-Graphics. The Scan-Graphics vector data format IDS, produced by its RAVE image conversion software, does not provide for any structuring of the picture data. However, an operator using their interactive vector editing software, IGMS, may organize the data into as many as 64 separate levels. The documentation also refers to an element type ASSORTED which may be used in the future to provide structure to the elementary data. Finally, there is an element USER-DEFINED SYMBOL that allows one to include symbols that have been previously defined and recognized by the RAVE software.

8.3 Comparison with CGM

The results are summarized in Table 3. The details follow.

Table 3: CGM Comparison

	ANA	**AutoD**	**Opti.**	**Scan-G**
POLYLINE	+	+	+	+
LINE WIDTH	+	+		
TEXT	+		+	+
TEXT FONT	+			+
CHAR SPACING	+		+	+
CHAR HEIGHT	+		+	+
CHAR EXP FACTOR			+	+
CHAR ORIENT	+		+	+
APPEND TEXT	+			
CLIP RECT/IND	+			
POLYGON	+	+	+	+
POLYGON SET	+		+	
RECTANGLE			+	
POLYMARKER	+	+		+
MARKER SIZE	+			+
CIRCLE	+	+	+	+
CIRCULAR ARC	+	+	+	
ELLIPSE	+		+	
FONT LIST	+			
SCALING MODE	+	+	+	
VDC TYPE		+		
VDC EXTENT			+	

ANA Tech. The SOF entity types and their Computer Graphics Metafile equivalent are given below:

END-OF-FILE	CGM END METAFILE
DRAW/MOVE	CGM POLYLINE
DATA WINDOW	CGM CLIP RECTANGLE/CLIP INDICATOR
LINE WEIGHT	CGM LINE WIDTH with LINE WIDTH SPECIFICATION MODE equal to "ABSOLUTE"
TEXT with attributes	CGM TEXT with attributes TEXT FONT INDEX, CHARACTER SPACING, CHARACTER HEIGHT, and CHARACTER ORIENTATION
TEXT CONT'N	CGM APPEND TEXT
RESOLUTION	CGM SCALING MODE equal to "metric"
AREA with no holes	CGM POLYGON with fill "solid"
AREA with HOLE	CGM POLYGON SET with fill "solid"
FONT FILE NAME list	CGM FONT LIST
LAYER	CGM BEGIN PICTURE
POINT	CGM POLYMARKER
POLYGON	CGM POLYGON with fill "hollow"
CIRCLE	CGM CIRCLE and CIRCULAR ARC CENTER
ELLIPSE	CGM ELLIPSE and ELLIPTICAL ARC CENTER

Two more elements do not map directly into CGM elements: GRAPHIC ITEM NUMBER and CHAIN/CONNECTION. These elements are used to store connectivity relationships between coordinates making up the picture. This information is included in the SOF only if needed and requested by the generator of the SOF. If the CGM were to serve as a replacement for the SOF, APPLICATION DATA elements of the CGM would need to be specified to contain this additional information.

Other Notes:

1. Each layer can be mapped directly into a CGM picture; one or more CGM pictures comprise a CGM metafile.

2. The SOF may optionally contain font tables, that is, character height and width information about each ASCII character in each font. Inclusion of this information can be suppressed during the generation process.

3. The SOF may also contain line width tables, that is, information describing how lines of various widths are normalized to a constant width. For example, a line width table of [1,3;6,8;] indicates that lines ranging in width from 1 to 5 units should be drawn at 3 units and those of 6 units or greater width should be drawn uniformly at 8 units wide.

4. The generator of the SOF may indicate whether the character height is measured from the baseline to the cap line (the default) or from the bottom line to the cap line. In the CGM, all character heights are measured from the baseline to the cap line only.

Autodesk. The vector file contents produced by CAD/camera map directly into CGM primitives as detailed in the following:

LINE	CGM POLYLINE with line type "solid" and line width "nominal"
POINT	CGM POLYMARKER with marker type "dot" and marker size "nominal"
CIRCLE	CGM CIRCLE with interior style "hollow"
ARC	CGM CIRCULAR ARC CENTER with line type "solid" and line width "nominal"
TRACE	CGM POLYGON with interior style "hollow"
SOLID	CGM POLYGON with interior style "solid"
POLYLINE with closure flag	No immediate effect on CGM
VERTEX	CGM POLYLINE
BULGE	CGM CIRCULAR ARC 3 POINT
WIDTH	Either (1) CGM LINE WIDTH if width is constant or (2) CGM POLYGON if width is not constant, as in an arrow
SEQEND	Nothing or CGM POLYLINE if closure flag is 1

SCALE FACTOR	CGM SCALING MODE "metric"
NEW LAYER	CGM BEGIN PICTURE
LINE EXTENSION	CGM POLYLINE
TRACE EXTENSION	CGM POLYGON with interior style "hollow"
BLOCK BASE	CGM POLYMARKER with marker type equal to block number
NUMBER MODE	CGM VDC TYPE.

Other Notes:

1. BLOCK BASE maps into CGM POLYMARKER only if the symbols denoted by block number are known to the receiving system as built-in markers.

2. No recognition of text primitives is performed by CAD/Camera.

Optigraphics. Information in the header section maps to the CGM elements SCALING MODE "metric" and VDC EXTENT. The maximum linewidth element cannot be represented directly in the CGM, but would be used during rendering to clamp the width of wide lines to some reasonable maximum.

Information contained in the Symbol Library Definition Section does not directly map to any concept contained in the current CGM specification. However, current work on extending the CGM to include the concept of segments is underway. When complete, these new CGM elements will be able to represent symbols well.

The geometric entities map directly to CGM entities with two exceptions as noted in the list below:

VECTOR STRING	CGM POLYLINE or POLYGON
RECTANGLE	CGM RECTANGLE
CIRCLE	CGM CIRCLE
CIRCULAR ARC	CGM CIRCULAR ARC CENTER [CLOSE]
ELLIPTICAL ARC	CGM ELLIPSE or ELLIPTICAL ARC [CLOSE]
B-SPLINE	No CGM counterpart; use GDP or reduce to POLYLINE's
ARROW	No CGM counterpart; use GDP or reduce to POLYLINE's or POLYGON

FILLED AREA	CGM POLYGON or POLYGON SET
TEXT STRING	CGM TEXT with attributes CHARACTER HEIGHT, CHARACTER EXPANSION FACTOR, CHARACTER SPACING, CHARACTER ORIENTATION
SYMBOL OCCUR'CE	INSERT SEGMENT under transformation or POLYMARKER only in very special circumstances.

Other Notes:

1. The rotation and scale parameters of SYMBOL OCCURRENCE are not yet supported.

2. Generalized Drawing Primitives (GDPs) for B-SPLINE and ARROW would have to be registered and supported for the CGM to perform well as a replacement for ODF.

3. All vector entities have a display type: solid (corresponding to CGM INTERIOR STYLE "solid"), hidden (corresponding to CGM interior style "empty" with no boundary visible), centerline (corresponding to "hollow" filled areas with "solid" borders), cutplane and phantom. These last two display types are not explained in the available documentation.

4. All vector entities have line width.

5. No vector entities have color.

6. Although text is recognized, specification of text font is not supported, unlike the ANA Tech and Scan-Graphics systems.

Scan-Graphics. Only seven element types are used by RAVE to represent the scanned image. These are listed below along with their correspondence with CGM elements.

SIMPLE VECTOR (centerline)	CGM POLYLINE
SIMPLE VECTOR (outline)	CGM POLYGON with interior style "hollow"
CIRCLE	CGM CIRCLE
CIRCULAR ARC	CGM CIRCULAR ARC CENTER

TEXT with attributes	CGM TEXT with the attributes CHARACTER HEIGHT, CHARACTER ORIENTATION, CHARACTER EXPANSION FACTOR, CHARACTER SPACING, TEXT ALIGNMENT, and TEXT FONT INDEX
FIDUCIAL	Not supported directly by CGM; would have to be represented by a registered GDP (a fiducial appears to be a text string representing a latitude and longitude)
CENTERED SYMBOL	CGM POLYMARKER with attribute MARKER SIZE and MARKER SIZE SPECIFICATION MODE equal to "absolute"
USER-DEFINED SYMBOL	Would correspond to INSERT SEGMENT under rotation and scale, when the extended CGM has been defined to include a segmentation facility.

Other Notes:

1. Color cannot be represented.
2. Several additional elements-ellipse, hyperbola, parabola, and dimension line-are planned to be used but are not yet generated by the RAVE software.
3. Line width information appears to be specified outside the IDS-at least the documentation provided did not seem to include a place for that information.
4. There was no indication in the documentation of how software reading the IDS would know whether a SIMPLE VECTOR represented a centerline or an outline.

8.4 Interface to IGES

ANA Tech. Only four of the SOF elements are mapped to IGES entities:

MOVE/DRAW	Maps to the IGES COPIOUS DATA entity (106) form 11.
TEXT	Maps to the IGES GENERAL NOTES entity (212).
CIRCLE	Maps to the IGES CIRCULAR ARC entity (100).
ELLIPSE	Maps to the IGES CONIC ARC entity (104) form 1.

What happens to the other graphic primitive information from POLYGON and AREA elements is unstated. Presumably the outline information is converted to lines (IGES COPIOUS DATA form 11), but what happens to the filled portion is not documented.

Autodesk. CAD/camera cannot directly output IGES files. However, because the CAD/camera vector files can be read by AutoCAD, IGES files can be produced if there is an IGES file generator available from Autodesk. The IGES entities so created are not described in the available documentation.

Optigraphics. Optigraphics sales literature states that vector data can be expressed in an IGES format optimized for the target CAD system. However, no documentation describing the actual IGES entities used was made available.

Scan-Graphics. RAVE IDS files can be converted to IGES formatted vector files according to the following mapping of IDS data types to IGES entities.

SIMPLE VECTOR (centerline)
IGES Line Entity (110) or Copious Data Entity (106 form 12)

SIMPLE VECTOR (planar outline)
IGES Plane Entity (108)

CIRCLE and ARC IGES Circular Arc Entity (100)

TEXT IGES General Note Entity (212)

DIMENSION LINE (when supported)
IGES Leader Arrow Entity (214 form 2).

9 Conclusions and Recommendations

9.1 Regarding the Process

As described earlier, three types of databases are typically created during the process of converting a physical document (paper, aperture card, etc.) to a digital form. These types are: (1) a **compressed bitmap** file with editing capabilities limited to cosmetic cleaning up of the digitized image; (2) a **CAD-compatible** vector database, which represents the drawing in an efficient manner and which permits easy modification and redisplay at different sizes, resolutions, and orientations on a wide variety of hardcopy and softcopy devices; and (3) a **CAD-accurate** geometric database, which is dimensionally accurate and consistent, permitting engineering analysis and redesign using a CAD/CAM system.

If the goal is to clean up and make a few minor changes to an old drawing, a bitmap database will suffice. Bitmap databases could be used:

- To provide images and photographs for technical publishing applications. Maintenance manuals and user's manuals, informative newsletters, and technical specifications are just a few of the end-products of the on-line computer-based publishing industry that has emerged in the past few years.
- To support purchasing; that is, drawings could be disseminated as part of bid packages.
- To support computer interactive training and maintenance delivery systems. Photographs, drawings, and even animated sequences could be displayed at a raster graphics terminal to explain how to use or fix a piece of equipment.

Resizing and rotating raster images is expensive and introduces distortions caused by statistical resampling of the image (known as **aliasing effects**). Similarly, aliasing effects appear if you need to display an image with a different resolution than the resolution at which it was scanned in and stored. Consequently, limited use can be made of these raster databases. Even if one were to standardize on, say, 200 dot per inch resolution for storing and displaying documents today, in the future, 300, 400, and even 600 dot per inch display technology will be affordable and commonplace. Indeed, already today in the technical publishing industry, 300 dpi is the laser printer standard; 400 dpi is available on some high-end large format electrostatic printers used for CAD/CAM, facilities management, and mapping applications; and 500 dpi and higher is used in the color pre-press and typesetting worlds.

Recommendation 1:

A formal raster image file format should be standardized upon. The standard should:

- Incorporate CCITT and other compression algorithms.
- Be based on the CGM file structure and encoding techniques.
- Support multiple bit-per-pixel images.
- Not be tied to any particular set of resolutions.

If the drawing will be used in other designs, will be changed often, is needed at various sizes and orientations, and will be displayed on a variety of hardcopy and softcopy devices with different resolutions, a CAD-compatible (vector and fill area) database is most useful. CAD-compatible databases could be used:

- In engineering design systems, to input older designs that are intended to provide a conceptual starting point for new designs or to input new conceptual designs developed on stand-alone CAD workstations (perhaps even PC-based).

- To support the technical publications process in all its phases. Pictures represented as CAD-compatible databases can be cropped, scaled, rotated, and composed to fit the needs of the documentation. They can be modified and enhanced by a graphics artist or technical editor to emphasize or illustrate certain features vital for proper maintenance or use.

- To support the purchasing process in all its aspects. Drawings can be manipulated just as in the technical publications process for similar purposes. In addition, diagrams, drawings, and displays represented as standardized CAD-compatible databases can be disseminated by the buyer to bidders to be used as benchmarks in the evaluation of the graphical speed, capacity, and capabilities of military components and subsystems. Conversely, a bid package may request that bidders submit standardized, CAD-compatible databases representing the display capabilities of their systems. The buyer's employees could then use these data to evaluate the technical merits of the proposals.

- To support computer-based interactive delivery of maintenance and training assistance. Pictures stored as CAD-compatible data are much more suitable for manipulation, enhancement, and animation than are images stored in raster form. Where photographs or high-density maps are needed, a hybrid approach with the raster data in the background and vectors, filled polygons, and text overlayed in the foreground is a very viable approach.

Converting drawings to CAD-accurate databases is needed in only two major situations:

1. When a major engineering design effort is undertaken and that effort is based on a previous design. For example, an improved design of an airframe would probably want to start from the complete geometrically accurate database of the current airframe.

2. When a part or subsystem needs to undergo extensive engineering analysis. For example, analysis for points of high stress or strain in a helicopter propeller.

Recommendation 2:

Suppliers of Raster-to-Vector Conversion systems should be urged to supply CGM files as a standard way of exporting both the unprocessed vector information (that is, the output of Steps 3 and 4) and the processed vector information (that is, the output of Steps 5 and 6). This would permit vector representations of drawings to be immediately usable in a wide range of publishing and drawing systems that plan on using ANSI/X3.122 (ISO 8632; FIPS 128), CGM, as their standard for importing pictures and diagrams. Publishing systems built around SGML and ODA/ODIF already specify the use of CGM.

9.2 Regarding IGES.

Exporting CAD-compatible information using IGES is an important feature of present-day systems. However, the weak conformance rules associated with the IGES standard (X3.110-1981) reduce its effectiveness. Only a few entities IGES seem to be used by any of the raster-to-vector conversion systems.

Recommendation 3:

Form an IGES task group to draft a minimum set of conformance guidelines for IGES interpreters. Work with industry suppliers to raise the level of intelligence that can be understood by all IGES interpreters. Then, develop a set of specifications for raster-to-vector conversion systems to meet. The specifications should indicate how different components of a drawing should map to IGES entities.

9.3 Regarding CGM.

Recommendation 2 suggests that CGM be used as the primary vehicle for exporting digital representations of drawings obtained from raster-to-vector conversion systems. Although CGM can be used in its present form as documented in the previous section, enhancements to CGM could be made to make the use of CGM more efficient and effective. In addition, several ESCAPE's and

GDP's should be specified and registered with the ISO Registration Authority. These elements should also be included in any future revisions and addenda to the CGM.

The recommended elements are:

An ARROW line attribute ESCAPE

This modal attribute would apply to all subsequent polylines and circular and elliptical arcs and would allow four enumerated values: (0) no arrows; (1) arrow at end; (2) arrow at beginning; and (3) arrows at both ends.

An ARROW SHAPE attribute ESCAPE

This modal attribute would control the appearance of any arrows drawn as a result of the ARROW attribute. Control over the length of arrowhead-from tip to base, its width at the base, and whether the arrowhead is filled or outlined should be provided as aspects of this attribute.

A FONT METRICS metafile descriptor ESCAPE

This element would contain at least the character width tables for all fonts included in the FONT LIST element. The specification should be compatible with the Font Description standardization work taking place in ISO/JTC1/SC18.

A SPLINE GDP element

The parameterization should probably be based on non-rational B-splines. However, experts from the CAD/CAM field should be consulted prior to this GDP's definition.

CLOSED FIGURE control ESCAPEs

The functionality should be based on the IGES and CGI (ISO DP 9636/dpANS X3.161) specifications.

A DISABLE CLEAR control ESCAPE

Specified as a two-state flag, this element when encountered in a metafile would disable or enable clearing of the viewing surface at the beginning of the next picture and all subsequent pictures. This functionality has been proposed in the TOP 3.0 CGM application profile and is needed to implement layers.

In addition, we should investigate whether there is a future need for representing fiducials, hyperbolas, parabolas, and dimension lines directly in the CGM.

Recommendation 4:

As outlined above, several proposals for Graphical Item registration should be prepared and sponsored according to the ANSI/X3 Sponsoring Body procedures. The extended CGM work now underway in ISO/JTC1/SC24 should also take these requirements into consideration.

The more sophisticated raster-to-vector systems support the creation of a Symbol Library for a drawing by recognizing instances of common geometric forms like diamonds, resistors, and arrowheads. In the current CGM, each instance of such a symbol would have to be described with its full geometry. No references to global definitions of symbols are possible. However, the extended CGM development work taking place within ISO and ASC X3H3 is considering adding a segmentation facility to CGM. The rules regarding where segments can be defined and the scope rules relating to referring to segments have not yet been decided.

Recommendation 5:

We advocate that the extended CGM permit segments to be defined outside a picture; i.e., in the metafile descriptor. Such segment definitions should be able to be referenced from within any of the pictures comprising the metafile. A facility comparable to GKS's INSERT SEGMENT under transformation (to permit scaling, rotation, and translation of the symbol) should be supported in the CGM.

10 Summary

Technology has advanced to the point that most raster-to-vector conversion problems can be solved by the application of some combination of automatic and manual methods, at an acceptable speed, with adequate accuracy. Each application requirement has its own price point; whether the price is cost-effective depends completely upon the application and the volume of work required. Where justified, the conversion process should begin now using current raster-to-vector conversion technology.

Three standards are relevant to the raster-to-vector conversion technology. Photographs and drawings may be scanned in and stored in one of the CCITT Group 3 or 4 facsimile formats. Similarly, previously generated raster images may be accepted by a raster-to-vector conversion system in one of the CCITT formats.

Unstructured vector data may be represented using the formats provided by ISO 8632 (ANSI/X3.122), the Computer Graphics Metafile (CGM). The CGM provides a standard syntax and semantics for storing and transmitting a broad range of color, gray-scale, and black-and-white pictures, represented as both vector drawings and raster images. Three encodings of CGM have been standardized. Each encoding meets different design objectives-compactness, speed of processing, and ease of understanding.

Structured and edited geometry data can be formatted for entry into CAD/CAM systems for subsequent modification and analysis using ANSI/Y14.26M, the Initial Graphics Exchange Specification (IGES).

Acknowledgements

The study reported in this paper is contained in a report, "Raster-to-Vector Conversion: A State-of-the-Art Assessment," delivered to the U.S. Department of Commerce National Bureau of Standards on April 2, 1987. It was provided under Contract Number 43NANB705617, ably administered by Daniel Benigni.

The descriptions of the various stages of raster-to-vector conversion borrow liberally from the various vendor descriptions; however, the total description represents a synthesis of all the products and does not necessarily represent the full capabilities available from any one vendor. ANA Tech, Autodesk, Optigraphics, and Scan-Graphics are especially thanked for their cooperation in providing technical material.

References

1. "A Comparison of Standards Relating to Graphics Picture Exchange-A Technical Analysis of the Compatibility of Product Data Definition Standards and Graphics Standards," Peter R. Bono Associates, *NBS Contract* No. 43NANB612434, 13 June 1986.

2. "Review and Analysis of CALS-related Requirements for Graphics Standards," System Development Corporation Report TM-HU-500/000/00, *NBS Contract* No. 43NANB613292, 31 July 1986.

3. "How the CALS Program Should Utilize Computer Graphics Standards," Peter R. Bono Associates Report, *NBS Contract* No. 43NANB615018, 10 October 1986.

Bibliography

Standards Documents

CCITT Terminal Equipment and Protocols for Telematic Services (the CCITT "Red Book"), Vol. VII - Fascicle VII.3.

- CCITT Recommendation T.4, Standardization of Group 3 Facsimile Apparatus for Document Transmission, 1986.

- CCITT Recommendation T.5, General Aspects of Group 4 Facsimile Apparatus, 1986.

- CCITT Recommendation T.6, Facsimile Coding Scheme and Coding Control Functions for Group 4 Facsimile Apparatus, 1986.

Computer Graphics Metafile for the Storage and Transfer of Picture Description Information (CGM), ANSI/X3.122-1986, August 27, 1986.

Initial Graphics Exchange Specification (IGES), Version 3.0, National Bureau of Standards Report NBSIR 86-3359, April 1986.

These documents are available from a variety of sources:

The published ANSI standard CGM can be obtained from ANSI, 1430 Broadway, New York, NY 10018. The CCITT documents may also be obtained through ANSI.

The IGES document can be obtained from the IGES Committee Chairman, Mr. Bradford Smith, National Bureau of Standards, Gaithersburg, MD.

Relevant Articles

"Optigraphics-Drawing Digitizing Price/Performance Leader," *F-M Automation Newsletter*, September 1985.

"Scanning Imager Offers Advantages Over Other CAD Input Methods", *Design Graphics World*, January 1986."

Baker, "Scanning/Conversion Systems Interface to CAD/CAM for Archiving," *Computer Technology Review*, Summer 1986.

Kogan and Stiefel, "Large-Format Document Conversion Enters Mainstream," The S. Klein *Computer Graphics Review*," Fall 1986.

"Scanning an E-Size Drawing," *Graphics Arts Monthly*, October 1986.

"Scanned Drawing Modification and Database Creation Made Practical," *A-E-C Automation Newsletter*, October 1986.

Automatic Digitizers-A Special Report, The Anderson Report, December 1986.

Extending CGM for Publishing and Technical Drawing Exchange

G. S. Carson

Abstract

The CGM was investigated to determine its suitability as a basis for graphics document transfer in the US Department of Defense (DoD) Computer Aided Logistics Support (CALS) System. CALS documents include technical publications, administrative publications, and technical drawings. It was determined that the general framework of the CGM was suitable, but a number of extensions were needed. These extensions are divided into 7 areas-lines, symbols, curves, hatch styles, text, images and naming/instancing. Initially, extensions will be done by registration mechanism, although the needed features are candidates for direct incorporation in future extended CGMs. The results of this investigation strongly suggest the suitability of the CGM for use in a variety of real-world applications by direct incorporation-with extensions as necessary-into application specific standards. Suitable application areas include office document transfer, publishing and product data exchange.

1 Overview

1.1 Introduction

The US Department of Defense (DoD) Computer Aided Logistics Support (CALS) System is intended to support the creation, storage, transfer, and production of a wide variety of documents related to the DoD logistics system. Its scope includes all technical and administrative documents related to operation, maintenance, and training for weapons systems. We were asked by the DoD to investigate the suitability of the CGM as a basis for graphics document transfer in the CALS program. This paper reports our findings, which are of general interest outside the DoD community. We determined that the general framework of the CGM was suitable for CALS document transfer, but a number of extensions-some involving significant new concepts-are needed. These extensions are summarized below. Registration proposals were developed to implement a number of them. They were derived by studying standards and draft standards (ISO, ANSI, and DoD) applicable to engineering drawings, product data exchange and publishing, and deriving required features for supporting graphical exchange mechanisms. In cases where no standards were available, features of the most widely used commercial products were used to define needed extensions.

1.2 Reference Model

For purposes of this study, a very simple reference model was adopted to define how the CGM is used in technical drawing production and publishing applications. One of the greatest deficiencies of the CALS program is its lack of an overall systems engineering effort that is capable of defining a reference model to serve as a framework for choosing and developing standards.

We assume that the CGM will be used in the following manner in CALS:

1 CGM pictures will be used to transfer engineering drawings.

2 CGM pictures will be used to transfer pages of office documents (potentially containing both text and graphics; the extensions we propose will allow the CGM alone to be used for transferring the content of documents including text, geometric graphics, and image (raster) graphics.) The CGM may also be used to transfer pictures which are then embedded in documents by some process outside the scope of this study.

3 All transfers are of "final" or "non-processible" form drawings or portions of documents that are ready for imaging on a graphics output device (perhaps following the resolution of external references).

We make no assumptions in the following areas due to the lack of a CALS reference model:

1 The manner in which graphical metafiles are transferred.

2 The embedding of CGM content in documents defined in other standards (e.g., ODA and SGML).

3 The manner in which descriptions of externally defined items are made available to a CGM interpreter.

4 Transfer of "processible" product definition data or "processible-form" office documents. (We assume IGES and/or ODA/ODIF are used in these cases).

1.3 Criteria for Selecting Extensions

We used the following criteria (based on our reference model) in defining required extensions:

1 Picture description must be as compact as is practical, consistent with ease of generation and interpretation. (This implies, in particular, that a "symbol" or "macro" capability is needed, as is access to external libraries of symbols.)

2 Only "presentation-related" relationships between objects and attributes of objects need be preserved in the transfer. This places the transfer at an intermediate level between that provided by IGES and by the (unextended) CGM. When (1) and (2) are considered jointly, they imply that transfer by "approximation with lower-level graphical entities"-such as approximation a curve with a sequence of line segments or a centerline with a set of polylines and/or marker types-is unacceptable. A local system is free however to make such approximations, consistent with accuracy restrictions, in the process of imaging a picture.

3 Extensions must be consistent with the philosophical basis of standards in the areas of Open Systems Interconnection (e.g. naming and addressing) and Office Systems (e.g. font architecture.)

1.4 Organization of the Paper

The remainder of this paper is divided into four sections. The first summarizes requirements for graphics in technical and administrative publishing and describes needed CGM extensions. The second summarizes requirements for graphics in technical drawings and describes needed CGM extensions. A final section summarizes needed extensions in both areas. Some extensions are described in more detail than others. This reflects the fact that, although needed extensions have been identified, not all the technical work is complete to define them.

2 Technical and Administrative Publishing

2.1 Introduction

It is widely recognized that computer graphics standards will need to be extended to properly support publishing. Such extensions will be initially developed in the form of GDPs and Escapes and the "folded into" the standards during their next revision cycles. Requirements for document exchange and production in this area include:

1 Rapid soft copy display of formatted composite documents.

2 Use of internationally standardized color models in interchange.

3 Use of standard methods for image compression.

4 General fill boundary specification.

5 Wide lines with join and end features, and patterns with anchoring.

6 Curves, including conics and Bezier curves.

7 General clip boundary.

Subsequent subsections of this paragraph describe first the methodology by which extensions in the publishing area were determined, and then general features that must be added to the CGM. These general features are given by way of example from current commercial products.

2.2 Required Capabilities

In the absence of standards in this area (the Text Presentation Metafile under development in X3V1 will not be available even in draft form until late 1987), we used the features of the most widely used commercial products to define the required capabilities. In particular, the PostScript Page Description Language [5,6] of Adobe Systems was selected to provide a baseline set of capabilities which the CGM must be extended to meet. In some cases, we used features from the Interpress Page Description Language [4] of Xerox Corporation in addition to or in place of those in PostScript. Defining required capabilities in the publishing area is more difficult than in engineering drawing, since format and presentation are determined more by artistic considerations than slavish adherence to format standards.

2.2.1 Lines.

"Lines" in PostScript are drawn through a two-step process. First, a path is constructed, corresponding to the line to be drawn. This is done by a sequence of moveto and lineto operators. (Relative operators, or curve operators can be interspersed.) Next, the stroke operator paints the path with the current color and line width.

The PostScript language gives complete control over how the stroke operator converts a path into a painted line or curve. The setlinewidth operators determines the width of the stroked line.

There are several operators that allows other characteristics of a stroked path to be precisely determined. Among these are:

1 setlinecap determines the appearance of line segment ends;

2 setlinejoin determines the method by which different line segments are joined;

3 setdash determines the pattern for dashed lines.

A final necessary capability is provided by the closepath operator. This operator adds a line segment to the current path connecting the current point to the last point addressed by a moveto operator.

Needed CGM Extensions. All of these capabilities, or their equivalents, must be added to the CGM.

2.2.2 Symbols.

Neither PostScript or Interpress provides an explicit modular symbol capabilities. Their program language-like structure however, allows graphical patterns to be defined once and positioned at various points to provide the necessary capability. This is discussed further below.

Needed CGM Extensions. Symbol capabilities-such as that provided by Polymarker-are of very limited utility in general publishing applications. No extensions in this area are appropriate. What is needed is a general object definition and instantiation capability as described below.

2.2.3 Curves.

PostScript provides the following operations to draw curve line segments:

arc - appends a counterclockwise arc of a circle to the current path, possibly preceded by a straight line segment.

arcn - behaves like arc, but builds it arc segment in a clockwise direction.

arcto - appends an arc of a circle to the current path, preceded by a straight line segment.

curveto - adds a Bezier cubic section to the current path.

moveto - starts a new subpath of the current path, sets the current point in the graphics state to the user coordinate without adding any line segments to the current path.

closepath - closes the current subpath by appending a straight line segment connecting the current point to the subpaths's starting point.

rlineto - appends a straight line segment to the current path in the same manner as lineto; however, the number pair is interpreted as a displacement relative to the current point rather than as an absolute coordinate.

rmoveto - starts a new subpath of the current path in the same manner as moveto, however, the number pair is interpreted as a displacement relative to the current point rather than as an absolute coordinate.

rcurveto - adds a Bezier cubic section to the current path in the same manner as curveto; however, the three number pairs are interpreted as displacements relative to the current point rather than as absolute coordinates.

stroke - paints a line following the current path and using the current color.

strokepath - replaces the current path with one enclosing the shape that would result if the stroke operator were applied to the current path.

setflat - sets the flatness in the current graphics state to a positive number. Flatness is used to control the accuracy with which curves are rendered on an output device.

clip - intersects the inside of the current clipping path with the inside of the current path to produce a new (smaller) current clipping path.

Needed CGM Extensions. All of these capabilities, or their equivalents, must be added to the CGM. The capability to construct an arbitrary closed or open figure-composed of more elemental primitive "segments"- is required. Associated generalized fill areas and clipping regions must also be supported.

2.2.4 Text.

Rather than draw the required text capabilities from PostScript-which represents only one of many technologies for defining and rendering text, we drew upon ISO DP 9541 Font and Character Information Interchange. ISO DP 9541 defines font referencing, positioning, and presentation.

Objectives and functional definitions. The objective of the Font and Character Information Interchange Standard is to define a common font resource architecture which can be used in a variety of development and application environments, for the purpose of supporting text (characters, symbols, ideograms) generation, interchange, and presentation. The font resources which are developed to this architecture may be used by: text and graphic editors, document formatters, utilities, device service programs, resource management programs, and presentation device drivers. Consistency of font resource information is a requirement for softcopy display of documents to be typeset, and interchange of documents between systems. The degree of consistency can be significantly improved through the use of a common font resource architecture.

A **font resource** is defined to be the total collection of information required to characterize and identify a font to compose blocks of text and to define the images of the characters, for use by an electronic data processing system. A font resource will contain information that:

1 identifies and describes itself to permit selection by users and application programs.

2 defines the character attributes required by a document formatting process to position the characters on a presentation surface.

3 defines each character's shape for generation of the character images on the presentation surface.

Font production is defined to be the process of designing the character images, converting those images into a digital technology format (bit image, vector drawing orders, outline algorithm, etc.), defining the various height, width, and escapement values for each individual character, assigning appropriate descriptive and identifying information (to the characters and the font resource in general), and creating a font resource that contains all of the required information in a format that can be used by a text processing system.

Text processing system is defined to be the total collection of hardware devices and software or firmware programs required to generate, modify, display, and/or print text.

Font storage and access is defined to be the process of storing the font file information on the appropriate media for use within a text processing system, and the process of accessing that information by the various components of a text processing system.

Font referencing is defined to be the process of identifying or characterizing a font.

Needed CGM Extensions. The manner in which text attributes are treated in the CGM must be completely changed to conform to this new architecture. (This can be done by registering new text primitives while keeping the old ones for compatibility.) In fact, a similar treatment of other primitives and their attributes should be developed for consistency. Such an architecture has numerous advantages over the simplistic indexed and directly specified attributes used in the current family of graphics standards.

2.2.5 Images.

PostScript includes a very minimal set of capabilities for handling images (raster bitmaps). The operators provided are:

image-renders a sampled image onto the current page. The sampled image is a rectangle array of sample values, each of which consists of bits sample bits of data (1, 2, 4, or 8).

imagemask-similar to the image operator, however, it tracks the source image as a mask of 1 bit samples that are used to control where to apply paint (with the current color) and where not to. It is most useful for printing characters as bitmaps. Such bitmaps represent masks through which a color is to be transformed.

These image capabilities are too limited to meet CALS requirements (or those of the publishing industry in general). More generally, compatibility with scanned images and with images communicated using standard CCITT facsimile standards is required.

Needed CGM Extensions. The CGM must be extended to incorporate standard raster formats and compression techniques used in scanners and facsimile communication. Further study is necessary to define the needed extensions.

2.2.6 Definition and instantiation of objects.

One capability that is sadly lacking in the CGM is the ability to define an arbitrary picture component (e.g. a symbol or non-primitive object) which can be instanced (repeated) multiple times within a single picture or shared amongst different pictures in a document. This capability is needed for both publishing and engineering drawing applications.

The capabilities of both PostScript (based on a programming language approach) and Interpress (based upon defining extended operators) are described below.

PostScript procedures. A PostScript procedure is a set of operations grouped together with a common name. This set of operations is stored with its key in a dictionary. When the key appears in a program, the associated set of operations is carried out.

Procedures are defined in exactly the same way as variables. The program must place the procedure name (preceded by a slash) on the stack, followed by the set of operations that make up the procedure. Then, the def operator is used to store the operations and name in the current dictionary.

Interpress symbols. The concepts of symbol and instance are provided in Interpress by composed operators and transformations. A graphical symbol can be defined as a composed operator. When an instance, or copy, of the symbol is to be printed, the current transformations will be applied to all coordinates as the symbol calls imager operators. The properties of the current transformation will thus determine the position, size, and rotation of the instance on the printed page.

The principal use of symbols and instances in Interpress is for printing characters. Each character is defined by a composed operator, called a character operator. These operators are invoked usually by SHOW, with a current transformation that achieves the proper size, orientation and position of the character.

Instancing can also be used for other purposes. Graphical objects that are repeated often on a page or throughout a document may be tracked as instances. A symbol is defined as a composed operator and called with an appropriate current transformation in order to generate each instance.

Needed CGM Extensions. A general naming and instancing capability is needed in the CGM. This should treat general objects in the same manner the ISO DP 9541 Font and Character Information Interchange treats fonts. Programmability in the Postscript sense is not a requirement. Further study is needed to define the required extensions.

3 Technical Drawings and Product Data

3.1 Introduction

It is widely recognized that some extensions to the CGM are necessary to properly support the creation of drawings and views of product model data. We developed requirements in this area from standards for product data description and drawings themselves, rather than limiting our attention to investigating the IGES standard [7] (which does not describe engineering drawings, per se, but rather the transfer of the complete information necessary to describe the representation of a product.) The methodology we used to define the capabilities required to define images of engineering drawings was:

1. Review requirements from ANSI and DoD standards for the production of engineering drawings, and extract the required representational capabilities.
2. Review the IGES standard to extract entities for which the CGM must be able to describe images.
3. Consider the CALS system level requirements in areas such as use of symbol libraries. Since no such requirements exist in explicit form and there is no defined CALS reference model, the capabilities of commercially available products were used to derive requirements.

As will be evident below, we found unique rendition requirements for graphical engineering drawings that could not be met by using the "standard" primitives and attributes.

3.2 Required Capabilities

Subsequent subsections define the requirements and needed extensions in the areas recognised.

3.2.1 Lines.

Lines are used in a very special and unique way in engineering drawings. This is described in the following material drawn from ANSI Y14.2M-1979 (Line Conventions and Lettering) which explains how "lines" are used in product definition drawings. Note the special rendition requirement that must be met, yet cannot be guaranteed by a CGM description of the line in many cases. Figures 1 and 2 illustrate many of these line styles.

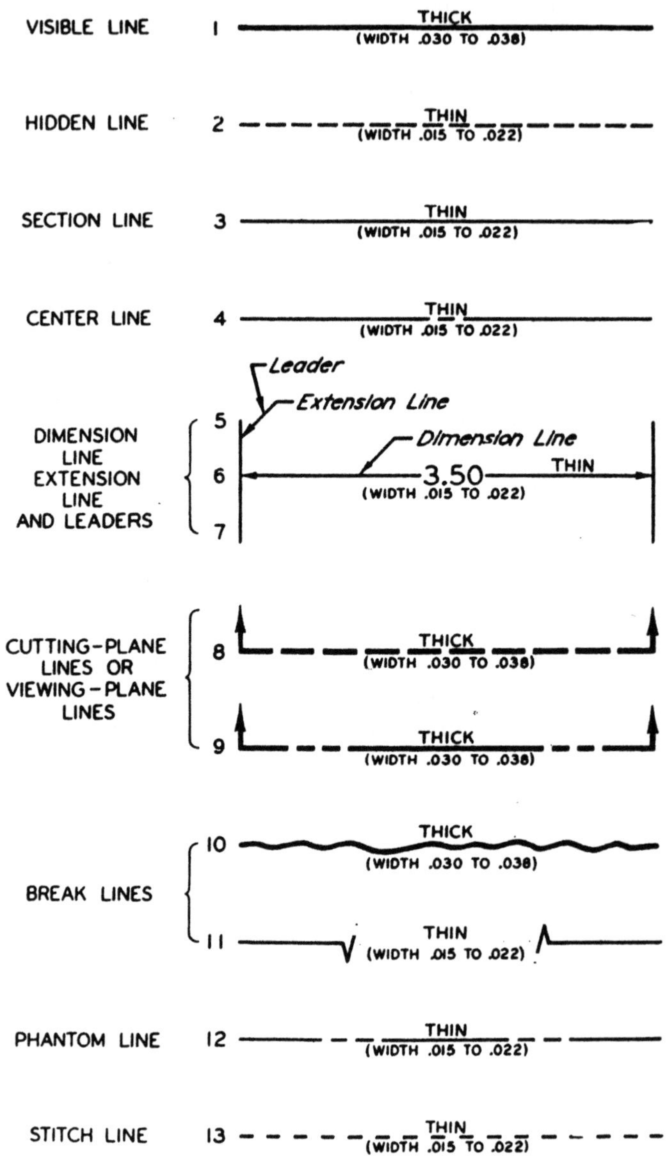

Figure 1: Line Styles and Widths

Note: These approximate line widths are intended to differentiate between **thick** and **thin** lines and are not values for control of acceptance or rejection of the drawings.

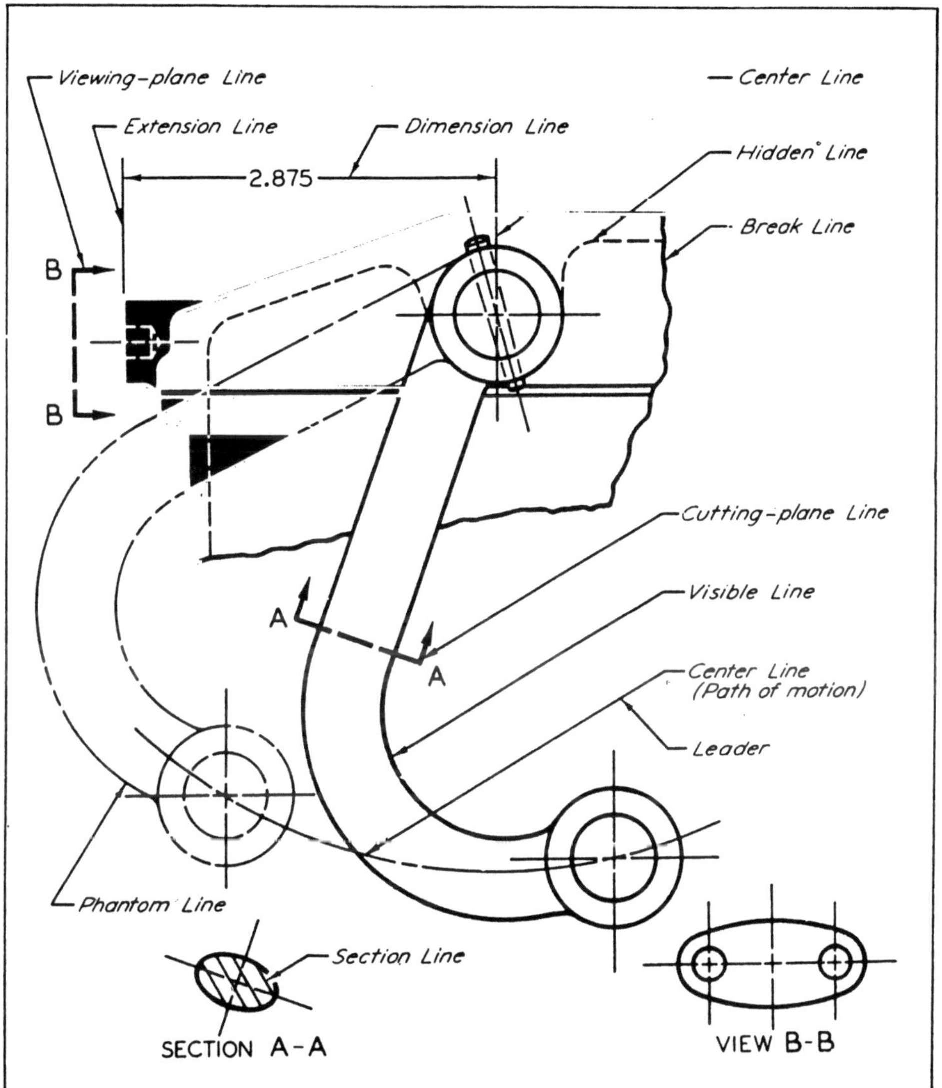

Figure 2: Lines in Engineering Drawings

Line widths - Two widths of lines are recommended for use on manually prepared drawings. One width of line is acceptable on drawings prepared by automated methods. The ratio of line thickness should be approximately two-to-one. The thin-line width should be approximately 0.35 mm or 0.016 inch and the thick-line width approximately 0.7 mm or 0.032 inch.

Line quality - All lines should be clean cut, opaque, uniform, and properly spaced for legible reproduction by all commonly used methods, including microfilming in accordance with industry and government requirements. When manually produced, there should be a distinct contrast between the two widths of lines. Contrast must be obtained only by variance in the relative widths of the lines. In no case should contrast be achieved by a difference in density, opaqueness or color.

Visible lines - The visible lines should be used for representing visible edges or contours of objects. Visible lines should be drawn so that the views they outline clearly stand out on the drawing with a definite contrast between these lines and secondary lines.
Hidden lines - Hidden lines consist of short evenly spaced thin dashes and are used to show the hidden features of the object. The lengths of the dashes may vary slightly in relation to the size of the drawing. Hidden lines should always begin and end with a dash in contact with the visible or hidden line from which they start or end, except when such a dash would form a continuation of a visible line. Dashes should join at corners, and arcs should start with dashes at tangent points. Hidden lines should be omitted when their use is not required for the clarity of the drawing. Although features located behind transparent materials may be visible, they should be treated as concealed features and shown with hidden lines.

Section lines - Section lines are used to indicate the cut surfaces of an object in a section view.

Center lines - Center lines consist of alternating long and short dashes. They are used to represent axes of symmetrical parts and features, bolt circles, and paths of motion. The long dashes of the center lines may vary in lengths, depending upon the size of the drawing. Center lines should start and end with long dashes. They should not intersect at the spaces between dashes or by crossing the long or short dashes. Center lines should extend uniformly and distinctly a short distance beyond the object or feature of the drawing unless a longer extension is required for dimensioning or for some other purpose. They should not terminate at other lines of the drawing nor should they extend through the space between views. Very short center lines may be unbroken if no confusion results with other lines.

Symmetry lines - This is a center line used as an axis of symmetry for a partial view. The line of symmetry is identified by two thick short parallel lines drawn at right angles to it. They are used in representing partially drawn views and partial sections of symmetrical parts. Symmetrical view visible and hidden lines may extend past the symmetry line if clarity would be improved.

Dimension lines - Dimension lines are used to indicate the extent and direction of dimensions and are terminated by neatly-made uniform arrowheads. The length of the arrowhead should be equal to the height of the dimension numerals if possible. If inadequate space is available, the arrowhead may be shown outside the dimension limit.

Extension lines - Extension (witness) lines are used to indicate the point or line on the drawing to which the dimension applies. A short gap is left where the extension line would join the object, so as not to confuse extension lines with the lines of the object. Extension lines are also used to indicate the extension of a surface to a theoretical intersection. When a point is located by extension lines, the extension lines should pass through the point.

Leaders - Leaders are used to direct notes, dimensions, symbols, item numbers, or part numbers to features on the drawing. A leader should generally be a single straight inclined line (not vertical or horizontal), except for a short horizontal portion extending to the center of the height of the first or last letter or digit of the note. This horizontal portion is optional and, if used, it should not underline the note.

Leaders should terminate as follows:

a Without symbol, if they end on a dimension line.

b With a dot 1.5 mm or 0.06 inch minimum diameter, if they end within outlines of an object .

c With an arrowhead, if they end on the outside of an object.

d With or without a dot or arrowhead on drawings prepared by computer automated techniques.

Leaders should not be curved in any way and should not cross each other unless unavoidable. Two or more leaders to adjacent areas on the drawing should be drawn parallel.

Cutting-plane lines - Cutting-plane and viewing-plane lines are used to indicate the location of cutting planes for sectional views and the viewing position for removed partial views. Two forms of cutting-plane and viewing-plane lines are approved for general use.

Break Lines - Two forms of break lines are approved for general use as follows:

a A freehand thick line.

b Long ruled thin dashes joined by zigzags.

Phantom lines - Phantom lines consist of long, thin dashes separated by pairs of short, thin dashes. The long dashes may vary in length, depending on the size of the drawing. Phantom lines are used to indicate alternate positions of moving parts, adjacent positions of related parts and repeated detail. These lines are also used for features such as bosses and lugs (later moved); for delineating machining stock and blanking developments; for piece parts in jigs and fixtures; and for bend lines on drawings or formed metal parts. Phantom lines should start and end with long dashes which may vary in length, depending on the size of the drawing.

Stitch lines - Stitch lines consist of short, thin dashes and spaces of equal lengths. The dots are approximately 0.016 (0.35 mm) in diameter and 0.12 inch (3 mm) apart. Stitch lines are used for indicating a sewing or stitching process.

Chain lines - The chain line consist of thick, alternating long and short dashes. This line is used to indicate that a surface or surface zone is to receive additional manufacturing treatment within limits specified on the drawing.

Arrowheads - Arrowheads may be prepared manually or mechanically. The length and width should have a ratio of approximately 3:1. The width of the arrowhead should be proportionate to the thickness of the lines used. Consistency of the style of an arrowhead should be contained throughout the drawing.

In addition to the generic line types defined in ANSI Y14.2M, ANSI and DoD standards in specific areas require the use of additional types of lines. Additional study is needed to fully investigate these and categorize them.

Needed CGM Extensions. Many additional linetypes are required to support engineering drawings. There are additional requirements on how patterns start and end within line segments beyond those that computer graphics standards alone can satisfy. Some of these restrictions may need to be stated in an application profile since they go beyond what can be specified through the registration process alone. For example, there are special rendition requirements for hidden lines that cannot be satisfied by a polyline primitive with the appropriate linetype alone. This happens because the conformance requirements for computer graphics standards do not specify how linetype patterns must be continued from segment to segment within a polyline, nor do they specify how such a line must end. We have written registration proposals for such items to include the additional conformance requirements, however they may be rejected by the standards committees.

We prepared a linetype registration proposal for each of the above linetypes, with the following exceptions:

- visible lines can be done with linetype solid;
- symmetry lines cannot be done with a single graphical line of any type; a symbol facility could be used, or a set of individual line elements;
- single and double arrow linetype can be used for leaders and dimension lines;
- cutting plane lines must be done as a set of individual lines since they can't be represented as a single linetype.

Some restrictions, such as allowable widths of lines and styles of text in engineering drawings, will need to be stated in the application profile(s) for engineering drawing applications.

3.2.2 Symbols.

The requirements for symbols in engineering drawings cannot be met by the polymarker primitives of the graphics standards. This is based on the following analysis of the applicable ISO (and derivative ANSI and DoD) standards.

International Standard ISO 3461 defines the general characteristics of symbols used in engineering drawings. This International Standard applies to graphics symbols which may be:

a placed on equipment or parts of equipment of any kind in order to instruct the persons handling the equipment as to its use and operation:

b placed on sites and ways where people may assemble or move, giving them instructions, such as prohibitions, warnings, rules or limits, regarding their behavior:

c used in pictorial reproductions, such as plans, drawings, layouts, guidelines and similar documents.

For the purposes of ISO 3461 a graphic symbol is a visually perceptible figure produced by means of writing, drawing, printing or other manufacturing techniques. It is used to transmit a message and represents it in an understandable manner, independently of any language. Graphics symbols stand for objects, concepts or states. (What a symbol stands for is usually known as the "referent.") This includes abstract references such as conditions, relationships, facts or actions.

As a rule, graphic symbols are used to:

a identify (for example to describe a piece of equipment or an abstract concept);

b qualify (for example to describe a variation or a secondary function);

c instruct (for example to describe an operation or method of use);

d command(that something must or must not be done);

e warn (for example of danger);

f indicate (for example direction, quantity).

Graphic Form. For each graphic symbol that is required, an original design is prepared. An original design is a symbol design drawn and presented in the manner described below, i.e.. drawn out on the basic pattern with due regard to the principles defined below. The basic pattern described below constitutes a frame in which the original design may be inscribed. The lines indicated in the basic pattern (circles, hexagons, octagons, squares, etc.) are intended as an aid to the designer in drawing up the original designs. The form of the graphics symbols should be suitable for economical reproduction by means of commonly applied techniques, such as etching, engraving, printing, and photographic means.

Basic Pattern. Graphic symbols are created on a basic pattern, consisting of sets of inscribed/circumscribed circles, rectangles and squares. The basic pattern is laid upon a 75 mm x 75 mm square subdivided by a 12.5 mm square grid which also coincides with the basic square. The original design of a graphics symbol should be fitted into the basic pattern according to the following principles:

1 for a symbol consisting of a single geometrical form, such as a circle or a rectangle, the corresponding geometrical forms of the basic pattern should be used, in which case the lines of the basic pattern should be the center lines of the .1 inch thick lines of the symbol being designed;

2 to achieve the impression of uniform perceived size among symbols, attention should be given in the equalization of surface areas; for example, a circle without external parts should be drawn upon the basic circle whereas a circle with external parts should be drawn upon the smallest circle.

Orientation of the Symbols. The majority of graphic symbols preserve their meaning in any position. However, when the meaning of a graphic symbol does depend on its orientation of position, this shall be explicitly stated. For example, the graphics symbol for a television receiver is not dependent on its position but the graphic symbol "bar" is dependent on its position.

Needed CGM Extensions. Typically, a large number of simple symbols are used repetitively in different locations to construct a drawing. Such drawings should not be transferred by building each symbol from primitives available in the CGM, nor is it feasible to make each required symbol a Generalized Drawing Primitive or marker symbol. It is absolutely essential that any technique used to transfer such drawings allow:

1 a symbol to be defined once in a picture and then instanced repetitively;

2 incorporation of externally defined symbols from standard libraries by reference.

This must be done for these reasons:

1 to reduce the required communication bandwidth;

2 to reduce the storage required for the picture;

3 to promote standardized appearance of drawings.

General naming and instancing extensions that support these requirements were described above.

3.2.3 Curves.

Further study is needed to investigate this area thoroughly. Engineering drawings are typically produced with a variety of conics and curved entities, such as splines and Bezier curves. Any of these can be added to graphics standards through the registration process. The problem is selecting a minimal and sufficient set of such curves to serve as a device and system independent transfer and description mechanism. There are substantial and non-trivial accuracy and stability problems to be overcome in defining this set.

Needed CGM Extensions. We assumed that the IGES entities represented a sufficient set and prepared registration proposals to render many of them through the CGM.

3.2.4 Hatch styles.

A wide variety of hatch styles are used in engineering drawings for purposes such as representing the nature of materials. Figure 3 illustrates some typical ones.

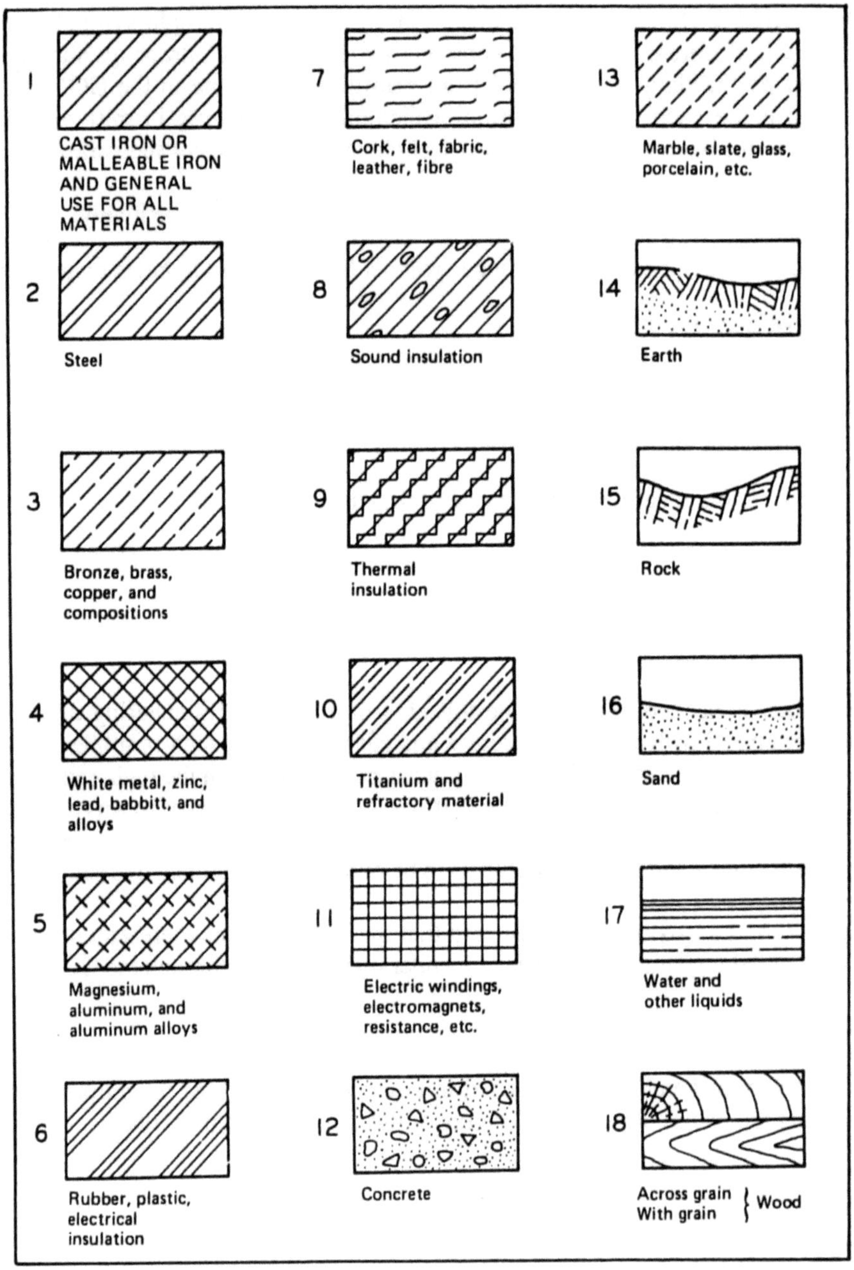

Figure 3: Hatch Styles from Y14.2M

Needed CGM Extensions. Based on preliminary observations, the following capabilities appear to be needed:

1 All necessary patterns must be made available as registered hatch styles (for reasons similar to those stated for marker symbols above, drawings containing these hatch patterns cannot be transferred between systems by decomposing the patterns using individual primitives available in the CGM.)

2 Arbitrary fill areas and clipping regions are needed to represent drawings containing such hatch patterns. These cannot be approximated by breaking them up into simpler areas since pattern continuity cannot be maintained.

Registration proposals were prepared for all types of section lining (hatch styles) except the following, which can be done with a built-in hatch style:

- electric windings, etc. (hatch index 6, horizontal/vertical crosshatch).

Registration proposals were prepared for the following hatch styles to support the more exact rendition requirements of engineering drawing standards from a similar type in the built-in CGM linestyles. In each case, the drawing standard requires "45 degree lines" while the built in hatch styles guarantee only "positive" and/or "negative" slope.

- cast iron, etc. (similar to hatch index 3, positive slope equally spaced parallel lines)
- white metal, etc. (similar to hatch index 6, positive slope/negative slope crosshatch)

3.2.5 Text.

Text capabilities required in engineering drawings are quite simple, although most drawing systems provide more advanced features. The requirements taken from Y14.2M-1979, are presented below. Then we describe needed enhancements to, for example, render IGES defined data without loss of quality.

Y14.2 Lettering Requirements

Single-stroke gothic lettering. Lettering on drawings must be legible and suitable for easy and rapid execution. These requirements are met in the recommended single-stroke gothic characters or adaptations thereof, which improve reproduction legibility. One such adaptation by the National Microfilm Association is the gothic style Microfont alphabet intended for general usage. Opaque and well-spaced lettering is required on the drawing for microfilm reproduction.

Inclined or vertical lettering. Either inclined or vertical lettering is permissible. Only one style of lettering should be used throughout a drawing. The preferred slope for the inclined characters is 2 in 5 or approximately 68 degrees with horizontal.

Use of upper-case letters. Upper-case letters should be used for all lettering on drawings. When additions or revisions are made, the original style of lettering should be maintained.

Lettering for titles, subtitles, drawing numbers, and other uses may be made free-hand, by typewriter, or with the aid of mechanical lettering devices such as templates and lettering machines. Regardless of the method used, all characters are to conform, in general, with the recommended gothic style and must be legible in full or reduced size copy by any accepted method of reproduction.

A type face comparable to light-line Pica Gothic, block numerals is preferred for typing on drawings.

Size and spacing of lettering. The recommended minimum freehand and mechanical letter height for various applications are defined in the standards as follows:

Letters in words should be spaced so that the background areas between the letters are approximately equal, and words are to be clearly separated by a space equal to the height of the lettering. For legible reproduction, a space between two letters of at least 0.06 inch (1.5 mm) is to be used whenever possible. The space between two numerals having a decimal point between them is to be a minimum of two thirds the height of the lettering. The vertical space between lines of lettering should be no more than the height of the lettering, and no less than half the height of the lettering used.

Notes should be placed horizontally on drawings and separated vertically by spaces at least equal to double the height of the character size used, to maintain the identity of each note.

The division line of a common fraction should be parallel to the direction in which the dimension reads and should be separated from the numerals by a maximum of 0.06 inch (1.5 mm) spacing. When fractions occur in notes, tables, and lists, the diagonal division line is permissible. Numerals in fractions should be the same size as other numerals.

Spacing between max/min dimensions should be one-half of the character height.

Lettering should not be underlined except when special emphasis is required. The underlining should not be less than 0.06 inch (1.5 mm) below the lettering.

Text in IGES. Product data exchange standards such as IGES define an entity called general note which consists of strings of text that are incorporated in other entities for producing drawing labels and annotation. IGES defines the following fonts for use with this entity:

0.	Symbol font (use longer recommended)
1.	Standards block
2.	LeRoy
3.	Future
4.	Fastfont
5.	Calcomp
6.	Comp 80
7.	Microfilm standard
8.	ISO standard
9.	DIN standard
10.	Military standard
11.	Gothic
12.	New gothic
13.	Lightline gothic
14.	Simplex Roman
15.	Italic
16.	APL
17.	Century schoolbook
18.	Helvetica
1001	Symbol font 1
1002	Symbol font 2

In addition, the IGES text model includes several capabilities that are not present in computer graphics standards such as the CGM.

IGES also includes a text font definition entity that enables a text font to be described as a sequence of strokes. This capability could be built on top of the CGM by stroking out the individual characters as required. A more general solution to compatibility is a common font definition mechanism, based on ISO 9541, for product data standards, graphics standards and publishing standards.

Needed CGM Extensions. If additional fonts are registered for use with engineering drawings, the CGM can easily support the simple text needed in engineering drawings. However, accomodating the more demanding features of IGES and many commercial products will require further extensions.

3.2.6 Images.

CALS will capture and store a great deal of existing engineering drawing data in raster form. Neither the CGM nor IGES adequately address this area. It is likely that a solution developed for the use of image (raster) data in the publications area will also effectively address the requirements of engineering drawings.

Needed CGM Extensions. The CGM must be extended to incorporate standard raster formats and compression techniques used in scanners and facsimile communication. Further study is necessary to define the needed extensions.

4 Conclusions

This section summarizes proposed extensions to the CGM. It is anticipated that most of these extensions can be implemented through the registration process. In several areas additional study is necessary to determine the precise nature of the required extensions.

4.1 Lines

A user defined linestyle is required. Linetypes that directly represent the presentation requirements of engineering drawings must be defined. Where the limited capabilities of the built-in polyline primitive-which allows a linetype to consist only of a sequence of line segments and gaps, without precise control over its rendition-are exceeded, GDPs may be needed. Some conformance data must be placed in the application profile. Extensions to line attributes to include line end styles and join options are needed.

4.2 Symbols

The polymarker primitive is not particularly useful for either publishing or engineering drawing. The registration of additional marker types has little utility. Instead, a general object definition and instantiation capability is needed. No registration proposals were completed in this area.

4.3 Curves

The following curves are required as GDPs:

1 Bezier curves,
2 B-splines,
3 Conics and conic arcs,
4 Other splines as determined by the future study.

Escapes are required to support their attributes: Registration proposals for the first three have been written.

In addition, a closed figure primitive is required, together with:

1 Arbitrary clipping regions,
2 Arbitrary fill boundaries.

No registration proposals were completed in this area.

4.4 Hatch styles

Registered hatch styles to support engineering drawing uses are required. Several registration proposals were written for these. Registered hatch styles to support technical and administrative publication are also required. Insufficient data is available to specify these now.

4.5 Text

The text model must be completely replaced through the use of GDPs and Escapes to adopt the model and architecture of ISO DP 9541. Some specific fonts for use in engineering drawings must be registered. No registration proposals were completed in this area.

4.6 Images

A raster "input" primitive to accept input from scanners and files stored on disc is required. The role of compression in the metafile must be clarified. It is best to adopt standard techniques for necessary compression (the lack of a CALS reference model again!), and it is necessary to add GDPs to cover both these and more sophisticated compression techniques in the CGM in the near term. The CCITT Group 3 and Group 4 facsimile standards included in MIL-STD-1840 do not provide either color or grey scale capabilities and are generally less than suitable for photographic images. Additional raster attributes are required to support image processing. No registration proposals were completed in this area.

4.7 Naming, Instancing and External References

The naming and definition of attributes and objects must be extended from a simplistic two-dimensional (positive and negative integer indices separating the space into registered and implementation-dependent types) name space to one consistent with the "resource" view of objects seen in most modern commercial systems and exemplified in the ISO DP 9541 font work. (A limited attempt was made in the CGM by including a list of font names that are then mapped to indices. This was a first step in the right direction.) This can be done fairly easily by defining GDPs and Escapes to replace the existing output primitives and attributes. It is absolutely essential that this be done to insure the long-term coherence of information processing standards. Neither the CGM nor other computer graphics standards will find acceptance in modern applications without these extensions. No registration proposals were written in this area.

4.8 Future Work

Additional work is needed to complete the definition of CGM extensions to meet CALS requirements. These extension are also suitable to allow the CGM to be used in general for the transfer of graphics in office documents and in engineering and technical drawings and illustrations. Such an extended CGM can be a basis for a Standardized Page Description Language (SPDL). Its adoption could halt attempts to standardize an SPDL based on commercial products-such as Postscript-that are incompatible with the family of ANSI and ISO computer graphics standards.

4.9 Registration Proposals

To implement the extensions defined here, we developed registration proposals for the following specific extensions and have submitted them for standardization:

1 Linetypes
   - chain line
   - center line
   - hidden line
   - phantom line
   - double arrow
   - single dot
   - single arrow
   - stitch line
   - user specified dash pattern

2 Hatchstyles
   - across grain wood
   - with grain wood
   - bronze, brass, copper, and compositions
   - cast iron or mallable iron and general use for all materials
   - steel
   - concrete
   - earth
   - magnesium, aluminum, and aluminum alloys
   - marble, slate, glass, porcelain, etc.
   - rock
   - rubber, plastic, and electrical insulation
   - sand
   - sound installation
   - thermal insulation
   - titanium and refractory material
   - water and other liquids
   - white metal, zinc, lead, babbitt, and alloys

3 Generalized drawing primitives
- Bezier curve
- conic arc
- parametric spline curve
- rational B-spline curve

4 Escape functions
- set line cap
- set dash
- set line join
- set miter limit
- set conic arc transformation matrix

Note:

This work was supported by the US Department of Defense (DoD), through the National Bureau of Standards (NBS) under contract number 43NANB705616.

References

1. G. Enderle, K. Kansy, G. Pfaff, *Computer Graphics Programming*, Spring Verlag, Berlin, 1984.

2. ANSI X3.122-1986, Computer Graphics - Metafile for the Storage and Transfer of Picture Description Information.

3. ANSI X3.124-1985, Computer Graphics - Graphical Kernel System (GKS) Functional Description.

4. Robert F. Sproul and Brian K. Reid, *Introduction to Interpress*, Xerox System Integration Guide 038404, Xerox Corporation, El Segundo, CA, April 1984.

5. Adobe Systems Inc., *Postscript Language Reference Manual.* Addison Wesley, Reading, MA, 1985.

6. Adobe Systems Inc., *Postscript Language Tutorial and Cookbook*, Addison Wesley, Reading, MA, 1985.

7. Brad Smith and Joan Wellington, *Initial Graphics Exchange Specification* (IGES), Version 3.0, National Bureau of Standards, April 1986.

8. *Modern Drafting Practices and Standards Manual*, Genium Publishing, Schenectady, NY, 1986.

9. ANSI Y14.2M-1979, Line Conventions and Lettering.

10. ANSI Y14.5, Dimensioning and Tolerancing.

11. Draft MIL-STD-1840A, Automated Interchange of Technical Information.

The CGM in the Presentation Graphics World

G. Silverman

Abstract

MAGICorp is a remote computer slide making service bureau which produces high quality 35mm slides, transparencies and prints. It can accept data of images created on a number of IBM PC/Compatibles software packages, graphics workstations and mainframe packages. Clearly, the adoption of a CGM standard offers us a tremendous advantage. It allows us to reproduce images from various sources without having to write separate drivers or conversion routines for each package. This paper discusses some general techniques we used in implementing the standard, as well as some of the problems we encountered.

1 Reducing the Data

In order to be filmed, most of MAGICorp's customers transmit their CGM files via modem. Therefore, reducing the size of the data for each image is very advantageous. It leads to faster transmissions and turnaround times, less expense for phone lines, less memory requirements, and the ability to process more files.

To obtain a more compact metafile, MAGICorp converts a binary encoded metafile into an output file with the following representation of CGM data:

First, each primitive keeps a distinct list of attributes. For instance, attributes of a polygon are stored separately from similar attributes of a circle. Attributes include fill color, edge color, edge thickness, horizontal and vertical reference points, style, start angle, end angle, etc. See Table 1 for a summary of attributes for all the primitives.

Table 1: Summary of Attributes for all Primitives

	BOX	ELLIPS	TEXT	LINE	POLY	WEDGE	ARC
Horizontal ref. pt.	X	X	X	X(1)	X(1)	X	X
Vertical ref. pt.	X	X	X	X(1)	X(1)	X	X
X-width, radius	X	X	X			X	X
Y-height, radius	X	X	X			X	X
Interior red color	X	X	X		X	X	
Edge red color	X	X	X	X	X	X	X
Line or edge width	X	X		X	X	X	X
Dropshadow Orient.			X				
Alignment	X	X	X			X	X
Text font			X				
Style				X	X	X(2)	X
Starting angle						X	X
Ending angle						X	X
Interior green	X	X	X	X	X	X	X
Edge green color	X	X	X		X	X	
Interior blue color	X	X	X	X	X	X	X
Edge blue color	X	X	X		X	X	
Rotation	X	X	X	X	X	X	X

Notes:

1 Reference Point Must be defined if T ne 0.

2 Wedge style is either pie slice or filled arc.

Next, when scanning the input metafile, the value of the particular attribute is passed to the output file only when it changes from its previous value. For example, suppose the first circle has a red interior, blue outline of thickness N1, radius of length N2, and center at (x1,y1). The next circle has similar attributes except its center is at (x2,y2). In this case the only attribute of the second circle written to the output file is the center point. Also, for the first primitive of each type, only the attributes which differ from the defaults are passed to the output.

This method often reduces the size of many files, especially those in which the primitives tend to have similar attributes. For instance, in a bar chart, each bar has the same width and horizontal reference point. With text, usually the same font and alignment are used. In a graph, each grid mark has the same width and color. Further, all the grid marks on the X-axis have the same vertical reference point and those on the Y-axis all have similar horizontal reference points. At worst, if all attributes of the primitives are different from the preceding primitives of that type, then the output should be approximately the same size as the input, as all the new values will have to be specified in both files.

2 Hatch Patterns

Monochrome devices (printers, pen plotters, terminals, etc.) can effectively use hatch patterns to represent objects of different colors. However, monochrome hatch patterns produce very poor quality slides, especially in contrast to color slides. Therefore, hatch patterns in the input metafile are converted into colors based on the following principles.

The color spectrum is divided up into regions, with the number of regions being one greater than the total number of hatch patterns. For example, if there are 9 patterns then there will be 10 regions. Further, if the color value extent is from 0 - 1000, then region 0 has rgb intensities of 0 to 99, region 1 has intensities of 100 to 199... and region 9 has intensities of 900 to 1000.

Each pattern is then assigned to a region. The denser, narrowly spaced patterns are assigned to darker regions and the broadly spaced patterns are assigned to lighter ones. Next, the highest value of the red, green or blue component of the pattern's color is then compared with its region's intensity. If the rgb component is greater or equal to the region's intensity, then the pattern is assigned to the next darker region. This insures the pattern does not map to its original solid color. Otherwise, it remains in the region.

At this point, the patterns and colors have been mapped into a range of color intensities, depending on the region assigned. The final color values chosen are based on the relative position of the highest rgb component within a region. For instance, if the color has an rgb value of (550,400,300), then the relative position of the red component in region 5 is 50. If the pattern was assigned to region 8 based on the procedure above, then the final red component is 850, to keep the same relative position in the new region. The green and blue components are changed proportionately. Although not a foolproof method, keeping the relative position allows for color variation in the output even in cases where the metafile uses the same hatch pattern with different colors.

3 Aspect Ratio

In 35mm slides, the aspect ratio is always 1.5, meaning that the X-axis is always 1.5 times as long as the Y-axis. Through the VDC extent code, a CGM image can have any aspect ratio. The aspect ratio of a metafile is maintained by the following procedure.

For aspect ratios which are greater than 1.5, the X-axis of the metafile is mapped to full horizontal range of the slide and the Y-axis is mapped to only a portion of the slide's vertical range. For aspect ratios less than 1.5, the Y-axis of the metafile is mapped to the full vertical range of the slide and the X-axis is mapped to only a portion of the horizontal range. In both cases, the images are centered in the dimension which is not fully utilized. The remaining unused space is filled with the background color.

4 Problems

In general, MAGICorp was able to produce many high quality slides from the metafiles sent by various customers. However, difficulties occurred in relation to text. MAGICorp's font libraries reduce the inter-character spacing of certain two letter combinations by a process called "kerning". Consider an "A" followed by a "V". Due to the structure of these letters, the appearance is aesthetically more pleasing if the "V" is shifted slightly to the left, rather than having a gap between the two letters.

Since kerned text enhances the quality, it is done automatically for the slide. The CGM standard, however, does not allow for any specification of how letters should be kerned, nor whether kerning is desired at all. Thus, the kerned text strings appeared to be misplaced on the slide. On the other hand, when kerning was left out, the strings appeared rather sloppy.

In addition, interpreting the font list was awkward. As there are literally thousands of copyrighted fonts, it would be unreasonable to expect one small slide service bureau to keep a library of point data for all of them. A more feasible option would be to keep a small subset of these. From this subset, the font which most closely matches the font requested by the metafile would be used. The matching could be based on characteristics such as sansserif, italic, bold, etc. However, since the CGM standard makes no provisions for specifying such characteristics, MAGICorp often could not predict which type of font was requested, when the names did not exactly match those in the font library.

5 Conclusions

By using the techniques discussed in this paper, MAGICorp adapted some of the CGM standard's provisions for slide output. The CGM metafiles thus created many fine slides. However, adding two more capabilities to the standard - the ability to specify kerning and the ability to list font characteristics - would result in better slides and more satisfied customers.

Part V

Encoding Issues

The CGM contains a functional description in Part I of the standard and this is followed by three parts detailing three possible encodings. As Mumford points out in the opening paper of this volume, there are different requirements for different applications. In some environments there may be a requirement for readability of the metafile, in others file size may be an over-riding issue and in others ease of generation and interpretation may be the most important factor. Because of these differing requirements there are the three encodings.

The binary encoding appears to be gaining much favour in this initial phase of CGM software development. Earlier in this volume we have seen that the binary encoding has been adopted for the MAP/TOP and the CALS profiles. In the future it is possible that there will be other encodings approved for work in these application environments. Initially though it is envisaged that this decision will have a wide impact in environments where binary transfer is straightforward.

In contrast to this important move, the three papers presented here are concerned with other encodings. Jepsen found that there were problems in using the binary encoding and adopted the character encoding for ease of transfer. Both he and Davison present comparisons of the CGM with other storage forms and find that the CGM compares favourably. There is a need for conversion utilities between the encodings.

Osland describes how the ideas and philosophy behind the CGM and its encodings can have a wider application. His concern is the storage of application data. He adopts two approaches: the first uses the CGM standard and the data are stored as APPLICATION DATA; his second approach uses the structure, data types and encoding of the CGM as a starting point for the storage of the data. Osland feels that this second approach is as useful for the transfer of application data as it is for the transfer of graphical data.

Protocol Comparisons: CGM and Others

G. S. Davison

Abstract

This paper provides a comparison of the file sizes (in blocks) generated by seven existing protocols used for the storage of pictures in files, or the transmission of pictures from the host to the graphics device.

1 Protocol Comparison

Protocol comparison was accomplished using a graphics standard to provide an easy method of comparison.

The Graphical Kernel System (GKS) is a standard subroutine library that provides a single software interface for application programs to access many devices. As such, it enables the user to easily switch back and forth from one protocol to another as devices become available within a lab, available at home, or when the latest graphics hardware arrives by truck.

The protocols examined are:

- CGM character encoding
- CGM clear text encoding
- GKS Metafiles (GKSM)
- PostScript (TM)
- Hewlett Packard Graphics Language (HPGL) (TM)
- ReGIS
- TEKTRONIX 4014 (TM)

Each protocol is a discrete method of storing pictures, and each can be used for:

- long-term storage
- transporting between computers
- transporting between operating systems
- transporting from one location to another
- transporting from one application to another

To switch between protocols, the Digital Equipment Corporation VAX GKS implementation of the GKS standard provides two logical names. One logical name (GKS$WSTYPE) tells VAX GKS which protocol to use. A second logical name (GKS$CONID) gives VAX GKS the name of the output file or device. The user simply redefines the logical names and re-runs the application program that uses VAX GKS subroutines.

2 Protocol Description

Following is a brief description of each protocol.

- Computer Graphics Metafile (CGM) is a standard protocol for storing picture information in a data file. Three different formats are provided for storing pictures: Storing them in the least amount of space (character encoding), storing them quickly (binary encoding), and storing them in a form that is easily readable (clear text).

- VAX GKS provides the CGM character encoding and the CGM clear text encoding as two of the many protocols that are available.

- GKS Metafiles (GKSM) are defined by the ANS/ISO GKS standard as a storage method for long-term filing of graphical information. It is most similar to the CGM clear text encoding because it is readable without being decoded.

- PostScript is best suited to printing formatted text and graphics. It is a favorite in industry for laser printing.

- Hewlett Packard Graphics Language (HPGL) is a mnemonic graphics language used for plotting. The instruction's mnemonic is suggestive of its role. For example, PU is used to pick up the pen from the drawing surface, and SP is used to select a pen.

- The Remote Graphics Instruction Set (ReGIS) is a graphics descriptor protocol for defining a graphics image.

- TEKTRONIX 4014 protocol is completely encoded.

In order to compare the protocols, seven GKS programs were run on each of the seven protocols. The files of output were stored and their sizes tabulated. In the first four tests, a single polyline, polymarker, text, or fill area primitive was repeated either 100 or 1000 times. The remaining three tests were short GKS applications which mix output in a typical fashion.

3 A Sample of the GKS Program Used

Below is a sample of the GKS program used. Only one of the four primitives was used in the loop.

```
      REAL X_ARRAY( 3 ), Y_ARRAY( 3 )
      DATA X_ARRAY /0.2, 0.7, 0.4/
      DATA Y_ARRAY /0.7, 0.5, 0.3/

      CALL GKS$OPEN_GKS( 'SYS$ERROR:' )
      CALL GKS$OPEN_WS( 1, 0, 0 )
      CALL GKS$ACTIVATE_WS( 1 )

      DO I = 1, 1000, 1
              CALL GKS$POLYLINE( 3, X_ARRAY, Y_ARRAY )
                          {or}
C     Use the "dot" style polymarker.
              CALL GKS$SET_PMARK_TYPE( 1 )
              CALL GKS$POLYMARKER( 3, X_ARRAY, Y_ARRAY )
                          {or}
              CALL GKS$TEXT( 0.5, 0.5, 'Sample String' )
                          {or}
C     Use "solid" filled areas.
              CALL GKS$SET_FILL_INT_STYLE( 1 )
              CALL GKS$FILL_AREA( 3, X_ARRAY, Y_ARRAY )
      END DO

      CALL GKS$DEACTIVATE_WS( 1 )
      CALL GKS$CLOSE_WS( 1 )
      CALL GKS$CLOSE_GKS()
      END
```

Notes:

1. The marker style is a dot of the smallest size the workstation can produce.
2. Filling an area was done using solid filled areas instead of hollow, pattern, or hatched.
3. The TEKTRONIX 4014 and HPGL fill areas are larger because they simulate solid filled areas by drawing many lines to cover the region.
4. The protocols were stored in black and white.

4 Blocks Used

		100 reps	1000 reps
CGM Character encoding	FILLAREA	8	63
	POLYLINE	8	63
	POLYMARKER	8	63
	TEXT	5	34
CGM Clear Text	FILLAREA	20	156
	POLYLINE	19	150
	POLYMARKER	20	154
	TEXT	13	87
GKSM	FILLAREA	25	222
	POLYLINE	25	222
	POLYMARKER	25	222
	TEXT	15	124
PostScript	FILLAREA	32	125
	POLYLINE	30	106
	POLYMARKER	31	114
	TEXT	27	78
HPGL	FILLAREA	1458	14579
	POLYLINE	7	69
	POLYMARKER	15	148
	TEXT	14	134
ReGIS	FILLAREA	33	317
	POLYLINE	6	56
	POLYMARKER	8	75
	TEXT	5	38
TEKTRONIX	FILLAREA	963	9629
	POLYLINE	4	34
	POLYMARKER	6	59
	TEXT	3	26

Note:

Each block is 512 bytes.

5 Application Programs versus Protocols Findings

The following table is a summary of running three application programs with each of the protocols presented above. BUDGET is a barchart using hatched bars. REVENUE is a stacked barchart. TRAJ is a line graph of some trajectory equations.

	Blocks Used
CGM Character encoding	
BUDGET	10
REVENUE	5
TRAJ	6
CGM Clear Text	
BUDGET	27
REVENUE	12
TRAJ	15
GKSM	
BUDGET	23
REVENUE	11
TRAJ	13
PostScript	
BUDGET	27
REVENUE	28
TRAJ	25
HPGL	
BUDGET2	6
REVENUE	23
TRAJ	11
ReGIS	
BUDGET	5
REVENUE	4
TRAJ	7
TEKTRONIX	
BUDGET	16
REVENUE	14
TRAJ	5

6 Summary

For each protocol, the following summary was derived by adding the blocks used by the three application programs to the blocks used by the four primitives repeated 100 times.

	Total Blocks with Fill Area	Total Blocks without Fill Area
CGM Character encoding	50	42
CGM Clear Text	126	106
GKSM	137	112
PostScript	200	168
HPGL	155	496
ReGIS	68	35
TEKTRONIX	1011	48

This comparison uses a variety of test programs and application programs that show some of the advantages of using each protocol, but the test base is limited, and may be biased in the direction of one protocol more than another.

In this comparison, out of seven possible storage methods, CGM character encoding uses the least number of blocks overall. This was the intent of its design. When the fill area test was removed, ReGIS used the least number of blocks. This may be accounted for by the way in which the protocol was implemented. The CGM character encoding has not been optimized as much as our ReGIS protocol. It has a longer initialization which is used to explicitly describe the environment of the picture and includes some unnecessary duplication of settings.

HPGL, CGM Clear text, and GKSM are similar in nature and are on the same order of storage. Each is readable without translation so they tend to occupy more space.

7 Conclusion

Measuring file size in blocks is a limited view of the potential of these protocols but it is a way of understanding the relative merits of each. Other analysis may be justified at a later date.

Note:

VAX is a registered trademark of Digital Equipment Corporation.
PostScript is a registered trademark of Adobe Systems, Inc.
HPGL is a registered trademark of Hewlett Packard.
TEKTRONIX is a registered trademark of TEKTRONIX, Inc.

A Need for Character

S. T. Jepsen

Abstract

A need for character-encoded CGM arose at Boeing Computer Services in order to view mainframe-generated graphics on a PC. The CDC InterActive Facility (IAF) prevents direct binary downloading to Cyber and Cray users, and file size rules out clear text: character encoding provides the one viable alternative in this environment. This paper gives a short history of Boeing's experience with CGM and current plans for expanding functionality and domain.

1 Introduction

About the time that CGM became an ANSI standard, a commercial product, The Petroleum Gallery [1] was being developed to facilitate a reasonably uniform PC environment for users of applications on machines/OSs including IBM-PC/MS-DOS [2] IBM/MAINSTREAM-CTS [3], CDC Cyber/MAINSTREAM-EKS [4] and Cray X-MP/MAINSTREAM-VSP [5]. Many of the applications produce graphics, but local viewing was only available via clumsy escape to a stand-alone Tektronix emulator. This left the user at the mercy of the particular operating system, which might vary for the "same" application, e.g. the size of a dataset being fed to an application might affect the choice of host. An integrated facility for local viewing was required.

Integrated Tektronix emulation/image-capture would perhaps have been the ideal solution, but the project was otherwise dependent on a second-party communications package [6]. A PC-based interpreter for "some kind of metafile" provided a more easily-implemented, albeit non-interactive, option. The existence of GSS*CGI [7] made the development of such an interpreter feasible, and of course encouraged the use of CGM.

Historically Boeing has used a clear text "CalComp neutral plotfile" as a standard interchange format. The following list shows approximate file sizes for one sample image in different encodings:

Encoding	**File Size**
CalComp neutral	133 K
Clear Text CGM <POINTLIST>	117 K
Clear Text CGM <INCRPOINTLIST>	83 K
Binary CGM	34 K
Character CGM <Displacement Mode>	33 K
Character CGM <Incremental Mode>	?? K

Since users would wait for file download, size was a critical issue, although the character-encoded size was not known until after development. The binary size was determined by using a simple clear-text interpreter on top of GSS*CGI and selecting the Metafile driver. Experiments with GSS*CGM [8] demonstrated its programmer's interface to be inadequate for our needs, and its binary format incapable of surviving transmission across required environments. In particular, the CDC InterActive Facility (IAF) [9] through which users access Cyber and Cray applications "looks for" 12 binary 0's on a 60-bit word boundary and trashes the file at that point.

Character-encoded CGM became the only alternative.

2 A First Implementation

CalComp neutral plotfiles are generated by postprocessors linked with a replacement CalComp library. A character-encoded CGM generator was created by modifying existing postprocessors and library. Since the initial target interpreter was to reside on GSS*CGI and performance on initial display of each image was paramount, considerable tailoring of the data was performed. Scaling Mode and VDC Extent were used to create the largest image centered in integer VDC space of extent 500 <= x <= 32267, 500 <= y <= 20000. The inadequate GSS*CGI text facilities (e.g., rotatable fonts) forbade the use of unvectorized text, so Polyline and Disjoint Polyline were the only output primitives generated; Line Colour was the only attribute.

Metafiles which assume only these interpreter capabilities contain -32767 as the parameter to Metafile Element List. With the exception of the second Scaling Mode parameter, all numeric parameters are integers encoded in Basic Format. Pointlists are encoded using Displacement Mode. Postprocessors map application-dependent color information into an indexed Line Colour parameter that assumes the following

Index	Color
0	Black (or background)
1	White (or default foreground)
2	Red
3	Green
4	Blue
5	Yellow
6	Cyan
7	Magenta
8	Dark Grey
9	Light Grey
10	Light Red
11	Light Green
12	Light Blue
13	Brown
14	Light Cyan
15	Light Magenta

The preceding table is targeted to support the Enhanced Graphics Adapter (EGA) PC display card, and function adequately with a Color Graphics Adapter (CGA). The interpreter [10] provides user control of background and default foreground colors for screen display, which then swap with Black and White in the table. With CGA, the background can be any of 16 colors, but the default foreground must be one of 1, 5, 9, or 13, each of which determines the other 2 indices available. Line Colour parameters are "modulo"-ed into device capability with background collisions resolved with default foreground.

The interpreter is a C program compiled with Microsoft C 4.0 and linked with the appropriate GSS*CGI library. Each picture in the metafile is displayed, and user options presented. Zoomed redisplay and hardcopy options are presented, with printer or plotter output scaled or unscaled.

3 CGM for CAD

The second use of CGM I am aware of at Boeing is hardcopy/plotfile support for an integrated CAE/CAD/CAM product, Axxyz [11]. Character-encoded CGMs are generated by the Axxyz graphics package and interpreted, if necessary, by a background process into the appropriate protocol. Output types include CalComp 907 and 925, CGM, Gerber, two flavors of HP-GL, PostScript and VersaPlot.

The generator's entry points reflect the structure of the Axxyz graphics package: Polyline, Polymarker, Line Type, Line Width, Line Colour, Marker Type, Marker Size and Marker Colour are supported. VDC Extent is a user-specified "paper size"; point lists are encoded in Displacement Mode with VDC Real Precision parameters (11, -14, -14, 1). Colour Selection Mode is "direct" with 10 bits of precision. Line Width Specification Mode and Marker Size Specification Mode are "absolute."

The generator uses two standardized line types ("solid" and "dot") plus five private ones ("dash" variations). All standardized plus two private marker types are used. The generator actually invents Marker Size in response to VDC Extent, but within a fairly narrow min/max range so as to produce recognizable but not oversized markers on a wide variety of paper sizes.

The interpreter needs to handle enough in the way of attributes and defaults replacement to require a "real implementation", minus bundle support. Output is tailored to device capability, although for the most part only PostScript is trusted to handle attributes (other than color) correctly.

Both generator and interpreter are written in APOLLO DOMAIN Pascal [12] and ported to other environments as required. A SunCGI [13] platform exists and should prove useful for future development, but Axxyz's currently perceived needs are fully met by existing functionality.

4 The Future

Expansion of CGM capability will occur as needs arise, and hopefully replace the CalComp metafile as a Boeing standard. Tools allowing higher-level access to generators are being considered as alternatives to GKS or other Application Program Interfaces. Although character encoding will probably continue to be viewed as the most portable and compact, interpreters will soon (?) recognize any Version 1 (no Addendum 1!) CGM and produce, if necessary, another encoding as output. In particular, the GSS*CGM and TOP [14] application-profile binary formats will probably soon require support. (Even CDC can handle binary if IAF is avoided.) If not, piecemeal enhancements will be made as projects require. At least the architecture is there.

Notes:

1. The Petroleum Gallery is a service mark of The Boeing Company.

2. IBM, PC are trademarks of International Business Machines Corporation.

   MS-DOS is a trademark of Microsoft, Inc.

3. MAINSTREAM-CTS is a registered service mark of The Boeing Company.

4. CDC Cyber is a trademark of Control Data Corporation.

   MAINSTREAM-EKS is a registered service mark of The Boeing Company.

5. Cray X-MP is a trademark of Cray Research, Inc. MAINSTREAM-VSP is a registered service mark of The Boeing Company.

6. RELAY Gold, which is a trademark of VM Personal .

7. GSS*CGI is a trademark of Graphic Software Systems, Inc.

8. GSS*CGM is a trademark of Graphic Software Systems, Inc.

9. Interactive Facility (IAF) is a trademark of Control Data Corporation.

10. PetroView, which is a service mark of The Boeing Company. This product is currently only available commercially to customers of The Petroleum Gallery.

11. Axxyz is a service mark of The Boeing Company.

12. APOLLO, DOMAIN are registered trademarks of Apollo Computer, Inc.

13. SunCGI is a trademark of Sun Microsystems, Inc.

14. Technical and Office Protocols, a trademark of The Boeing Company.

Bridge that GAP (The CGM at the Real Applications Interface)

C. D. Osland

Abstract

The CGM built on the graphical concepts of GKS and provides a means of exchanging pictures. It does this simply, unambiguously and concisely. The structure of the standard, with a single functional specification and multiple encodings, addresses the needs of a wide range of different applications.

For most users, its benefits are mainly indirect: more of their application programs drive more of the devices available to them. Users do not have direct contact with the CGM: it is generated and interpreted by the packages and systems they use. It is however possible to employ much of the same design ideas that went into the CGM - and the identical encoding mechanisms - to provide a system truly at the applications interface (as distinct from the basic drawing interface of GKS or the workstations interface of the CGI). This may be termed a Graphics Applications Protocol (GAP).

This paper explores this idea. It is seen as a departure from a strictly graphical system, borrowing ideas from spreadsheet and report writing systems as much as from conventional graphics thinking. It lends itself to both batch and interactive methods of working and even addresses the needs for scripting graphical output to video.

Two methods of communicating applications data are shown. In the first, the framework of the CGM and its application data elements provides for an evolutionary path. In the second, the ideas and techniques in the CGM are preserved but used in a way that is more appropriate and efficient.

1 Introduction

The Computer Graphics Metafile (CGM) was designed to communicate information. Specifically, it communicates graphical information. It does not aim to transmit models (concrete or abstract) or to reflect the underlying structure of the object it is displaying.

The different forms of encoding (character, binary, clear text) that are specified in the CGM document encourage its use with applications that require highly compact data, quickly generated files or easily edited data. It is therefore invaluable as a graphical interface in a large installation with many computers and many different output devices.

At the Atlas Centre, the installation of a Cray X-MP/48 computer significantly increased the requirement for graphical output. The speed of the machine - and the type of projects using it - demand graphics facilities with which the researcher can explore the results of a calculation. A large fraction of the workload consists of simulation of 3D phenomena in which the area of interest is not known before the program is run.

The additional graphics facilities for the Cray system were considered under two main headings: improved permanent output, including video tape, and high power graphics workstations.

Increasingly, graphical workstations are being used to display the results of computer calculations. These workstations have considerable computational power, disk storage, bandwidth to their screens and graphical rendering capability. Such workstations are now becoming available at (or below) the price of highly intelligent, but passive, terminals a couple of years ago. Some of them provide their maximum performance when handling 3D data, since dedicated graphics hardware is tuned to this task. This implies that a 2D metafile, like the current CGM, will not exploit the system fully.

For the scientific user who wishes to use a variety of devices, the advent of these powerful workstations is a mixed blessing. They tempt with the promise of electrifying response, but threaten to entrap the user into the environment (packages and operating environment) of a single manufacturer.

One ray of hope on the horizon exists with the work by ANSI and ISO towards higher levels of graphics standard than GKS; in particular the PHIGS+ project aims to provide a level of interface to graphics that can make good use of such workstations.

However, these workstations can be used, for graphics, in ways that any graphics standard cannot hope to describe. This is because they can be used not just to present but also to select data, at a stage well before that data is rendered graphically.

This paper explores some ideas on how this form of communication can be organized and how the ideas at the base of the CGM can be used, almost intact, in the structuring and encoding of the information. The design of the system is currently being developed, so in many cases a broad-brush description is given of our current intentions.

2 The GAP Scheme

2.1 A Model of a Large Application

Programs in the Cray - typically very large, pre-existing codes - need to be able to produce graphical output on screens, hardcopy devices, video and film. For the last three targets, the sequence of pictures to be produced has to be specified as input to the Cray program. For viewing on screens, there is no need for this and every desire by the users to select data to be displayed after the program had run. This selection might happen after the Cray job ends or while it is in progress.

Many of the applications are research simulations of complex 3D systems such as oceanography, seismology, atmospheric physics and material science. The results of these simulations are usually large, multi-dimensional arrays. The users require a system that simplifies the storage of such Application Data and the presentation of results on the workstation screen.

This leads to the idea of the mainframe program, in effect, communicating a database to the workstation. Application data, not graphics data, is passed from the mainframe to the workstation. One immediate advantage of this, to the programmer who has to modify the original code, is that the modifications consist almost entirely of adding requests to export data, a simple, relatively safe task.

Correspondingly, the users' session at the screen - the sequence of commands that select the data and display the pictures - may be viewed as a Script. The same model can be used for hardcopy, video and film output. In this case the Script would be supplied with the job.

2.2 Is this the Re-invented Wheel?

Any number of systems have many of the elements described so far. For two decades, physicists have relied on systems that started as histogramming mechanisms to display, in a methodical way, the results of vast numbers of accelerator events. In many cases, the programmer requested particular graphical output by means of a command file (a script). Examples are the ENPLOT, FAPLOT, HBOOK, HPLOT and ZBOOK. Similarly, astronomers work with organized systems of data in which commands are available to select and display telescope (and other) images. Examples here are the Starlink system and suites from JPL. Such systems are very common in every discipline, arising naturally with large collaborations and providing a valuable unifying tool for those involved.

The idea of selecting data dynamically is central to spreadsheet systems, typified by systems like CricketGraph, and is also to be found in mainframe presentation graphics systems like DataManager. It is of course the basic method in all report writer systems such as SAS and EasyTrieve.

The idea of scripts for graphical work is as old as the idea of animated output, whether on screens, pen plotters or films. It is central to the structure of the majority of current packages for animated output. Examples are MOVIE-BYU, Abel and Oasis.

The system described in this paper is thought to be unique in a number of ways:

Application Independence

the type of data supported is independent of any scientific discipline;

Openness

data is communicated between parts of the application in a single, deterministic format and all data elements are self-describing, allowing complete open communication;

Distribution of Function

the act of producing the data and presenting it may be - to borrow a phrase from the CGM - separated in time and/or space.

Figure 1. Characteristics of GAP

1. Application Independence

   To refer back to the high energy physics systems, they provided many options, but would tend to have a primary key which might be the experiment number, the event number, the beam energy or some other hook into their particular environment. Similarly, for obvious reasons, packages originating in astronomical spheres would have more concern for 2D image data than perhaps vector functions in 3D. Each worked well for workers in its own discipline but would be strained if required to work outside that area.

2. Openness

   The report-writer and spreadsheet systems mentioned above tend not to have a single format used for communication. Many, because of their remit, accept dozens of different formats while perhaps using a single internal format. Also, they tend to handle datasets rather than individual data items.

3. Distribution of Function

The majority of graphics systems are either run within one computer system (not distributed) or are split somewhere at a graphical interface (GKS user interface, CGI, CGM or ad hoc device interface). None of these allow the viewer to select the data to be viewed, although some may permit the viewing conditions to be manipulated.

2.3 The System in Outline

The system being proposed is exceedingly simple. It is a means of communicating data of absolutely arbitrary type and dimensions from one part of an application to another. There is no conceptual hierarchy; each data element is completely self-contained and consists of its data prefixed by a header that identifies it and describes its dimensions and type.

Name	Descriptor	Data

Figure 2. Basic Data Item: The Application Data Stream Principally Consists of a Sequence of these Data Items.

In the same way as the data stream is independent of the application, so the script is independent of the graphical system. It contains instructions for selecting data from the data stored in the workstation and for presenting the data in the desired way. The way in which these instructions will actually be executed will vary from one system to another, depending on the (high and low level) graphics systems installed. The extent to which hardware, firmware and software are used will vary enormously.

2.4 A Concrete Example

Let us consider a trivial example. Suppose that an application analyses the results of a calorimetry experiment. The results may be available in the application in two arrays, of the same length: the temperature and pressure in a vessel at a number of equally spaced times.

The researcher, not knowing the results of the experiment in advance, does not know what he wants to view. The application is therefore told to output both arrays, possibly calling them calor.temp and calor.press, respectively.

When the data has arrived on the workstation, he can request

DISPLAY calor.temp

or

DISPLAY calor.press

or

PLOT calor.press VERSUS calor.temp

as he wishes. In this example, DISPLAY and PLOT are being assumed as primitives in the script language. They are being used as analogues of any equivalent operation such as selecting PLOT on a menu and indicating the data to be plotted on a menu list of eligible data. The above form would, naturally, be preferred for stored scripts used for hardcopy, video and film production.

It can be seen that, given this style of working, the "script interpreter" is free to use any facility on the workstation to achieve what is requested. This may be built-in hardware, commercial software or specially developed software. The important concept, for our application, is that the same system can be installed on workstations whose power may differ by a factor of a thousand without the user having to change his method of working.

2.5 Data Elements in Detail

It was stated above that each data element consists of a header and the data. The header records the name, type and dimensionality of the data. All data in one data element must be of the same type; the way in which data of different types can be associated is described below.

1. The Name

The name is an arbitrary character string. If required, the format of the name may become significant to the "script interpreter," as described below under Data Structures.

2. The Descriptor

The descriptor consists of the data type, the number of dimensions and the actual dimensions. For example, the descriptor for an array of real numbers of length 10 would therefore be (in abstract)

REAL 1 1:10

The data types supported include obvious types from standard programming languages and others included so that pictorial information - such as colour - can be communicated in an appropriate way, without mapping to primitive data types. The list of data types is shown in Figure 3.

BIT
COLOUR INDEX
COLOUR
REAL
COMPLEX
nD POINT
STRING

Figure 3. List of GAP Data Types

The 'nD POINT' data type covers 2D (as in the CGM), 3D (as in GKS-3D and PHIGS) and 4D (3D + time) and higher dimensions (such as 6D + time for robot manipulator data).

The dimensioning information consists simply of the number of dimensions and the lower and upper bounds for each dimension. Since what is being communicated is data, there is no requirement for any other form of bounds information, as happens in some programming languages.

By way of a more complex example, the header for the wind speed at 2.30 pm over Texas at 1 degree intervals in longitude and latitude might be

"WindSpeed/Texas/14.30" REAL 3 1:2 108:93 26:37

The pair of values at each location represent the wind speed as a vector.

3. The Data

It can be seen that the types of value required in the header are all fundamental types employed in the CGM, extended from 2D points to 'nD' points. The data can therefore be encoded in exactly the same was as the CGM.

2.6 Data Structures

Each data element consists of elementary data values that are all of one type (INTEGER, REAL, STRING etc..). This does not allow data structures within a single data element. However, the naming of data elements allows a very natural form of structure specification, equivalent to that of PL/I or COBOL. Thus, the application might output data elements called

```
"Bin.14/Energy"   REAL      1 1:50
"Bin.14/Count"    INTEGER   1 1:50
"Bin.14/Name"     STRING
```

and a display macro could be set up which, called up as

BinPlot Bin.14

could generate something like

```
PLOT Bin.14/Energy VERSUS Bin.14/Count CAPTION Bin.14/Name
```

The idea is that, while the user is completely free to use any appropriate or memorable names, it is also possible to have the effect of data structures through organized use of names. In PL/1 terms, the above data could be regarded as:

```
DECLARE 1 Bin14,

    2 Energy   (1:50)     FLOAT BINARY,
    2 Count    (1:50)     FIXED BINARY(31),
    2 Name     CHAR (*);
```

Obviously much more complicated data structures can be achieved through this mechanism.

2.7 File Format

So far, we have only considered the format of individual data elements. While these are the most frequently occurring elements in GAP, the complete "file" of information has a structure very close to that of the CGM.

The GAP data is organized into **Groups**, in very much the same way as the CGM is organized into pictures. No fixed interpretation is placed on groups. In a very large number of cases, GAP is going to be used for simulations where the application generates a number of successive sets of data. These will often correspond to timesteps in the simulation but could equally be steps in steps or some other dimension. The Group structure in GAP allows this structure to be maintained.

The GAP file consists of an arbitrary number of groups enclosed in a file header and file trailer. The file header serves the same purpose as in the CGM. It identifies the file and establishes conventions for the rest of the file. In particular, it indicates how groups are to be handled. The options are:

- only the most recent group is retained;
- the most recent 'n' groups are retained;
- all data is retained.

As for the CGM, the file header will also specify the form of encoding that will used, leaving some aspects (such as method of compression - see Data Efficiency below) to be clarified on an element-by-element basis. This will be done via control elements, rather than by extending the data element headers.

2.8 Data Storage

Although the graphics workstations expected to be used with GAP will have adequate memory for processing the data, it is unlikely that all data sent from the Cray to the workstation can be held in real memory. The name of the data - or the root name of a large data structure - could be used to file the data on the workstation's disk. It is however safer to assume that the name is mapped to a filing system name, since the user is free to use any character string for the name and the filing system is unlikely to be as relaxed about file names.

2.9 Data Efficiency

Large application codes, such as those for which GAP is designed, tend to generate large quantities of information. Tens of megabytes are common. While this poses no great problem when the user requires permanent (hardcopy) output, it places considerable strain on both network resources and disk space, since many of these files may have to be held concurrently.

Since the majority of users of the Cray at the Atlas Centre are located at UK universities (typically 100 miles from the centre), and most links to the centre have a maximum bandwidth of 48 Kbaud, compression of data is essential if results are to be viewed even the same day as the Cray program ran.

The basic encoding scheme for GAP, being modelled very closely on that of the CGM, achieves very good results for integer data. This general efficiency can be further improved, for many applications, by the use of a predictor system.

Normally, the application program would ask the GAP system to transmit a complete array of data. However, in many cases the data to be transmitted might be very similar to a previous array. This would typically be the case for a finite element mesh that was being gradually distorted: most points would only move a short distance at each step of the simulation. GAP could be instructed always to compare an array with its previous value and could then decide whether to transmit the complete data or change data.

2.10 Implementation

Two methods of implementing GAP have been considered. In the first, the CGM is used as it stands, except that the only picture elements to be included are Application Data Elements. In the second, the overall structure of the CGM is maintained but GAP uses the whole of that scheme.

1. Using CGM Application Data Elements

The CGM was designed to allow applications data to be imbedded in the body of the metafile. While it was not germane to specify what such applications data should be used for in the standard, it was expected that one use would be to insert data relating to the model of which the metafile was the picture. For example, the angular and positional description of a molecule might accompany a view of that molecule.

The data being communicated in GAP could be seen as a description of the model; the irony is that it would accompany zero pictures! The structure of the CGM is perfect for GAP, with the exception that a large number of graphical attributes would have to be set which will have no effect (since there are no pictures). For this reason, the second method, described below, is preferred.

2. Using the ideas that shaped the CGM

The CGM has a simple, classical structure. Each CGM starts with a header that relates to the file as a whole and ends with a positive 'end of CGM' trailer. Similarly, each picture starts with a header that relates to just that picture and ends with a positive 'end of picture' trailer.

Looking at the headers in more detail, it will be seen that the file header ensures (as much as can be done in an output-only situation) that the interpreter knows in advance that it will be able to process the file. It does this by enumerating the facilities that may be used and by specifying the forms of encoding for a variety of data types.

Exactly the same form of establishment of communication is required for GAP data; the only change is that the values communicated refer to aspects of the GAP data (such as how data may be compressed) rather than to aspects of the CGM (such as how linewidth will be specified).

The details of each element have yet to be determined.

2.11 Advantages of the Scheme

1. Minimum Disturbance of Application

   Since the selection of data to be presented has been kept separate from the application, the application program is unlikely to be affected by changing display requirements. The form of modification to the application is very safe, unlikely to add logic errors into a working program.

2. Full Use of Power of Graphics Workstation

   The graphics workstation can be used properly, not just as a graphics display but as an autonomous computer. This allows the user to decide (rather than guess) what data is to be viewed.

3. Freedom of Choice in Type of Presentation

   Alternative forms of display can be tried at a screen without any disturbance to the application program.

4. Data Compression

   Methods of data compression can be provided which are transparent to the user.

2.12 The Debt to the CGM

For a paper presented at a conference devoted to the CGM, it may be thought that GAP is an intruder, like a cuckoo in the nest that fed it. In fact, the CGM is really the parent (real not foster) of GAP, as can be seen from a number of parallels.

- GAP aims to provide communication of applications data between systems separated in time and/or space; CGM provides the same facility for graphical data;
- GAP aims to provide an interface between application and graphical processor that is independent of the application and the processor; CGM provides independence between the generator and interpreter of the metafile;
- GAP maintains exactly the same form of overall structure as CGM, first announcing the desire to communicate, then the method of communication and finally the data communicated;
- GAP uses the same basic data types as CGM;
- GAP uses the same encoding schemes as CGM, only extended to deal with arrays of data and point data of dimensions beyond 2 and 3.

Use of Trade Names

In the body of this paper, a number of product names are referred to. They are only used by way of examples, as being systems with which the reader may be familiar, and no praise or criticism, of the systems mentioned or of those omitted, is implied or intended.

Acknowledgments

The basic idea of GAP came from discussions with Trevor Daniels, Head of Software and Development at the Atlas Centre. All the work on CGM, which will be re-used in GAP, has been done by Craig Alsop in Graphics Group. I have been much assisted by discussions with Roy Platon, project leader for graphics on the Cray, also of Graphics Group.

Part VI

Testing Considerations

The CGM has very limited conformance requirements in the standard. The only requirement is for a particular metafile to conform to the functional specification and, where required, to conform to one of the three standard encodings. There are no requirements imposed by the standard for the software which generates and interprets the metafiles. When we considered application profiles earlier in this volume we found that this was not acceptable in many environments where it was necessary to ensure transfer of pictures and, in some cases such as CALS, to ensure that the picture could be accurately reproduced.

There seems, therefore, to be an expectation that testing, both to the standard and to important application profiles, will be necessary. The adoption of application profiles by a wide range of companies may also make testing of these profiles commercially viable.

This part of the proceedings include three papers from people with experience in testing standards. The three take different perspectives. They include proposals for a possible approach to testing the CGM and to implementing a test service within the US Government.

Pink suggests that the methodology should be adopted from Open Systems Interconnection (051) testing. She refers to the strategy which has been adopted at the National Computing Centre (NCC) in the UK. This is endorsed by Carr who has been involved in using this strategy for developing document testing for ODA. This work is a parallel to the CGM work. There are places, however, where the work does overlap, particularly in the area of the Geometric Graphics Content Architecture of ODA. The difficulties for both ODA and CGM of comparing manual output when testing interpreters and of developing automated tests are considered.

The need for a testing service is recognized by NBS for graphics standards including CGM. Kemmerer outlines a proposal for a testing procedure for the US Government. This procedure could be used within the graphics arena for those standards which are adopted by the Government.

Testing of the Computer Graphics Metafile

A.E.J. Pink

Abstract

This paper proposes a method of providing third party testing for implementations of the Computer Graphics Metafile (CGM). Formal third party Testing Services, which are currently being operated, are considered and the possibility of CGM Testing being set up within a similar framework. Two aspects of testing are considered, conformance testing, which tests for conformance to the standard and evaluation, which tests beyond the scope of the standard with the aim of providing more practical information on the usefulness of a particular product.

1 Testing Services at the National Computing Centre Ltd.

NCC first became involved in conformance testing, or validation as it is often known, in the early 1980's. Funding was made available by the Department of Trade and Industry (DTI) to establish a COBOL 74 Compiler Validation Service in the UK, based on the service already offered in the USA. An NCC staff member underwent a period of training at the Federal Software Testing Center (FSTC), as it was then known, in COBOL compiler validation. The service was launched by NCC in February 1983 and used the same tests and procedures as used in the USA. In addition, a reciprocal agreement was signed between NCC and FSTC, meaning that each organization would recognize compilers validated by the other. NCC launched a FORTRAN 77 compiler validation service in November 1983, again based on the tests and procedures used in the US. Over 100 COBOL and FORTRAN compilers have now been validated by NCC.

NCC was appointed the UK Ada[1] Validation Facility in 1985 and a large proportion of the work of Testing Services now involves Ada Compiler validation. The Graphical Kernel System (GKS) Test Service, which is described in the next section, was launched

1 Ada is a registered trademark of the United States Government (Ada Joint Program Office)

in July 1987. In addition NCC runs an OSI Testing Service for the Transport and Session layers of the 7 layer model.

NCC is also involved in test development. The project to write the new COBOL 85 test suite was led by NCC and the programming and maintenance of this test suite has all been done at NCC. Also, there is a heavy commitment to OSI test development. Test Systems have been developed for the Transport and Session layers and we are also involved in FTAM and MHS test development.

NCC is continually looking for new areas into which testing services can expand. Office Document Architecture (ODA), Unix and CGM are currently the three areas in which initiatives are being taken.

2 The European Commission GKS Project

In 1985, NCC became involved in a 2 year project funded by the European Commission, in partnership with the Gesellschaft fuer Mathematik und Darenverarbeiting (GMD) and Bureau d'orientation de la Normalisation et Informatique (BNI), to establish a harmonized testing service for GKS within Europe. Using the GKS tests developed by the University of Leicester and TH Darmstadt as a basis, the project aimed to enhance and extend the tests and establish procedures and documentation for a test service. This work was completed in July 1987 when version 2.0 of the GKS test suite and associated documentation was released. Third party testing services for GKS are now available from NCC, GMD and AFNOR (BNI merged to become AFNOR) within Europe. A major object of this project was to ensure harmonization, of tests, of operating procedures and of test reports. This will ensure that the results of testing a GKS implementation will be identical, whether the testing is carried out in the UK, France or Germany.

A Control Board has been established within the GKS Testing project to deal with queries from clients of GKS testing. It is likely that the process of testing GKS implementations will uncover areas within the standard which are open to interpretation and upon which a ruling will be required. The Control Board consists of a representative from each Testing Laboratory and two representatives of ISO/TC97/SC21/WG2 - Computer Graphics.

It is hoped that the GKS testing service established within Europe will be available in the United States from the end of 1987.

3 An Overview of the Operation of Existing Testing Services

The test suites, used for COBOL, Fortran, Ada* and GKS testing, check the relevant compiler for conformance to the corresponding standard. The methods used are not exhaustive and cannot guarantee the absence of errors. The methods can only expose instances where a compiler fails to meet the requirements of the standard. However, a large measure of confidence can be felt in a product which successfully withstands the rigors of the validation suite.

The COBOL and Fortran test suites consist of conforming test programs, which the compiler should be able to compile and execute correctly. The majority of test results are produced automatically, a very small number of tests requiring operator intervention.

The Ada test suite is similar, but in addition has a series of non-conforming test programs, which the compiler must reject. In addition the Ada test suite contains tests which evaluate the capacities of a compiler, for example, the number of levels of nesting supported, the maximum floating point precision. These tests provide extra information, of an evaluation nature, beyond the scope of the standard.

The GKS test suite consists of five series of test programs. Data consistency test programs check the consistency of values in the GKS description table and the workstation description tables. Data structure test programs examine data in the GKS state lists, using Inquiry Functions, before and after specified actions have taken place. Error handling test programs, generate error situations and check that the correct error handling mechanism is invoked. These first three series of tests all produce automatic reports of the results. The final two test series require manual intervention and checking of graphical displays by the test operator. The metafile test programs check that the GKS metafile is implemented correctly. The input/output test programs provide a test of graphics system as a whole and cover all the input and output capabilities of GKS. For each test program, a series of graphical displays must be checked and a series of actions must be carried out by the test operator. The GKS Evaluator's Manual, which is supplied with the GKS test suite, describes the items to be checked via a comprehensive check-list.

There are three major stages in performing third party testing of a product:

- pre-testing
- formal testing
- preparation of report.

At the pre-testing stage the client is supplied with the test suite and is able to run the tests on his product until he is happy with the results. A date is then set for the formal testing to take place and the client provides the testing laboratory with pre-validation material. Pre-validation materials includes the results from the execution of some, or all, of the test programs, details of the exact configuration to be tested and a description of the procedures to be used for formal testing (command procedures for reading the tape, compiling etc).

The Testing Laboratory then conducts formal testing at the customer's site on the specified day. Another copy of the test suite is brought on-site by the Testing Laboratory and this must be used for the validation. An alternative method to this is if an approved integrity checking method can be used to ensure that the copy of the test suite used for pre-testing has not changed. All the test programs are compiled and executed under the supervision of staff from the Testing Laboratory, who then check all the results.

On return to the office a draft Test Report is produced and sent to the client for approval. This Test Report provides full details of the validation and gives a description of any error found. When agreement is reached with the client a final Test Report is produced and a certificate may be issued, if the requirements of the certification scheme have been met.

4 What can be Achieved with CGM Testing?

So far, this paper has examined third party testing services which already operate successfully. It now goes on to look at how a CGM Test Service might be operated and what format the tests would take. Many of the ideas have also come from analysis of the methods used within OSI testing, where the aim is to check for the correct transfer of data between two systems.

The CGM standard describes a file format for the storage and transfer of picture information. Section 0.2 of the CGM Standard identifies the reasons for the Standard:

- to allow picture information to be stored in an organized way on a graphical software system;
- to facilitate the transfer of picture information between different graphical software systems;
- to enable picture information to be transferred between graphical devices;
- to enable picture information to be transferred between different computer graphics installations.

If we consider these objectives in relation to testing a CGM implementation it becomes clear that three areas need to be addressed by a test system:

1. checking that the file format in which the picture data is stored is syntactically correct;
2. checking that the file format is correctly generated;
3. checking that the file format can be interpreted on the same, or another system, to give the expected results.

The first two areas above can be extended to provide interoperability testing between two or more graphical systems containing CGM implementations.

The next important point to consider is exactly what testing can be achieved within the framework of the CGM standard. Section 7.1 'Forms of Conformance' in the CGM standard states that:

> 'the standard specifies functionality and encodings of Computer Graphics Metafiles; it does not specify operations or required capabilities of metafile generators or metafile interpreters.'

General guidelines for Metafile Generators and Interpreters are however given in Annex D of the Standard. An Annex is for information only and as it is not part of the Standard could not be used as the basis for conformance testing.

Since the conformance section clearly states that the CGM standard is not concerned with the capabilities of metafile generators and interpreters, it follows that a conformance test system can only address the first area identified above (ie. checking of the static file format). Such testing can tell us nothing about the metafile generators and interpreters. The implication is that out of the four 'reasons' given for the metafile standard only the first of these can be tested. The three most important reasons for creating a metafile standard i.e. those concerned with the capability of transfer of graphical data, cannot be considered within a conformance test system. This is a serious deficiency in the CGM Standard.

Section 7.2 and 7.3 of the CGM standard go on to describe two ways in which a metafile may conform to the standard. In brief, full conformance occurs when the metafile conforms exactly to the functional specification described in Part 1 of the Standard and to one of the encodings described in Parts 2-4 of the Standard. Functional conformance occurs when the metafile conforms exactly to the functional specification described in Part 1 of the standard, but a private encoding is used.

The concept of full conformance means that it should be possible to provide conformance testing for the syntax and structure of a metafile encoded using one of the three standard encodings. Functional Conformance is more difficult. The Testing Laboratory has a metafile to test which is in an encoding not defined in the standard. Each metafile would have to be dealt with on a case by case basis, with specific test programs being written. This is unlikely to be either economic or feasible. In Annex B of the CGM Standard guidelines for private encodings are given. The guidelines given include the suggestion that designers of private encodings ensure:

- the ability to translate a metafile encoded in one of the standardized encodings into the private encoding;

- the corresponding ability to translate a privately encoded metafile to one of the standardized bindings.

Again, it is important to note that an Annex is not part of the Standard and hence cannot be considered valid input to a conformance test system.

The only way in which a Testing Laboratory could viably test a metafile using a private encoding is if the implementor, in following the guidelines in Annex B, could also supply the metafile in one of the standard encodings. The Testing Laboratory is then testing the metafile for full conformance.

The concept of functional conformance defined in the CGM standard, would therefore appear to be of little value. The CGM Standard, as indeed any standard, should not include a concept such as this which cannot be tested.

In conclusion to this section, one area has been identified where conformance testing can be achieved for the CGM, that is testing for full conformance of a Metafile. Testing of interpreters and generators cannot be addressed by a conformance test service.

Since Conformance testing of the CGM will be limited to checking that the metafile is stored in the correct file format, it is likely that there will be a need for extended testing beyond the scope of the standard to provide more practical information about implementations. This testing could examine metafile generators and interpreters.

The next sections examine, firstly conformance testing of the metafile and secondly, testing of generators and interpreters.

5 Testing a CGM for Conformance

As explained in the last section testing a CGM for conformance is limited to doing static checks on the metafile to ensure that the file format conforms to the rules in the standard.

Some work has been done on such a syntax checker at GTS-Gral in West Germany with funding received from the European Commission. The result of this work will be an elementary checker, capable of checking metafiles encoded in any of the three standard encodings. It is likely that this work will provide a good basic set of conformance tests for the CGM.

The following list gives the minimum set of checking to be achieved by such a syntax checker:

- check that the structure of the metafile is correct. (The CGM State Diagram provides a basis from which to start); [Note: This would ensure that metafile delimiter elements were present and in the correct position.]
- check that all classes of elements are encoded according to the syntax defined in the Standard;
- check that all non-standardized elements are encoded using the ESCAPE element or the external elements APPLICATION DATA and MESSAGE;
- check for consistency between the Metafile Descriptor Elements and the content of the metafile;
- check for consistency between the Picture Description Elements and the parameter modes which are used.

The checker must be capable of analyzing metafiles encoded in any of the three encodings defined in the standard. The checker should provide an automatic report of the results. This would need to specify the following details for each metafile element found to be in error:

- location within the metafile;
- brief description of the error;
- a reference to the section of the standard in error;

A summary report should indicate the total number of errors and should also indicate the number of metafile elements processed. It is also important to report if any elements were not processed or skipped over. Such results reports should be kept as short and concise as possible. It is likely that some type of trace facility, built into the checker, would be invaluable to the implementor who was involved in debugging.

6 Testing of CGM Generators and Interpreters

Conformance testing of a CGM, as described in the last section, gives very limited information and it is likely that further evaluation of the metafile generator and interpreter software will be requested of a Testing Laboratory.

There are four areas of testing possible:

1. Check that the generator produces a syntactically correct metafile
2. Check that the interpreter produces a correct realization of the metafile on some device
3. Check both the generator and interpreter on a given system
4. Check the interoperability between a generator and an interpreter on different systems.

All of these four areas are dealt with below. Many of the ideas for testing of generator and interpreter software have come from an analysis of the methods used for OSI testing. OSI Testing checks that data is correctly transferred between two systems at some layer of the 7 layer model. A Test System for the Transport layer, layer 4 of the 7 layer model, has been developed and is operated by NCC. An interesting feature of this test system is that testing can be carried out remotely, with the Testing Laboratory sending tests via a network link to the implementation under test and receiving results back for analysis. This is an area where the scope of testing has been extended beyond that defined in the standard to allow interoperability testing to be carried out to ensure that two conformance tested products can interwork correctly.

The approach to testing described below assumes that the Testing Laboratory will have an encoder and decoder capable of generating and interpreting any Conforming Metafile.

6.1. Testing the Generator

In order to test a generator some method of defining the test metafiles to be generated is required. This problem was discussed in some detail at a workshop held in March 1987 on CGM Testing and the following possibilities for defining the test metafiles were identified:

1. Let the client of testing choose an appropriate set of metafiles;

2. Provide sample programs to the client written using some application programs for example GKS which produce metafiles if a metafile device driver is available;

3. Provide a set of pictures to the client, illustrating the metafiles to be generated;

4. Provide a more formal description of the picture to the client. For example, using the clear text encoding of the CGM.

Option number 1 does not provide a fair test. For any formal third party test service a precisely defined set of test data is required to ensure uniformity of results.

Option number 2 provides a better means of defining the test metafiles. In this case, the Testing Laboratory can describe the test metafiles to be output using an application program. This method is reliant on the client supporting the given application interface. The code to generate the test metafiles could be made available to support all application interfaces where a standard was available or under development.

Option number 3 again provides a simpler means of defining the test metafiles for the Testing Laboratory. However, it will require a lot of work on the part of the client to code the pictures into metafiles. This method would also enable the comparison of output at the operator interface to be easily carried out. However this would be reliant on the client also having an interpreter on his system.

Option number 4 would involve a considerable amount of work to produce a range of test metafiles.

None of those options are totally satisfactory. Option 2 is the best provided that the client supports one of the standard application interfaces on his system. Option 3 would appear to be the best back up alternative.

The test service would operate in the following way:-

- the Testing Laboratory supplies the client with either application programs or pictures as a description of the test metafiles

- the client uses his CGM generator to generate the metafiles The CGM test metafiles are then sent to the Testing Laboratory

- the Testing Laboratory interprets the metafile using the encoder/decoder and analyses the result.

Figure 1 demonstrates the process.

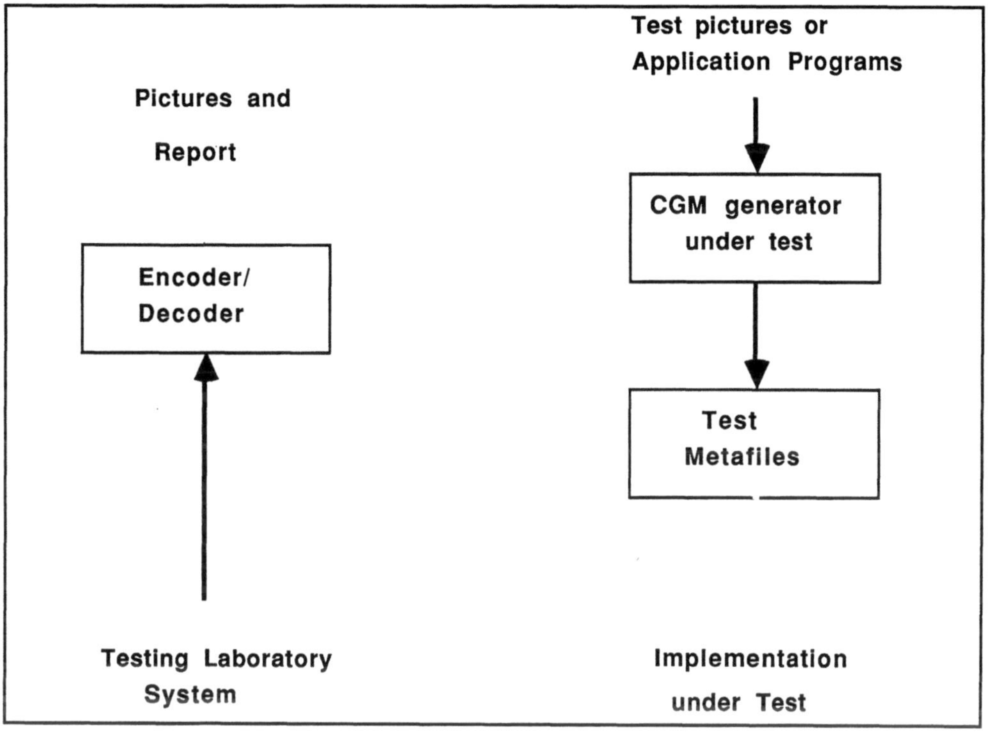

Figure 1. Generator Test Process

6.2. Testing the Interpreter

The test service would work in the following way:-

- the Testing Laboratory asks the client to provide details of his CGM implementation and its capabilities. The Testing Laboratory then generates test metafiles to examine all the claimed capabilities of the implementation
- these test metafiles are sent to the CGM implementation under test and interpreted on the test system
- the pictures produced by the interpreter are checked for correctness against reference pictures.

Figure 2 demonstrates the process.

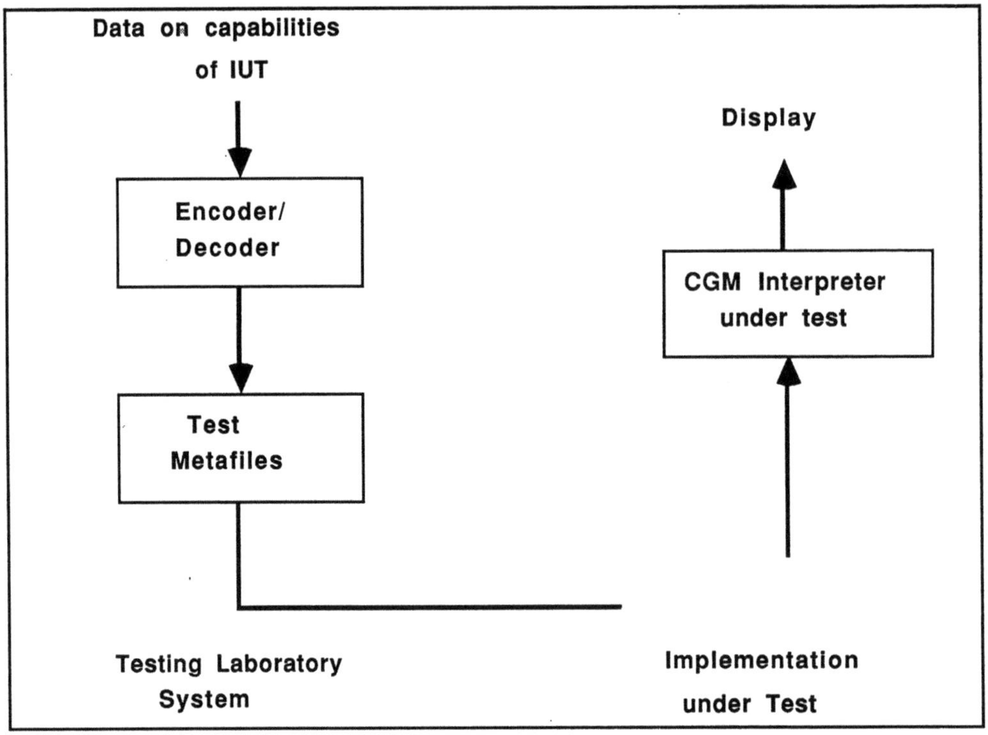

Figure 2. Interpreter Test Process

6.3. Testing the Generator and Interpreter

The process described in items 1. and 2. above can be easily extended to carry out a test of both the interpreter and the generator. The process would be as follows:-

- the Testing Laboratory generates test metafiles according to the claimed capabilities of the implementation under test
- the interpreter at the test site interprets the metafiles
- the pictures produced can be checked for correctness
- in addition, the implementation under test produces metafiles which are sent back to the Testing Laboratory
- the Testing Laboratory decodes the metafiles and checks the pictures produced.

Figure 3 demonstrates the process.

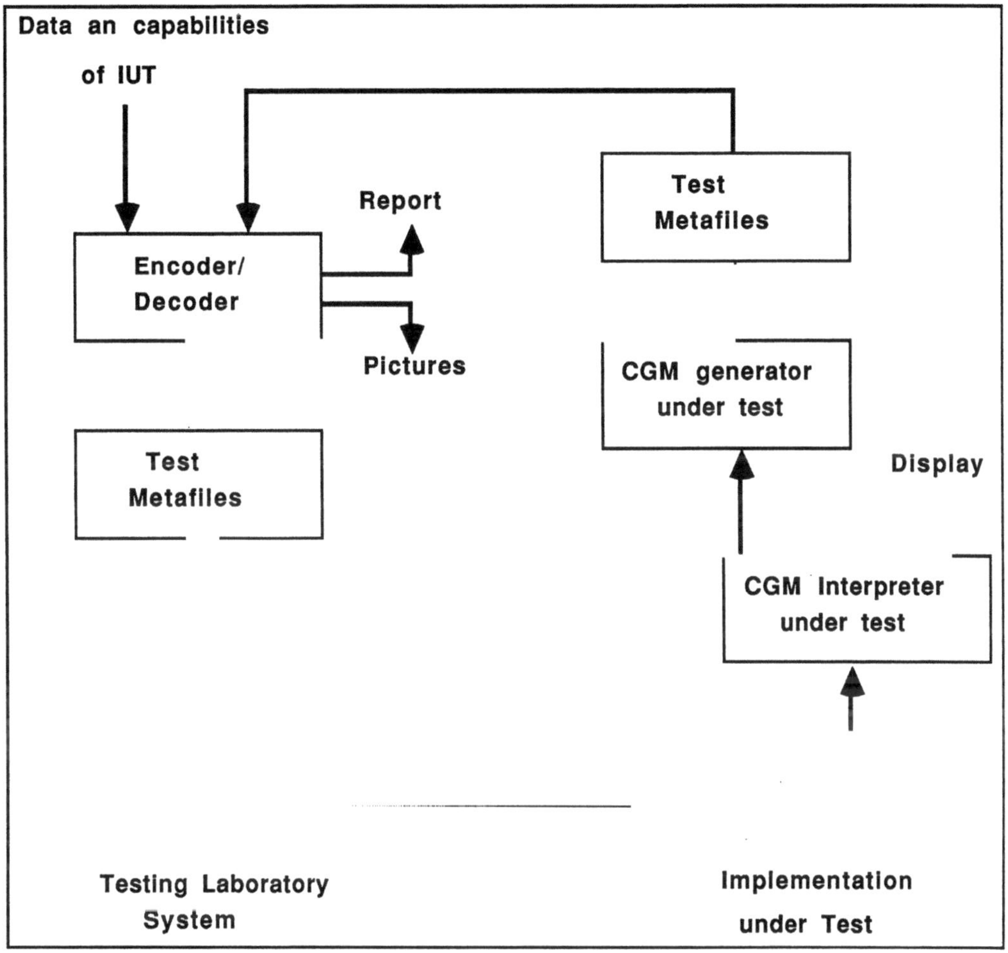

Figure 3. Generator and Interpreter Test Process

6.4. Testing the Generator and Interpreter on Different Systems

This testing is an extension of item 3. in which the two systems are the Testing Laboratory system and the system under test. A service could be provided by the Testing Laboratory to test whether two CGM implementations could transfer metafiles successfully. Such testing would only be performed on two systems which had already passed the previous tests. Such a service would provide information on a practical level in situations where it was important that two systems were able to transfer graphical data successfully.

7 Establishing a Test Service

The previous section has described in detail the type of testing which can be carried out for the CGM. The level of testing which can be achieved as a conformance test service is very limited, unlikely to be a viable exercise for the Testing Laboratory and the results produced would be of little practical use. The evaluation testing of generators and interpreters provides a much more useful exercise both for the Testing Laboratory and for the user of the CGM.

Carrying out tests for conformance to the CGM standard is a simple exercise for the Testing Laboratory. The client is asked to send a series of metafiles, demonstrating the full capabilities of the implementation to the Testing Laboratory. The metafiles can be sent over a network link or via some data medium, such as magnetic tape. The Testing Laboratory performs syntax checking on all the metafiles and produces a report. The report details the results and lists the features supported by the implementation. The Testing Laboratory requires only the syntax checking software.

Evaluation testing of CGM generators and interpreters requires that the Testing Laboratory has a more sophisticated test system.

The Testing Laboratory would require a full reference implementation of the CGM consisting of a generator and interpreter. This 'encoder/decoder' as we shall call it must have the following capabilities:

- ability to generate a metafile in any of the three standard encodings;
- ability to, on instruction from a utility program, generate incorrect metafile elements;
- ability to produce, via a reporting program a report of the test process, giving details of any errors detected and a log of the test protocol.

A Utility Program would be required as part of the system. This would read details on the capabilities of the implementation under test and use this information to select test metafiles from a database. This program would also control the reporting mechanism, reading responses from the encoder/decoder and produce a report.

The test data required is:

- a database of test metafiles, utilizing the full requirements of the standard;
- a set of application programs capable of generating these test metafiles, and for use when testing generators. It is likely that the existing input/output test programs in the GKS test suite could be used as the basis for these application programs;
- a set of invalid test metafiles.

Figure 4 demonstrates the test system.

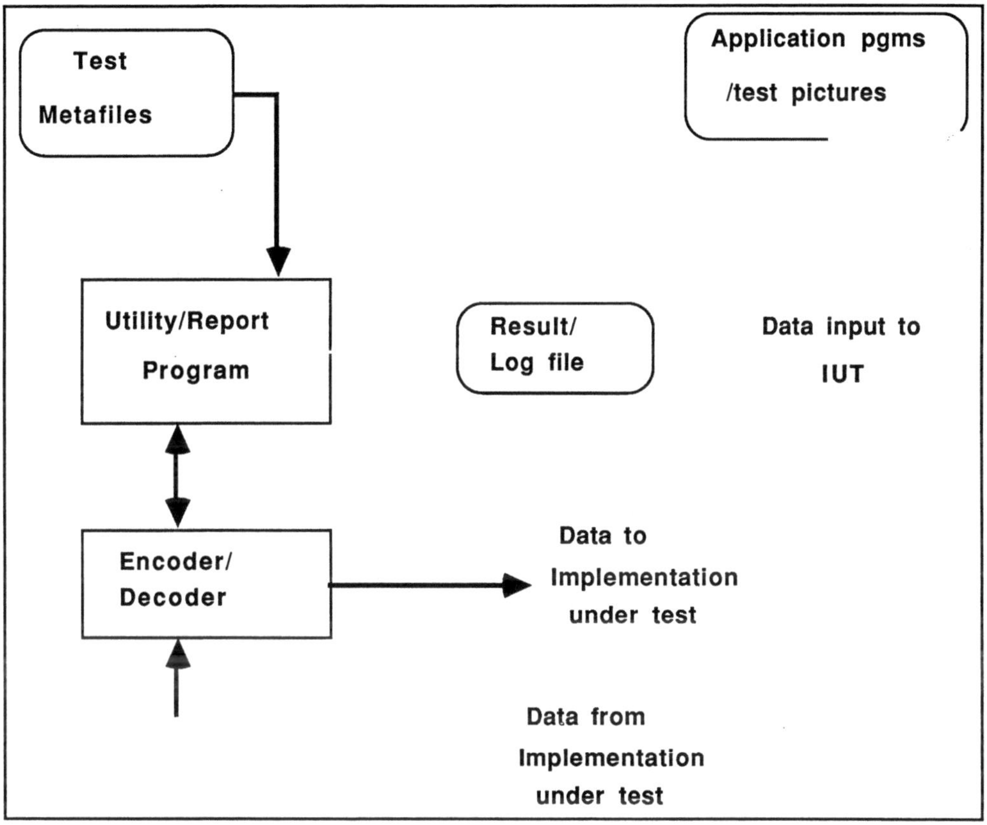

Figure 4. Test System

As a result of carrying out evaluation testing on interpreters or generators or both, the Testing Laboratory would produce a report. This report would list the capabilities of the implementation, provide details of the tests applied and the results obtained. It is important to note that such a report would be made available to provide evaluation information on the implementation. No pass/fail criteria can be applied to such testing - all that can bc done is to supply all the information to the users so that they can determine the best implementation for their requirements.

8 Conclusions

It has been determined that very little testing for conformance can be carried out on a CGM implementation. Such testing is limited to checking the file format of a given metafile. However it is likely that useful information could be provided by an evaluation service, providing for testing of generators and interpreters. An ideal design quality for a set of tests is that they should be self-checking with automatic reporting facilities. This is possible for the simple syntax checking of a metafile. However for testing generators and interpreters the only way of ensuring the metafiles have been transferred correctly is to manually check the pictures produced on a device against a set of reference pictures. This is also the case with the input/output test programs and metafile test programs in the GKS test suite. Human judgement is introduced into the checking process and this increases the possibility of an error being missed. The GKS Test Service operates on the basis of a very manually intensive operation and it is likely that this is a fact we will have to accept when testing graphics standards.

The question remaining is whether such a service would be economically viable for a Testing Laboratory to operate. If we assume that funding can be found for development of the test system required, then it is likely that the demand from users of CGM implementations will force the implementors to submit their products for testing.

The CGM has been included in the TOP (Technical and Office Protocol) Application Profile and it is likely that tests for conformance to this profile will be required.

A major aim of any initiative to develop tests and establish a test service must be to ensure that the tests and test procedures are accepted on an international basis. It is towards this aim that the future work in the UK on CGM Testing will be directed.

Acknowledgement

I would particularly like to thank Anne Mumford of the University of Loughborough Computer Centre. Many of the ideas in this paper are as a result of discussions with Anne.

References

1. *Open Systems Interconnection - Computer Graphics Metafile* - DTI Opportunity Study, Anne Mumford.

2. *Testing the Computer Graphics Metafile*, Report on the workshop held at Disley, 2-4 March 1987.

3. *OSI Testing*, Vony Gwillim, NCC.

4. Computer Graphics Metafile for the storage and transfer of picture description information, Part 1. Functional Specification (ISO/DIS 8632/1).

5. *An Elementary Syntax Checker for the CGM,* Peter Schloendorf, GTS-Gral.

An Overview of ODA and ODA Conformance Testing

R. Carr

Abstract

The Office Document Architecture Standard (ODA) is expected to become a full ISO International Standard (IS 8613) at the end of 1987. It is currently (June 1987) at the 2nd Draft International Standard (DIS) stage and as such can be considered technically stable and suitable for implementation. Collaborative projects in the European Esprit and UK Alvey programmes have been underway for some time with the aim of demonstrating the usefulness of the standard. Manufacturers are already developing ODA editors and translators for both future and existing systems to comply with emerging application profiles such as those defined in TOP and UK-GOSIP that will be used in user procurement specifications. This paper gives an overview of ODA and shows how the architectural model can be used to facilitate document interchange between open systems. It also includes an outline of a proposed methodology for ODA conformance testing.

1 What is ODA?

ODA is an ISO Standard for interchanging 'what you see is what you get' integrated text and graphics documents between dissimilar systems in an Open Systems Interconnection (OSI) environment. The ODA Standard provides for the interchange by prescribing an independent model of the content, logical and layout sub-structures found in typical office documents. Although initially designed for office systems, ODA is now viewed as being appropriate for the interchange of complex workstation documents such as those found in the aerospace industries.

ODA's abstract model caters for documents such as memos, newsletters, technical reports, manuals, presentations etc. where the content might include mixtures of character text, facsimile and drawings. Importantly, ODA provides for processable document interchange where the paragraphs and page layout information can be transferred between previously incompatible systems, edited and reformatted by these systems and make round trips between systems without losing information the users did not intentionally delete.

2 Why We Need ODA

Without a common model for interchanging documents the solution usually adopted for electronic transfer is the use of filters between each pair of different systems. This involves writing software to convert system A's documents into system B's and if two way working is needed, writing a B to A conversion. Although this approach is adequate for a small number of systems where it might offer a low level of conversion degradation the method presents a serious disadvantage if more systems are added to the set in use. In the case of n different document systems, each will require n-1 conversion programs for transfer to and from the n-1 remaining systems i.e. n times n-1 programs in all. The cost of this approach grows exponentially with the number of interchange systems. Fifty-six pieces of software would be needed for eight systems, three-hundred and eighty for twenty systems! A standard intermediate form keeps the cost to the software industry linear at two converters per system. However, it is important that whatever intermediate form is used, it should not simply be a common subset of the n document structures but be powerful enough to avoid the information loss that is present with any non-trivial conversion. ODA with its clear separation of document and content architectures and with its powerful set of attributes satisfies such a requirement.

3 Elements of the ODA Model

3.1 Document Profile

The ODA model describes a document in terms of a document profile and a document body (see Fig. 1). The profile is used for document management, specifying those characteristics of the document that apply to is as a whole such as filing and retrieval details, security aspects and external references. It also details the type of structures and content present in the document body and for this reason may be interchanged on its own. This allows a recipient system to interpret the information in the profile and subsequently determine whether it wants to receive the document body.

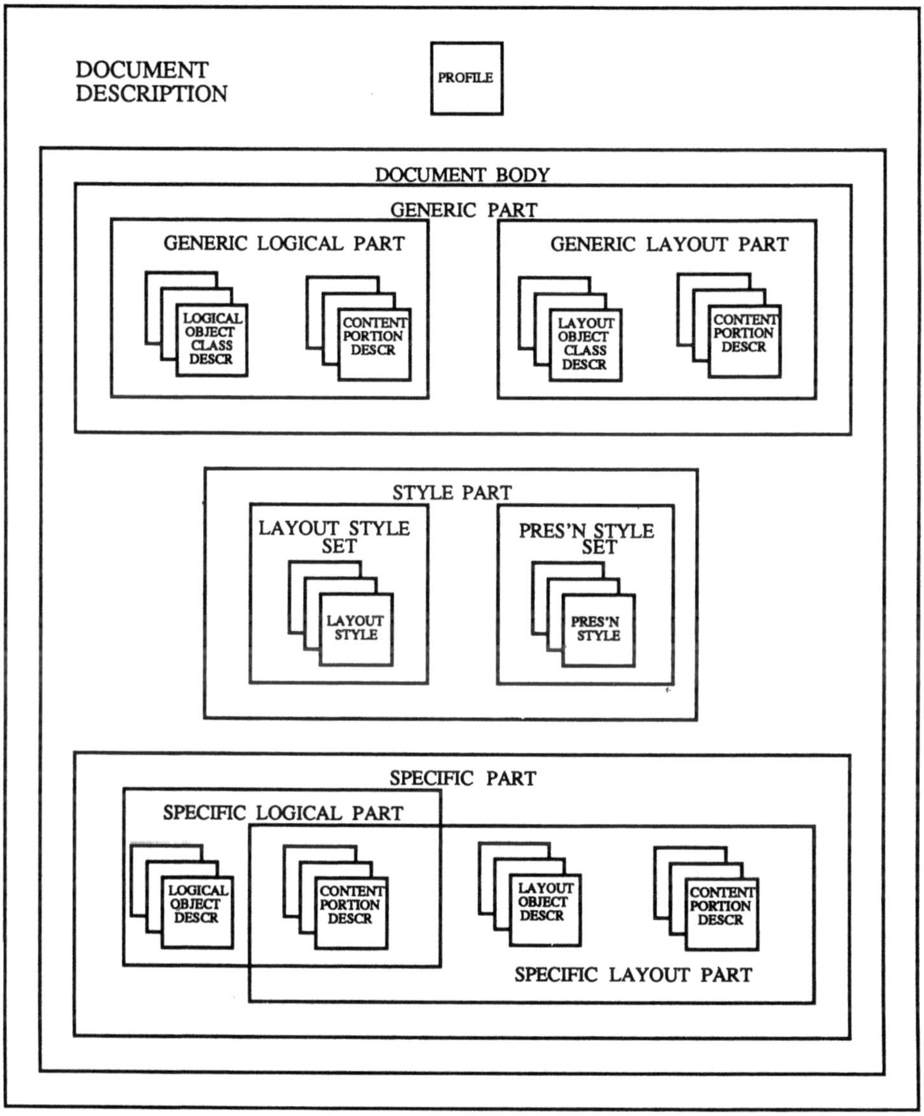

Figure 1: Descriptive Representation of a Document

The ODA Standard allows the profile to identify which particular application profile (DAP) an originator has used. A DAP defines a subset of the structures and features available in ODA and is used to tailor ODA to a particular user's or organisation's needs. Currently, DAP's are being defined by such organisations as ISO, CCITT, TOP, NBS, SPAG, the UK and European Governments, etc. It is envisaged that these DAP's will be functionally equivalent within classes; two types have already been fairly well defined by the groups. These being an application profile for existing wordprocessors and one for the integrated text and graphics documents found on desktop publishing systems. All application profiles will be registered, so any receiving system will know what type of document to expect from the identity of the application profile. It is thought that most implementations of ODA will configure the interchange systems to handle one or more particular application profiles.

3.2 Document Body

An ODA document body can contain up to three parts: a specific structure, a generic structure and a document style. A document's specific structure represents a particular document such as a technical journal; the logical elements being the contents list, individual papers with their titles, abstracts and sections etc. The layout structure of the journal could be seen as the page-sets for each contribution and the areas of the pages used for headings, paragraphs and figures. The content of the specific structure is the character text in the paragraphs and the objects in the figures. The generic structure for a document provides information that describes a class of documents which, in the case of a journal, might reflect all the general properties of the type of document such as the requirement for each author's name and organisation to appear on the first page of each contribution.

3.3 Document Style

A Document Style refers to the collections of attributes that are used to direct the layout and control presentation of the document's content. There are two types: layout style and presentation style. An example of a layout style requirement might be the directive to keep a figure and its caption on the same page. A presentation style might specify that the footnotes in a paper are to use an 8pt italic font and that the section titles are to be underlined. By extracting the common style elements it is possible for ODA to save on the transmission costs of interchanging a document since it would not be necessary to send the same information for text which had the same layout or presentation characteristics.

3.4 Specific Structure

ODA views the content in a document's specific structure in two ways. The specific logical structure associates the content of a given document with the document's logical elements. These might be sections, footnotes, paragraphs,figures or any other object a system may use to logically partition a document's content. ODA also provides the specific layout structure of a document to associate the same content with elements related to the presentation media such as pages and columns. Depending on the application and whether or not further editing of the document is required,a system can transfer either or both of the structures. If the specific logical structure is transferred alone then, although the content can be subsequently altered, its layout will be determined by the recipient's system. Transferring just the specific layout structure will ensure that the layout is "as intended by the originator" but the content will be in image form only and as with facsimile image this inhibits further logical processing.

3.5 Generic Structure

ODA uses a generic structure to describe a class of documents. As previously mentioned a document class is a set of documents that exhibit common characteristics such as pages with the same headers or standard paragraphs with consistent presentation features. These may be such elements as the layout of a company memo or particular clauses in a legal contract. If an organisation wants a logo to appear on each page of an interchanged document then there is no need to transmit more than one content portion containing the logo or one layout object describing its position etc. on the page. As well as improving transmission efficiency by factorising such information that would be common to a document, the generic structure can also be used to maintain the internal consistency of documents since it inherently provides an editing guide and page template for the recipient system. This can be used to preserve an organisation's own particular format for documents.

4 Attributes

One of the ways in which the richness of ODA can be seen is examination of the particular attributes that model the properties of a document and its structures. If one considers all the logical requirements that might be needed when laying out and presenting a document then the attributes offered by ODA adequately cover the needs of current wordprocessors as well as features envisaged for the more sophisticated text and graphics systems that have recently entered the market as desktop publishing systems. The following list describes a few of the layout directive attributes that might be required by a logical object such as a paragraph.

Attribute	Sample application for paragraph
block alignment	specifies alignment of paragraphs within the page;
indivisibility	specifies that a logical object is to be contained within a particular layout object, for example, specifying that a paragraph is not split across two pages;
layout category	specifies a particular layout object for elements in the paragraph so that, for example, the text of layed out at the end of a report;
same layout object	specifies that two logical objects, such as a figure and its reference within a paragraph are to be layed out on the same page;
separation	specifies the minimum distance between logical objects such as a figure, its caption and the following paragraph;
synchronisation	specifies paragraph alignment for multi-column working;
new layout object	specifies that a logical object is to be layed out in a new object, for example, that a section is to start on a new page.

5 Example Document

An example three page document is shown in Fig. 2 through 4. This example has been developed by members of a special working group in ISO TC97/SC18/WG3 responsible for examples of ODA documents. The full specification and interchange format for this document are contained in Annexes to the current Draft International Standard. The example contains raster graphics content in the form of a logo on the first page and a signature on the last page. The second page contains some geometric graphics in the form of a figure with axes, curve and text objects. The rest of the document uses the character content architecture coded to ISO 6937. The second page of the document could be considered to contain four logical objects. These being paragraph AAAAA..., paragraph BBBBBB....., a composite logical object consisting of a graph and its associated caption and paragraph CCCCC...., which is split across the second and third pages. The second page could also be viewed as a composite layout object consisting of areas holding paragraph A, paragraph B, the graph, the caption and the first part of paragraph C. The areas within a page that hold the content are termed frames in ODA. Frames can be composite to nest other frames and can overlap with other frames. On the first page there could be frames defined in the layout structure to hold the logo, date, summary etc. On the last page the formal ending might be a common piece of content that might appear on all such documents and for this reason could be held centrally by an organisation.

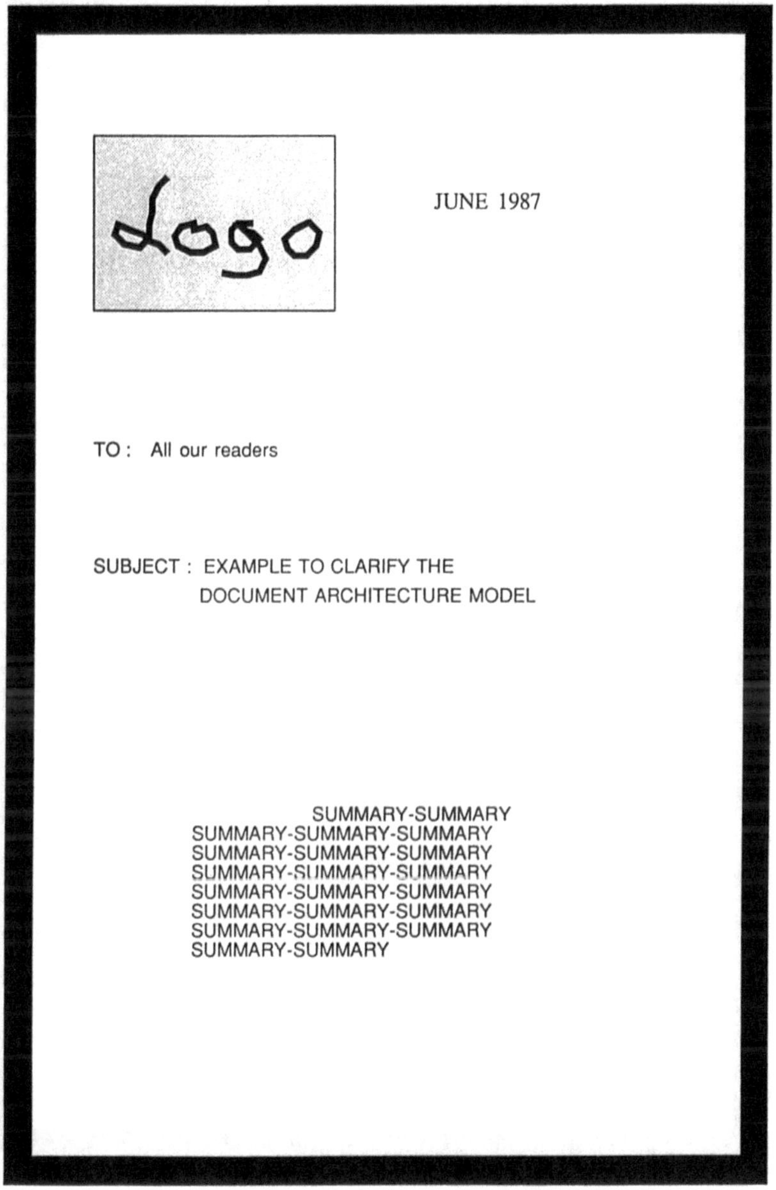

JUNE 1987

TO : All our readers

SUBJECT : EXAMPLE TO CLARIFY THE
DOCUMENT ARCHITECTURE MODEL

SUMMARY-SUMMARY
SUMMARY-SUMMARY-SUMMARY
SUMMARY-SUMMARY-SUMMARY
SUMMARY-SUMMARY-SUMMARY
SUMMARY-SUMMARY-SUMMARY
SUMMARY-SUMMARY-SUMMARY
SUMMARY-SUMMARY-SUMMARY
SUMMARY-SUMMARY

Figure 2: First Page of Example Document

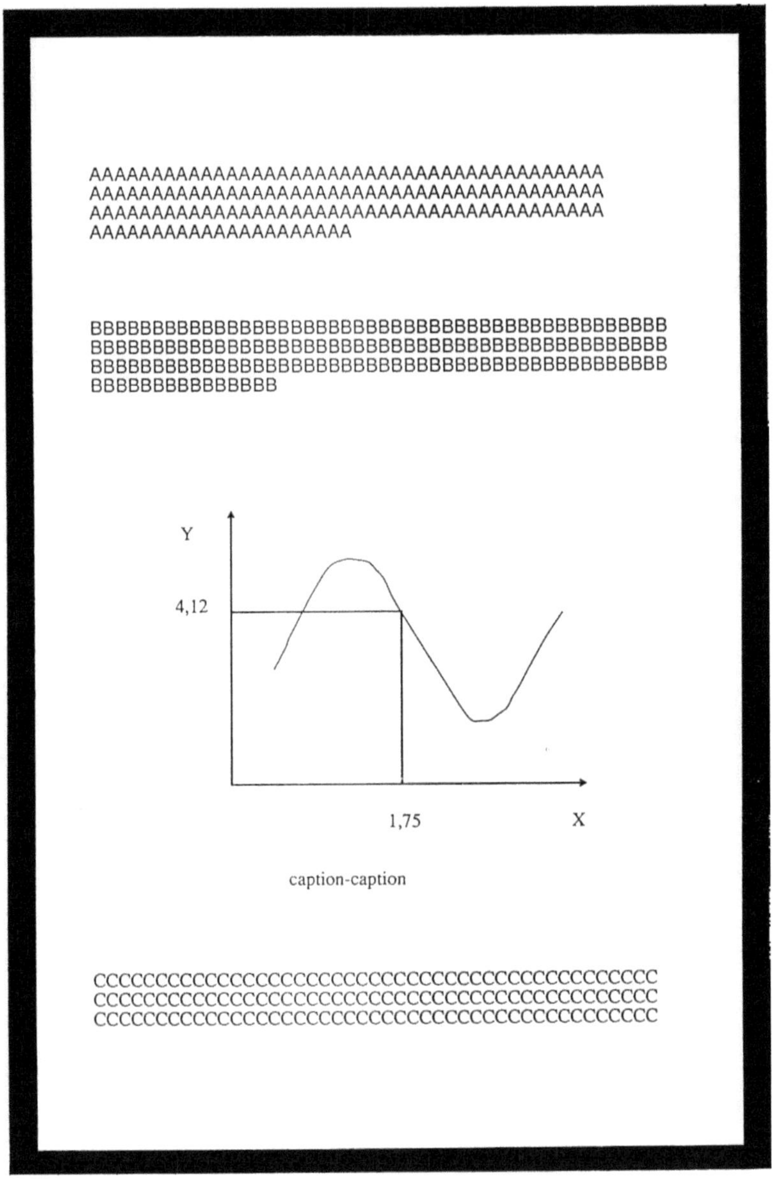

AAAAAAAAAAAAAAAAAAAAAAAAAAAAAAAAAAAAAAAAA
AAAAAAAAAAAAAAAAAAAAAAAAAAAAAAAAAAAAAAAAA
AAAAAAAAAAAAAAAAAAAAAAAAAAAAAAAAAAAAAAAAA
AAAAAAAAAAAAAAAAAAAAA

BBBBBBBBBBBBBBBBBBBBBBBBBBBBBBBBBBBBBBBBBBBBBB
BBBBBBBBBBBBBBBBBBBBBBBBBBBBBBBBBBBBBBBBBBBBBB
BBBBBBBBBBBBBBBBBBBBBBBBBBBBBBBBBBBBBBBBBBBBBB
BBBBBBBBBBBBBBB

caption-caption

CCCCCCCCCCCCCCCCCCCCCCCCCCCCCCCCCCCCCCCCCCCCC
CCCCCCCCCCCCCCCCCCCCCCCCCCCCCCCCCCCCCCCCCCCCC
CCCCCCCCCCCCCCCCCCCCCCCCCCCCCCCCCCCCCCCCCCCCC

Figure 3: Second Page of Example Document

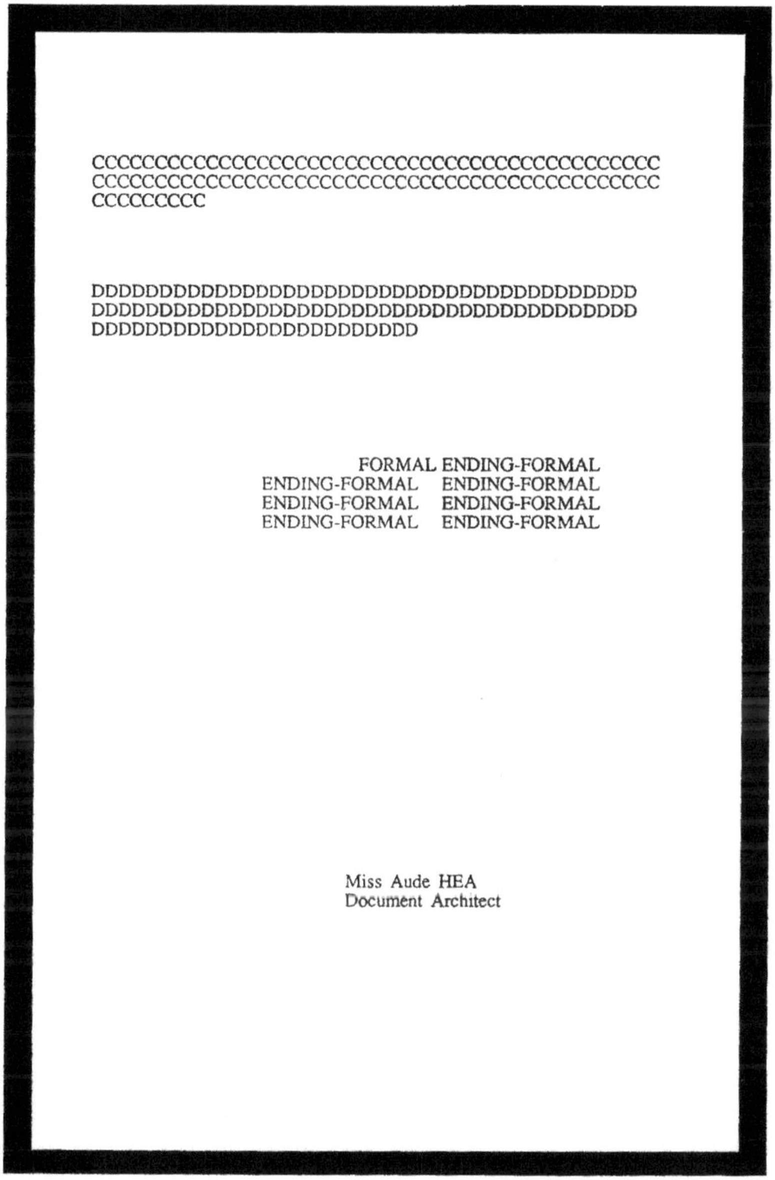

CCCCCCCCCCCCCCCCCCCCCCCCCCCCCCCCCCCCCCCCCCCCC
CCCCCCCCCCCCCCCCCCCCCCCCCCCCCCCCCCCCCCCCCCCCC
CCCCCCCCC

DDDDDDDDDDDDDDDDDDDDDDDDDDDDDDDDDDDDDDDD
DDDDDDDDDDDDDDDDDDDDDDDDDDDDDDDDDDDDDDDD
DDDDDDDDDDDDDDDDDDDDDDDD

FORMAL ENDING-FORMAL
ENDING-FORMAL ENDING-FORMAL
ENDING-FORMAL ENDING-FORMAL
ENDING-FORMAL ENDING-FORMAL

Miss Aude HEA
Document Architect

Figure 4: Third Page of Example document

6 Interchange Mechanisms

ODA documents can be interchanged between open systems in a variety of ways. It will be possible to specify an ODA document as a body type using the CCITT X.400 Electronic Mail Standard or as a document type using the ISO FTAM Standard (ISO 8571). It will also be possible to transfer ODA documents on flexible disk using the File Structure and Labelling for Information Interchange Standard (ISO 7665). Whichever mechanism is used, Part 5 of the ODA Standard specifies the interchange format (ODIF) which is expressed in the ASN.1 notation (ISO 8825).

7 ODA Testing Requirements

7.1 Conformance Testing

Any proposed ODA Conformance Testing Methodology should be based on providing a tester capable of testing conformance to registered document application profiles (DAP's) as well as testing conformance to the full ODA standard.

Two types of tests are distinguished. Tests where an Implementation Under Test (IUT) generates data streams for analysis by the tester and tests where an IUT receives and images documents sent from the tester. These are known as IUT Generation Tests and IUT Reception Tests respectively. Combinations of these two types of tests are also possible.

In the case of IUT Generation Tests an IUT is instructed to produce documents containing a number of test features required for analysis by the tester. In the case of IUT Reception Tests the tester creates documents exhibiting particular test features that an IUT is expected to receive and image.

Fig. 5 shows the major processes and data structures in the proposed testing environment.

The test case generator process produces abstract and executable test cases from the ODA Standard, a particular document application profile (DAP) conforming to 8613 and the Formal Specification of ODA (FODA). The test case generator process modifies the test cases in consideration of the particular options chosen by an implementation which can be declared in the Implementation Conformance Statement. For each implementation a series of test cases is produced, each containing a number of required test features.

The IUT generator process receives each test case in the form of instructions to produce a document exhibiting required features. The features are specified using an ODA-document specification language. The IUT generator process then produces the required documents and transmits the ODIF encodings to the document analysis process.

The document analysis process uses 8613, FODA and the particular DAP together with each test case to analyse the received ODIF and produce imaged documents, diagnostics, and verdicts.

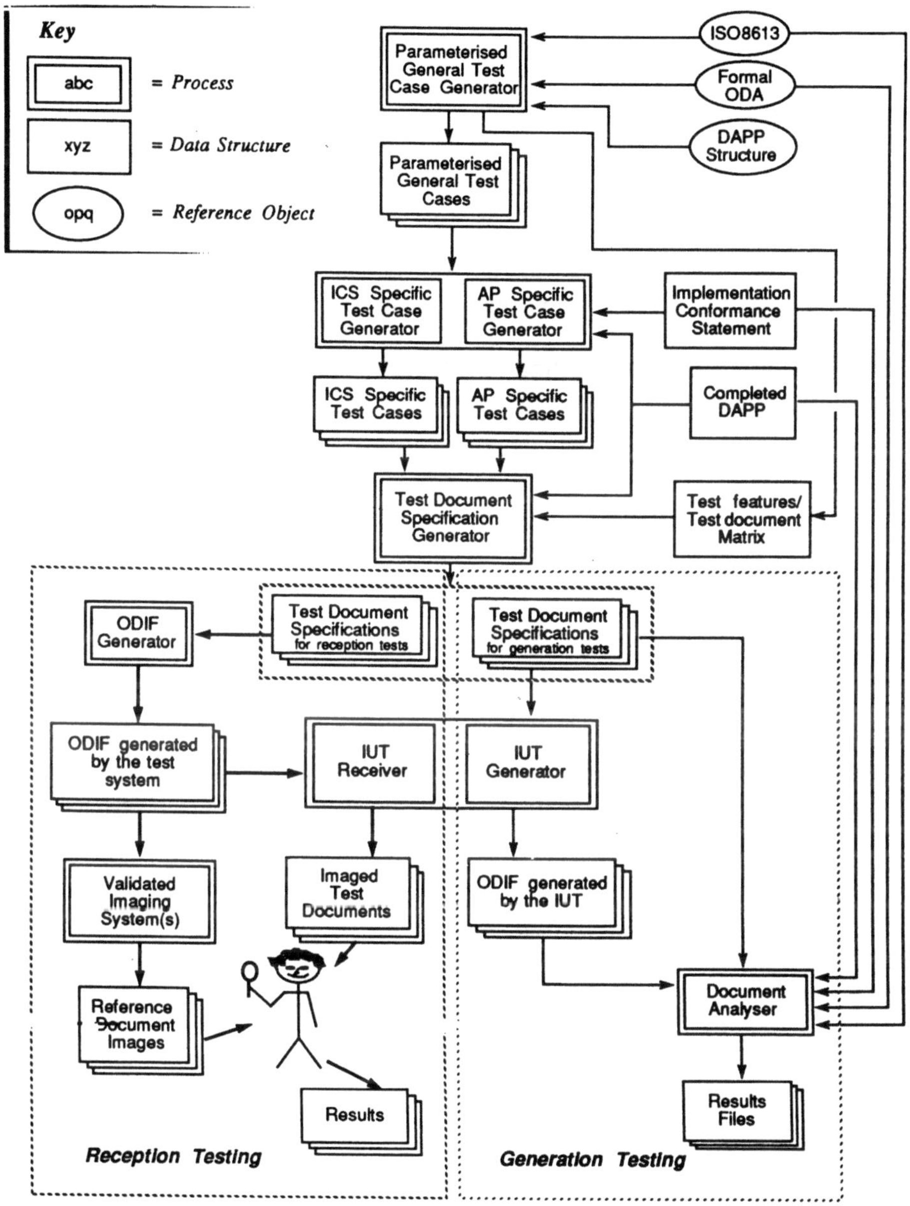

Figure 5: ODA Testing Environment

The document generator process uses a number of 8613 documents and test cases to produce ODIF encodings for the IUT receiver process to image.

7.2 Development Testing

Conformance testing is understood to be testing for conformance to the full 8613 standard or to an 8613 document application profile. However the proposed methodology should also cater for the use of the tester for development testing.

Development testing is understood to be testing during the process of implementation for the purpose of verifying the implementation or partial implementation.

In support of development testing, test tools are proposed which can determine the various characteristics of an ODA implementation under a number of headings:

- conformance to the 8613 standard
- conformance to the 8613 registered document application profile
- conformance to a private use document application profile
- conformance to an 8613 fragment or feature
- functional range

It is the intention that these tools would be available for use by product developers. By selecting the relevant tests, particular features of a product can be selectively tested. In some cases it should be possible for developers to define and run their own tests.

These same test tools could additionally be used :

- to ensure ongoing product assurance
- in preparation for acceptance testing
- for maintenance testing

8 Summary

An overview of ODA has been presented showing the structures and some of the attributes found in its architecture model. ODA can easily describe the average document found on current wordprocessing systems. ODA application profiles are already being specified by large user groups which the European Commission and TOP. NBS Implementor Agreements will be finalised before the end of 1987 and as a result a number of implementations of ISO 8613 seem likely to appear in demonstrations during 1988. To ensure user confidence in the resulting ODA products it is essential that test services are available to adequately exercise implementations. A conformance and development testing methodology has been proposed that the author believes answers this need.

AN NBS Conformance Testing Program: Ideas and Procedures for Graphics Testing

S. J. Kemmerer

Abstract

One of the primary missions of the National Bureau of Standards, Institute for Computer Sciences and Technology is the development and promotion of national and international standards for use by the U.S. Federal Government. Those standards which promise the biggest payback to the Government are developed into Federal Information Processing Standards (FIPS). These FIPS and the standards they are promoting are implemented into hardware, software and communications products for commercial use. Without conformance testing of the product to the standard, correct representation of the standard in a product can only be assumed. This is not an optimum way to operate, since many products which "conform" are not able to transfer data between dissimilar systems. The intent of this article is to suggest a process to follow to develop a conformance testing program for the NBS FIPS currently published for GKS and CGM. A consistent application of testing processes and specific test suites will help align commercial products to conform to the standards; the application of such a process will become more critical as Federal Agencies begin to request procurement of software implementing these two standards.

1 Introduction

Technically sound national and international standards are needed to preserve open competition in international markets and to support increased productivity and delivery of services at reduced cost. Through standards, users are provided with off-the-shelf, compatible software products. Validation of computer products claiming conformance with standards further reduces risks and uncertainties to vendors and users. Uniform testing procedures should be employed to perform this validation of conformance.

Conformance testing constitutes the evaluation of a candidate product or service for the existence of specific characteristics required by a standard. The Institute for Computer Sciences and Technology (ICST) at the National Bureau of Standards (NBS) assists in developing U.S. Government-wide standards for computer software, hardware, data management, networks and security. ICST works through voluntary industry standards organizations to develop standards which will meet the needs of Government users and be implemented in off-the-shelf commercial products. Standards that promise sizable benefits to the Government are issued as Federal Information Processing Standards (FIPS). These FIPS and the standards they are promoting are implemented into software products for commercial use. Through past experience in research and testing, ICST sees a need for expansion of its efforts in structuring conformance testing to these FIPS, and is in the process of formulating a program.

ICST is developing an initial structure and approach for uniformity in conformance testing programs Government-wide for appropriate FIPS PUBs. The overall ICST conformance program and individual conformance tests for any given standard, will evolve as more experience is gained.

Long term ambitions include finding working solutions for the many questions raised when one mentions conformance testing. This paper is an adaptation from the initial documentation generated on a "conceptual conformance testing program framework" here at ICST.

The following outlined process offers one approach for developing an NBS/ICST conformance testing program for FIPS PUBs covering graphic standards. The main thrust of this paper deals with the accreditation, role and responsibilities of a testing laboratory. Depending on U.S. government need, NBS may or may not perform conformance testing to its FIPS onsite. Variations to this process are assumed since testing requirements and programs will be based on the maturity and complexity of the standard, available resources, and public demand. It is broken down into the following sections:

- Accreditation Program Development
- Testing Methods
- Certification and Reporting Considerations
- Testing Administration
- Testing Laboratories
- Mutual Recognition of Validation/Certification
- References

2 Accredition Program Development

2.1 Standards Identification.

The first step in developing a conformance testing program is to identify those FIPS which have an importance to commerce and consumer well-being, as well as strong user interest. Currently FIPS PUB 120, Graphical Kernel System (GKS), and FIPS PUB 128, Computer Graphics Metafile, have been identified as having such an importance.

2.2 Guide for Developing an Accrediting Program.

The following issues need to be addressed in developing a new accreditation program for graphics; guidelines and recommendations to solve these issues follow in the remainder of the text.

1. If multiple test methods are currently available, establish assessment techniques and priorities to decide which test method(s) should be offered for accreditation.

2. Decide what the units of accreditation should be, i.e., individual tests, a test suite testing a specific function, or all the test suites available to test the graphic standard.

3. Identify the critical elements (environmental, test equipment, procedures), for each test method, e.g., quality assurance checks.

4. Determine the applicability of proficiency testing for the test method and the means for implementing new or available proficiency testing programs.

5. Recommend selection criteria and nominate technical experts who could scrvc as assessors and evaluators.

6. Recommend any other special technical requirements beyond what follows, which should be considered as necessary for accreditation.

2.3 Application for Accreditation.

1. Any laboratory may request an application for accreditation under the graphics accreditation program following the instructions provided in notices announcing the formal establishmcnt of thc program.

2. Upon receipt of the laboratory's application, the Certification Body shall:

    a. acknowledge receipt of the application;

    b. request further information, if necessary;

c. confirm any payment of fees before proceeding with the accreditation process; and

d. specify the next steps(s) in the accreditation process.

3. In accepting an application from a foreign-based laboratory, consideration shall be given to the policy of the host government regarding the acceptance of test data from laboratories accredited by ICST or other foreign accreditation systems.

3 Testing Methods

3.1 Commonly accepted conformance test methods.

Tests for FIPS 120 and 128 will initially employ falsification testing as the testing method. Unfortunately, use of falsification testing will only determine non-conformance to the standards, it can never assure complete conformance. As the testing program matures, other methods of testing may be evaluated and considered.

3.2 Guidelines for development of test method approaches.

The test method should be specified in a way that is easy to understand and to implement. The resulting test suite should be useful to implementors, and the following steps followed when developing a test method:

1. **Management Plan.** Describes the overall scheme for the testing. It should include a specification of the technical objectives to be achieved, a description of the test strategy, and an outline of the procedures to be used for testing. This management plan should be publicly available.

2. **Non-Testable Features.** Although the objective is always to test all functions in a standard, there are sometimes parts of a standard which are non-testable. For example, some error conditions, depending on their nature, cannot be included in a standardized test method to check conformance. A list of all areas explicitly not tested should be available as part of the documentation of the test method.

3. **Test Strategy.** A full description of the test strategy to be used for the standard should be produced and made publicly available. This should include a specification of the structure of the proposed test suite, an indication of the number of tests, and an identification of the elements of the standard to be tested.

4. **Test Procedures.** The test method should be automated and include consideration of the procedures used to carry out testing. The setting up and execution of the test suite on a system under test, and the analysis of the output

produced should be carried out in accordance with clearly defined procedures. These procedures should be documented in a manual to accompany the test suite, and should give criteria for the analysis of all acceptable outputs for each test in the test suite. Specific assumptions for failure of test should also be stated.

5. **Levels of Testing**. The development of the test method should take into account all possible levels and/or options specified in the standard. The test method should allow for modularity so that tests for a specific level or option can be easily identified.

3.3 Existing test methods.

The following areas should be examined when selecting the appropriate test method:

1. Standard Specification:

   a. Definition of conditions for conformance with FIPS 120 and 128 (conformance clauses).

   b. Specification requirements. The requirements of GKS and CGM will be evaluated to identify the test method necessary for determining conformance. This method might include tests for determining that the implementation:

      - rejects illegal structures;
      - accepts data and other constructs permitted by the standards, and processes them in accordance with the standard;
      - docs not include extensions to a standard;
      - properly flags usage of standard requirements options or levels;
      - properly processes implementation dependent specifications in accordance with the standard;
      - handles optional implementation features of the standard correctly.

2. Written test procedures supporting the test suite to identify:

   a. test objective;

   b. personnel responsible for test;

   c. necessary equipment;

   d. input materials, e.g., support software;
   e. input data;
   f. expected output;
   g. constraints;
   h. required test preparation, setup;
   i. operator actions, console setups; and
   j. step-by-step execution instructions.

3. The test suite to see if it is:
   a. easy to understand and manage;
   b. portable between different hardware configurations and designed to take into account any implementation-dependent criteria allowed by the standard;
   c. designed in such a way that there are no restrictions in using the test method or implementations on the size machine on which it can be executed.

4. Documentation Requirements for inclusion of:
   a. description of test cases;
   b. notation used to define test;
   c. test method implementation/user guides; and
   d. evaluation guides for qualifying pass, fail, or inconclusive test verdicts.

5. Requirements, if any, for specially designed test equipment training.

3.4 Test Suite Structure

The following guidelines should be followed when writing test suites:

1. Clear documentation should be incorporated into the tests and this documentation should include:

a. comments, which are clear and concise. No redundant comments should be included.

b. a reference to the clauses in the standard which are under test.

c. clear statements of any assumptions made in the test suite design.

d. a list of any tests which are performed for information only, and will not be used to determine conformance.

2. The test suite should be split into a series of independent test programs or scenarios, such that each test program tests only one specific requirement of the specification document.

3. Each self-contained test should use the same format, and:

   a. list all test tools necessary;

   b. provide the test environmental data, including display of setup instructions to operator;

   c. include program documentation section;

   d. initialize its own workspace;

   e. perform the test;

   f. provide a verification section;

   g. check whether passed/failed;

   h. report result;

   i. have the pass/fail path clearly defined;

   j. include a simple comment describing the task performed by the test and a reference to the section of the standard under test; and

   k be kept as simple as possible.

4. Only simple features of the selected programming language(s) should be used.

5. Translating the Test Suite to Other Languages. If possible and when applicable, the test suite should be written in a common format, which can then be converted, by the use of translators, to each of the programming languages. Updates to the test

suites across languages must be kept in line at all times by strict use of the change control procedures.

3.5 Maintenance of Test Methods.

1. **Responsible Party.** The Certification Body is responsible for ensuring maintenance of current test methods, authorizes changes, defines the procedures for approving changes, and indicates when any changes become effective for validation purposes.

2. **Procedures.** A published change control procedure should be established for both the test software and the associated documentation. The change control procedures should provide a formal mechanism for the following:

   a. reporting errors in the test software;

   b. logging changes to the test software;

   c. reporting errors in the documentation; and

   d. logging changes to the documentation.

3.6 Interim Procedure

An interim procedure available for testing FIPS 120 and 128 is to model the procedural direction of the National Computing Centre Ltd., United Kingdom. Testing procedures are already in place for GKS and likely require no change to be used for FIPS 120. This similarity between programs would also foster international continuity for conformance testing.

4 Certification and Reporting Considerations for FIPS

4.1 Certification Body.

1. **General Requirements.**

   a. Access to the Certification Body shall not be conditional upon membership in any association or group, nor shall there be undue financial conditions to restrict participation.

   b. The procedures under which the Body operates shall be administered in a non-discriminatory manner.

c. ICST will identify the members on the Certification Body.

Responsibilities.

a. Approve test methods to be used by the testing laboratories when they are not included in the standard itself. Ensure the test method is technically correct before using it as the basis for issuing certificates.

b. Collaborate with the testing laboratory in drafting a contract for testing services to include regulations which define rights and obligations in detail.

c. Determine accreditation of testing laboratories and keep lists of all accreditations. Since technical requirements for accreditation are specific for each standard, technical requirements for accreditation should be developed using expert advice in that given field.

d. Notify any testing laboratory that it is no longer accredited.

e. Issue certificates at the request of the Client, based on the certification criteria defined by the Certification Body.

f. When applicable, define the requirements and procedures of a Manufacturer's Declaration of Conformance testing program.

g. Define Client/testing laboratory dispute procedures. Arbitrate appeals in cases of dispute. Include procedures for disputed tests as well as disputed testing results.

h. Determine if there is a need for a Certified Computer Products List. If there is a need, identify who should maintain and what information should be reported.

i. Determine what process should be followed in recognizing other published Certified Computer Products Lists.

j. Notify the public by advertising new accreditation programs when the technical requirements and test methods are developed for the standard(s). Publish a notice in the FEDERAL REGISTER announcing the establishment of the program, requirements, or methods. The notice will:

- Identify the scope of the accreditation program; and
- Advise how to apply for accreditation.

k. Develop criteria and procedures for evaluating, modifying and accepting test methods for use in conformance testing to the standards. Keep in mind such test methods sources as:

- Industry
- Government
- Other Countries
- Universities

l. Publish the effective date for modifications to test methods.

4.2 ICST Role in Conformance Testing As Government Agent.

1. Assist and educate the agencies with regard to the scope and purpose of the test method as a measure of product quality.
2. Assist agencies in developing solicitation document requirements with regard to product testing for determining conformance to standards.
3. Identify publicity and announcement sources for informing national and international industry, Government and product users on the availability of conformance test methods and validation services.
4. Work with other government agencies as required, to incorporate requirements within the procurement regulations (i.e., General Services Administration's Federal Information Resources Management Regulations) concerning use of conformance testing and certification of products offered to the Government.

4.3 Role of Standards Bodies (National and International).

1. Consider conformance testing aspects in the development of standards.
2. Provide advice and give technical committee or subcommittee recommendations for the approval of a test method.
3. Provide technical advice when necessary, on interpreting a standard under conflict.

4.4 Test Report.

1. **Content.**

   a Includes a complete test report and a statement citing laboratory accreditation.

   b Includes complete identification of system under test (SUT).

   c Provides a description/identification of the test environment, and any incidents contrary to routine process.

2. **Format.**

   The following guidelines should be followed when writing the software tools to produce the test program reports:

   a The volume of output produced by each test program should be kept as concise as possible. Tabular summaries are encouraged.

   b The following details should be given in the test report for each test: test number, brief description of the test, reference to the standard and implementation under test (IUT), and message indicating pass/fail/inconclusive, or not executed.

   c Test discrepancy summary complete enough to repeat the process.

3. **Style for Test Reporting.**

   a. Each test report should provide a summary of the results giving the following information: number of tests passed, number of tests failed, number of inconclusive tests, number of "information only" tests, number of tests not executed, and total number of tests.

   b. Wherever possible, the output of test programs should be structured in a way which is easy to check both manually and automatically, e.g., tabular.

   c. If test programs produce visual output on a graphics display, then this output should be kept as simple as possible to ease the checking process, while still examining all necessary features.

   d. All tests which produce visual output should be accompanied by a comprehensive check list in the form of an operator script and a set of reference samples.

e. Particular care and attention shall be paid to the arrangement of the test report, especially with regard to presentation of the test data and ease of assimilation by the reader. The format shall be carefully and specifically designed for each type of test carried out, but the headings shall be standardized as far as possible.

4.5 Certificate of Validation Format, Content and Presentation.

1. Identifies the standard(s) tested.

2. Includes a statement of the fact that the product(s) or service(s) meets the standard(s) or an applicable portion(s) thereof, clearly identifying that which is being certified.

3. Includes a clear reference to the testing laboratory and test report produced.

4. States the product name and version tested.

5. The certificate only applies to the product version operating in the SUT.

6. Certificate validity depends on the set of standards, and the specified period of time.

7. Laboratory accreditation by NBS/ICST is indicated.

4.6 Applicability of Certificate of Validation on product tested.

Some of the criteria to consider include:

1. The system configurations that require testing for the product for which conformance is claimed.

2. The number and type of errors discovered during testing.

3 Use of the validated product under different operating environments e.g., different hardware configurations and operating systems.

4 New software releases.

5 Testing Administration

5.1 General Guidelines for Test Method Administration.

1. Test methods need to be approved by the Certification Body with technical guidance of the responsible standards committee as necessary.

2. Test methods for which accreditation is offered are made available to everybody through adequate specified conditions.

3. Test methods for which accreditation is offered are official for and binding on conformance testing.

4. The same test methods derived from the standards specification should be used by all ICST accredited testing laboratories.

5. Test method upon which certification is based is:

   a. acceptable to buyer or governmental regulator if mandated.

   b. used in its entirety unless limitations are fully disclosed.

   c. is based on a FIPS (which is based on a national or international standard) available to the public.

   d. suitable for use as a basis for conformance testing.

7. Declaration of conformance is indicated by a statement, certificate, label or mark which:

   a. includes information on the product, standards, producer, and procedures used.

   b. presents clearly the intent of the certification.

5.2 Criteria and Procedures for Alternative Testing Sources.

1. Manufacturer's declaration of conformance (Self testing). Requirements for Vendor include:

   a. manufacturer's quality management system and documentation;

   b. technically appropriate resources for testing and inspection;

   c. use of a test method approved by the Certification Body;

d. retention of complaint records against product or service; and

e. any dispute resolution is in accordance with the Certification Body for that standard.

2. Third-party testing. Requirements include:

a. products to be tested are fully identified;

b. procedures by which the laboratory is operated include provision for:

- fiscally responsible management and appropriately
- participation on a non-discriminatory basis.
- resource commitment to both initial and continuing validation activities.
- selection and retention of qualified testing and inspection services.
- notification of participants on changes in standards and procedures.
- confidentiality of proprietary information.
- maintenance of records.
- safeguarding use of official declaration of conformance.

c. Documentation required by the laboratory includes:

- availability of published program directory listing products, standards, licensees, and other parties.
- file of legally binding agreements for licensees.
- availability of published statement of operating procedures.

d. Accreditation by Certification Body.

3. Government-managed testing. The same criteria and procedures for third-party testing would apply.

5.3 Associated Costs.

Identify costs associated with developing and maintaining conformance test methods and responsible source of funding. Typically, costs associated with conformance testing will be on a cost-reimbursable basis.

5.4 Resource and Overhead Requirements.

Examine:

1. Where and what type of facilities are required to perform validations.
2. What staff, equipment and office facilities are required to support a validation service.
3. What are the retention and storage requirements for validation materials, project folders and financial accounting records.
4. What is the anticipated volume of Clients and tests conducted over a year.

5.5 Criteria and Procedures for Requesting Validation Services

The table below provides example timeframes associated with first time validation. These times will vary according to complexity of tests requested, and number of tests being performed.

1. **Requesting validation.** The Client must provide the following information/material to the Accredited Testing Laboratory in a Letter of Request:

    a. desired and alternate month of testing;

    b. product identification, including version;

    c. host and target configurations, operating systems, program language and other appropriate information necessary for the testing laboratory to carry out the test;

    d. site locations and addresses;

    e. a point of contact for validation, including full name, address, and telephone number; and

    f. which test(s) the Client desires to take.

Table 1: Schedule Expectations for Validation

T - 120	Contact Accredited Testing Laboratory, Negotiate agreement; vendor testing
T - 90	Submit disputed tests, if any
T - 60	Prevalidation test information/material received by the testing laboratory
T - 30	Resolve all outstanding issues
TEST	Laboratory testing
T + 4-7	Testing complete
T + 60	Final Conformance Summary Report available

Key
T = Testing Day 1; '-' or '+' = Before/Beyond Test Start

2. **Revalidation Requests.** The Client requests revalidation by the appropriate testing laboratory. The request includes:

   a. date of current certificate of conformance.

   b. a statement clearly confirming the computer product which is certified was not modified from the computer product described in the Conformance Summary Report.

3. **Revalidating.** When a modification has been made to the computer product previously certified, which is beyond continuing maintenance, it should be recertified.

4. **Scheduling Validations.** These times apply to the Client's responsibilities directly with the testing laboratory; the specific month in which the testing takes place is established by the laboratory.

   a. Any prevalidation information/material must be received 60 days prior to the month of the scheduled validation.

b. For products not previously offered to the Government, request for validation should be submitted at least 120 days prior to the desired testing month. Data collection dates will not be established for first time validations until after a successful review of prevalidation materials has been made by the testing laboratory.

c. Requests for changes to an existing test date should be submitted no later than 60 days prior to that date.

d. Priorities. Priority is given to the scheduled annual validations. Requests from Clients for special, procurement-related validations are given second priority. Third priority is given to requests for official validation of new products. All other requests are given a lesser priority.

5. **Appeal Process.**

a. Disputed tests. If a Client believes any tests are in error, or not appropriate, the Client shall contact in writing the testing laboratory, and provide associated justification for the dispute. A copy of this letter shall be forwarded to the Certification Body as well.

b. The Client shall follow the procedures defined by that Certification Body which accredited the testing laboratory for any appeals over disputed tests or disputed validation testing decisions by the Accredited Testing Laboratory.

6 Testing Laboratories

6.1 Conditions for Accreditation

To become accredited and maintain accreditation, a laboratory shall agree in writing to:

1. Be assessed and evaluated initially and on a periodic basis.

2. Demonstrate, on request, that it is able to perform the tests representative of those for which it is seeking accreditation.

3. Pay any relevant fees.

4. Participate in proficiency testing as required.

5. Be capable of performing the tests for which it is accredited according to the latest version of the test method within one year after its publication or within the time limit specified by the Certification Body.

6. Limit the representation of the scope of its accreditation to only those tests or services for which accreditation is granted.

7. Limit all its test work or services for Clients to available capacity.

8. Limit advertising of its accredited status to letterheads, brochures, test reports, and professional, technical, trade or other laboratory services publications.

9. Inform its Clients the laboratory's accreditation or any of its test reports in no way constitutes or implies product certification, approval, or endorsement by NBS/ICST.

10. Maintain records of all actions taken in response to testing complaints for a minimum of one year.

11. Maintain an independent decisional relationship between itself and its Clients, affiliates, or other organizations so that the laboratory's capacity to render test reports objectively and without bias is not adversely affected.

12. Report to ICST within 30 days any major changes involving the location, ownership, management structure, authorized representation, approved signatories, or facilities of the laboratory.

13. Return to ICST, the certificate of accreditation for possible revision or other action should it:

    a. be requested by ICST,

    b. voluntarily terminate its accredited status, or

    c. become unable to conform to any of these conditions or the applicable criteria for accreditation and related technical requirements.

6.2 Criteria for Accrediting Testing Laboratories

The criteria addresses a laboratory's quality system, staff, facilities, and equipment, test methods and procedures, records, and test reports. At a minimum, the following criteria must be met following ISO/IEC Guide 25, in order for a testing laboratory to be accredited:

1. **Quality System**

    a. The laboratory shall operate an internal quality assurance program appropriate to the type, range, and volume of work performed. The quality assurance program shall be documented in a quality assurance manual which is available for use by the laboratory staff. The manual shall be maintained relevant and current by a responsible member of the laboratory staff. A person or persons having responsibility for quality assurance within the laboratory shall be designated by the laboratory management and have direct access to top management.

b. The quality assurance manual shall contain information regarding:

- the structure of the laboratory (organizational charts);
- The operational and functional duties and services pertaining to quality, so that each person concerned will know the extent and the limits of his responsibility;
- general quality assurance procedures;
- quality assurance procedures specific for each test, as appropriate;
- where appropriate, proficiency testing, use of reference material, etc;
- satisfactory arrangements for feedback and corrective action whenever testing discrepancies are detected;
- procedure for dealing with technical complaints.

c. The quality system shall be systematically and periodically reviewed by or on behalf of management to ensure the continued effectiveness of the arrangements, and corrective action initiated. Such reviews shall be recorded together with details of any corrective action taken.

2. Staff

a. Staff shall have the necessary education, training, technical knowledge and experience for their assigned functions.

b. There shall be a job description for each senior technical position category, which includes the necessary education, training, technical knowledge and experience.

c. The proportion of supervisory to non-supervisory staff shall be such as to ensure adequate supervision.

d. Suitable staff shall be nominated to deputize for the senior technical and quality system management staff in their absence.

e. Information on the relevant qualifications, training, and experience of the technical staff shall be maintained by the laboratory.

NOTE: In small laboratories, one person may fulfill more than one function.

3. **Testing Equipment**

a. The testing laboratory shall have access to all items of equipment required for correct performance of the tests for which it is recognized.

b. All equipment shall be properly maintained to ensure protection from corrosion and other causes of deterioration. Instructions for a proper maintenance procedure for those items of equipment which require periodical maintenance shall be available.

c. Any item of the equipment which has been subjected to overloading or mishandling, or which gives suspect results, shall be taken out of service and clearly labelled until it has been repaired and then shown by test to be performing its function satisfactorily.

d. Records shall be maintained on each major item of equipment. Each record shall include:

- The name of the item of equipment.
- The manufacturer's name and type identification and serial number.
- Date received and date placed in service.
- Current location, where appropriate.
- Details of maintenance.

4. **Test methods and procedures**

a The testing laboratory shall have adequate documented instructions on the use and operation of all relevant equipment, on the handling and preparation of test items (where applicable), and on standard testing techniques, where the absence of such instructions could jeopardize the efficacy of the testing process. All instructions, standards, manuals, and reference data relevant to the work of the testing laboratory shall be maintained up-to-date and be readily available to the staff.

b. The testing laboratory shall use methods and procedures required by the specification against which the test items are to be tested. The specification shall be available to staff performing the test.

c. Where it is necessary to employ test methods and procedures which are non-standard, these shall be fully documented.

d. All manual calculation and data transfers shall be subject to appropriate checks.

e. Where these results are derived by electronic data processing techniques, the stability of the system shall be such that the accuracy of the results is not affected. This generally implies an ability to detect malfunctions in the hardware during program execution and to take appropriate action.

5. **Environment**

a. The environment in which the tests are undertaken shall not invalidate the test results or adversely affect the required accuracy. The testing premises shall be protected as required from conditions such as excessive temperature, dust, moisture, steam, vibration, electromagnetic disturbance, interference, and shall be maintained accordingly. There shall be sufficient space to limit the risk of damage or danger and to allow operators to make practical and precise movements. The premises shall have the equipment and energy sources needed for the testing.

b. Access to and use of all test areas shall be controlled in a manner appropriate to their designated purpose and access entry by persons external to the laboratory shall be defined.

6. **Records**

a The testing laboratory shall maintain a record system to suit its particular circumstances and comply with any existing regulations. It shall retain on record all original observations, calculations and derived data, and the final test report for an appropriate period. The records for each test must contain sufficient information to permit satisfactory repetition of the test.

NOTE: In some countries it may be necessary to maintain records for a period specified by law.

b. All records and test reports shall be held secure and in confidence to the Client, unless otherwise required by law.

7. **Test Reports**

a. The work carried out by the testing laboratory shall be covered by a report which accurately, clearly, and unambiguously presents the test results and all other relevant information.

b. Each test record shall include at least the following information:

- name and address of testing laboratory;
- unique identification of report (such as serial number), and of each page of the report;
- name and address of Client;
- description and identification of the test item;
- date of receipt of test item and date(s) of performance of test, as appropriate;
- a statement to the effect that the test results relate only to the items tested;
- identification of the test specification, method, and procedure;
- description of sampling procedure, where relevant;
- any deviations, additions to, or exclusions from the test specification, and any other information relevant to a specific test;
- disclosure of any non-standard test method or procedure utilized;
- measurements, examinations and derived results, supported by tables, graphs, sketches, and photographs as appropriate, and any failures identified;
- a statement on test performance uncertainty where relevant;
- A signature and title of person(s) accepting technical responsibility for the test report and date of issue;
- a statement that the report shall not be reproduced except in full without the approval of the testing laboratory.

c. Corrections or additions to a test report after issue shall be made only by a further document suitably marked, e.g., "Supplement to test report serial number . . . (or as otherwise identified," and shall meet the relevant requirements of the preceding paragraphs.

8. **Role of Certification Body in Accrediting Laboratories.**

a. Ensure the testing laboratory is accessible to anyone, including foreign Clients.

b. Develop a model contract (e.g., order form) to serve as agreement between Client and testing laboratory.

c. Ensure the amount of accredited laboratories is consistent with the Client needs, without over saturating the market. Any Client requesting testing for a given standard, should be able to have his product tested within one year after his letter of request to an Accredited Testing Laboratory.

d. Establish standard specific criteria for assessing competence of laboratories to perform CGM and GKS testing. (Information contained in this document should assist in the generic aspects of assessment plan development.) On-site assessment can be carried out by the Certification Body or by independent assessors approved by the Certification Body.

e. Construct the test method management plan with enough flexibility to accommodate technological developments.

f. Select any/all technical experts, assessors and evaluators necessary for accrediting a testing laboratory.

g. Prepare an administrative recommendation that the laboratory either be granted or denied accreditation. This recommendation is based on a review of the evaluation and other records to ensure that all ICST technical, financial, and administrative obligations have been satisfied.

6.3 Testing Laboratory Assessment

Figure 1 is a pictorial explanation of the procedures for testing laboratory assessment.

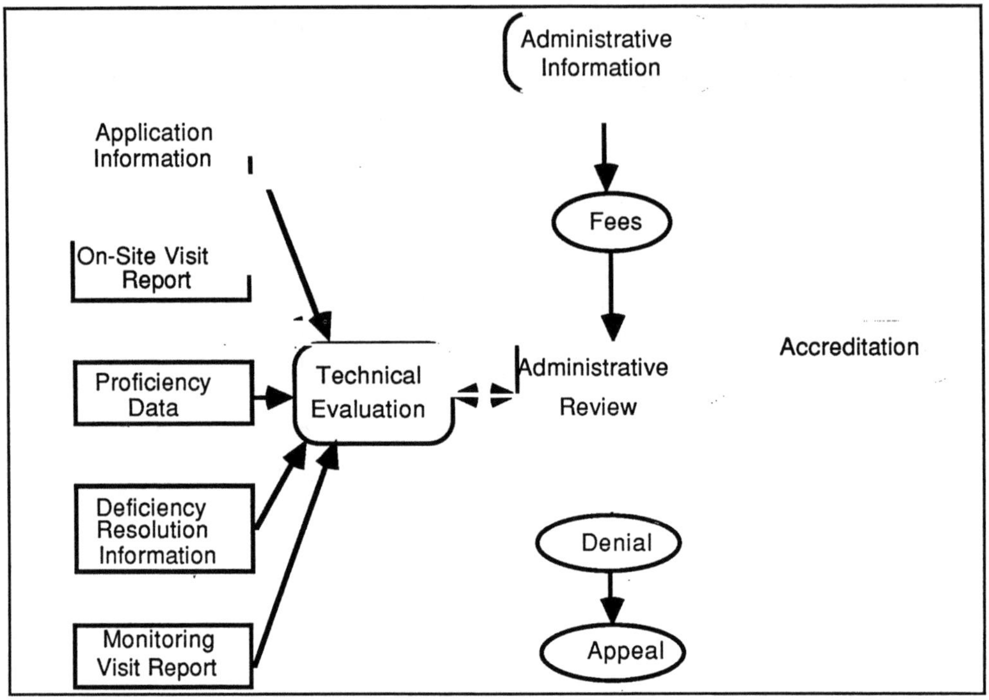

Figure 1: Accredition Process

1. **On-Site Assessment**. Before initial accreditation and about every two years thereafter, an on-site assessment of each laboratory is conducted to determine compliance with the criteria. Assessors use standardized checklists so each laboratory receives a fair assessment in relation to others; however, assessors have considerable latitude in judgments about each laboratory's compliance with the criteria depending on their experience and the unique circumstances of each laboratory. The assessors are selected and assigned on the basis of their expertise in the testing techniques to be reviewed. The time needed to conduct an assessment varies, but generally two days is the norm. Every effort is made to conduct an assessment with as little disruption as possible to the normal operations of the laboratory. The assessors:

   a. Meet with management and supervisory personnel responsible for the laboratory's activities for which accreditation is being sought to acquaint the individuals involved and to set the assessment agenda.

b. Examine the quality system employed by the laboratory. The history of one or more samples from receipt to final issue of test reports is traced. Assessors thoroughly review the laboratory's quality manual or equivalent, examine technician notebooks for records pertaining to the samples, check sample identification and tracking procedures, determine whether the appropriate conditions are maintained, and examine copies of completed test reports.

c. Review records of periodic internal audits, use of check samples or participation in round robin testing or other similar programs.

d. Review representative records including competency evaluations for all staff members who perform the tests, verification records, and sample control records.

e. Observe demonstrations of testing techniques and discuss them with the technical personnel to assure their understanding of the procedures.

f. Examine major equipment, apparatus, and facilities.

At the conclusion of the assessment, an exit briefing is held to discuss assessment findings with laboratory management and identify any deficiencies uncovered. A written summary of all identified deficiencies is left at the laboratory. If independent assessors were used, the assessment forms and a written report is submitted to ICST for further evaluation. The laboratory is asked to respond within 30 days of the date of the exit briefing and provide documentation or certification that the specific deficiencies have been corrected or that specific actions are being taken. Any laboratory applying for initial accreditation may request a delay in responding.

If any deficiencies are noted at laboratories which are currently accredited, such deficiencies must be corrected within 30 days after the exit briefing or the laboratory may face possible suspension, revocation or expiration of its accreditation. When test systems are identified as malfunctioning, it must not be used until corrective action has been completed. Any deficiencies noted for corrective action will be subject to thorough review and verification during subsequent assessments.

2. **Monitoring Visits.** In addition to regularly scheduled assessments, monitoring visits can be made at any time during the accreditation period. Monitoring visits serve to verify reported changes in the laboratory's personnel, facilities, and operations, or to explore possible reasons for poor performance in proficiency testing. The scope of a monitoring visit may range from checking a few designated items to a complete review. Failure to cooperate with NBS assessors may be grounds for adverse accreditation action.

3. **Proficiency Testing.** Proficiency testing is an integral part of the NBS accreditation process. While the existence of facilities, equipment, and personnel which satisfy the criteria indicates a laboratory's overall capability to obtain good results, an analysis of actual test results for certain test methods is also necessary to determine if the overall capability does in fact produce the desired results. A laboratory's failure to participate fully in the conduct of required proficiency testing is grounds for adverse accreditation action.

4. **Evaluation.** Evaluation of a laboratory is conducted by ICST with technical experts who review records on the applicant laboratory and base their decision on:

   a. Information provided on the application;

   b. On-site assessment reports;

   c. Actions taken by the laboratory to correct deficiencies;

   d. Results of proficiency testing; and

   e. Information from any monitoring visits performed on the laboratory.

   If the technical evaluation reveals additional deficiencies, written notification describing them will be made to the laboratory. The laboratory must respond within 30 days of such notification and provide documentation or certification that the specified deficiencies have been corrected. Clarification of some issues may be requested by telephone. All deficiencies must be corrected before accreditation can be granted or renewed.

5. **Accreditation Actions.**

   a. Recommendation. When accreditation is recommended, the recommendation forms the basis for granting accreditation. A certificate of accreditation is issued to the laboratory.

   b. Denial. In cases where denial is recommended, the laboratory is notified of a proposal to deny accreditation and the reasons for denial.

   c. Appeal. When denial has been proposed. the laboratory may request a hearing, under United States Code (U.S.C.) 556, within 30 days of the date of receipt of the notification. If a hearing is not requested, the denial becomes final upon the expiration of that 30 calendar day period.

   d. Renewal. Accreditation is granted annually or biennially with renewal occurring on the same anniversary date every year or every two years.

e. Termination. A laboratory may voluntarily terminate its accreditation by written request at any time. The accreditation certificate must be returned with the request. If a laboratory elects not to renew its accreditation, a notification of such intention should be forwarded to ICST in writing. It is the laboratory's responsibility to complete any previously scheduled testing obligations for Clients prior to termination.

f. Suspension. If an accredited laboratory develops problems or deficiencies which are of a temporary nature, its accreditation may be suspended until such time as the deficiencies are resolved.

g. Revocation. In cases where a laboratory is found to have violated the terms of its accreditation, the accreditation can be revoked. The laboratory may, however, be given the option to voluntarily terminate accreditation. The laboratory has 30 days from the date of receipt of a notice of proposed revocation in which it may appeal the proposed revocation by requesting a hearing. If a hearing is not requested, the revocation becomes final upon the expiration of that 30 calendar day period. When revocation is final the laboratory must return its certificate of accreditation and cease to reference its ICST accreditation on any of its reports, other correspondence, or advertising.

6. **Public Notification**. ICST will publish accreditation actions and a directory of accredited laboratories on a routine basis.

6.4 Responsibilities of Testing Laboratories.

1. Carry out conformance testing and provide test reports to the Client.
2. Fulfill contractual commitment to the Certification Body.
3. Record technical test details.
4. Communicate the approved test method to the Client for conformance testing preparation.
5. Treat all test results and documents confidentially, except those which are explicitly stated as public.
6. Comply with all requirements for accreditation.
7. Comply with existing laws. Accreditation does not relieve the laboratory of the need to observe and comply with existing Federal, State, and local statutes, ordinances, or regulations that may be applicable to its operation, including consumer protection and antitrust laws.

8. Accredited laboratories are encouraged, within specified limits, to publicize their accredited status. The major restriction is that advertising must not imply product certification by NBS or the U.S. Government. (Laboratories and their Clients may not reference their accredited status in consumer media, in product advertising, or on product labels, containers, or packaging.)

7 Mutual Recognition of Validation/Certification

Mutual recognition of validation means issuing a national certificate solely on the grounds of a test report, without testing anew. The layout of both test reports and certificates should be harmonized to improve mutuality among testing laboratories and certification bodies, and to ease translation.

It is necessary to examine bilateral agreements on mutual recognition of certificates which exist for other conformance testing programs, e.g., language compilers.

To help achieve common recognition (at both the national and international level) for test methods, interface is encouraged through:

1. The certification system to provide the right for every testing laboratory to attend the testing by any other laboratory once a year in order to allow reciprocal observation for the sake of identical results.

2. Any Client worldwide, shall be able to address national or international certification bodies.

Considerations and issues need to be resolved in order to achieve common recognition of validation test reports for products offered by multi-national companies who trade with other countries.

8 References

1 Wood, H., "Emerging Software Standards: Opportunity and Challenge", *Proceedings of Computer Standards Conference* - 1986, IEEE Computer Society Press, 1986.

2 Kruckeberg, F., Conformance Testing and Certification for Information Processing Systems, *Computers & Standards* (4), North-Holland, pp 21-32, 1985.

3 ISO/IEC Guide 2, 1983-07-01.

4 ISO/IEC Guide 38, 1983-12-01.

5 *Certification - Principles and Practice*, ISO, Geneva, 1980.

6 Berger, Harvey (X4016), *The National Voluntary Laboratory Accreditation Program*, American Laboratory, November 1986.

7 ISO/TC 97/SC 22/WG 12 N45 - Test Methods for Programming Languages Processors - Guidelines for Their Development and Procedures for Their Approval.

8 *Validation Guide*, LSAR ADP Systems, USAMC Materiel Readiness Support Activity, Lexington, Kentucky 40511-5101, January 1987.

9 ISO/IEC Guide 40, 1983-12-01.

10 Institute for Computer Sciences and Technology *Compiler Testing Procedures*, NBS/ICST-87/010, February 1, 1987.

11 ISO/IEC Guide 25, 1982-12-15.

12 *Planning for Software Validation, Verification, and Testing*, NBS Special Publication 500-98.

13 *An Overview of Computer Software Acceptance Testing*, NBS Special Publication 500-136.

14 ISO/IEC Guide 28, 1982-12-15.

15 ISO/IEC Guide 7, 1982-12-15.

16 ISO/TC 97/SC 21, Information Processing Systems - OSI Conformance Testing Methodology and Framework - Part 1: General Concepts, 1986-12-09.

Part VII

Further Considerations on Using the CGM

This final part of the book summarizes the discussions which took place following the presentations of the papers. There were four groups which considered:

- technical barriers to using the CGM
- using and defining application profiles
- user requirements beyond those in the standard
- testing

The CGM leaves environmental considerations as implementation dependent. It is a virtual metafile (the original name of the standard when it was being developed was Virtual Device Metafile). Bundle settings, screen position, font definition are all left open in the standard. There is often a requirement to tie these down more precisely. The discussions reported here were concerned with this need. The CGM is of little value unless it can be transferred with ease. It is hoped that the experiences reported here will be of value to other implementors. The MAP/TOP Profile is a very significant move in the use of metafiles and it is likely that other application profiles will emerge. It is important that such application profiles are complete and unambiguous and result in a conforming CGM.

There was some dissatisfaction with the capabilities of the CGM and a strong feeling that further primitives and attributes, in particular, need to be added. These user requirements are listed and many of the ideas have been forwarded, in some form, to the standards making process.

Testing is certainly very difficult and the group discussing this area developed the ideas presented in the papers given to the workshop. The testing requirement is always going to be market driven and must be economic. It will be interesting to see which forms of testing emerge during the next year or so.

The final chapter of this part lists some of the errors which exist in the standard. It is hoped that these will help implementors who are finding difficulty in these areas.

Technical Barriers to Interchange Using the CGM

1 Introduction

This group considered technical barriers that occur when people use the CGM as a means of exchanging graphical data. The group suggested ways the CGM should be used and proposed future extensions to the standard. This section is useful to CGM implementors.

2 Application Profiles

All agreed that a CGM conforming to any defined application profile must be a conforming CGM. This implies that an application profile must not specify different (implicit) defaults than 1S0 8632. This allows interpreters to handle a range of application profiles. Information in a metafile must be self-explanatory and complete.

Information in an application profile must be clearly defined. This need is also endorsed by the testing group. There is a danger in defining too many application profiles. Developers of profiles should seriously consider whether their needs are different from the needs of the developers of earlier profiles.

3 Text

Problems arise interpreting metafiles since there is a lack of knowledge about font metrics. For example: the text is expected to be evenly spaced; there is no information about justification or kerning. The problem is solved in theory at least if:

a font names in the font list are registered together with their complete font metrics and

b all interpreters support all fonts.

Current font work in the 1S0 arena being carried out in SC18 addresses this requirement. The graphics community to be aware of, and contribute to, this work. If SC18 standards are not timely it may be appropriate to register font descriptions within the 1S0 graphics registration procedures. There could be informal agreements within the graphics community, for example by an NBS implementors agreement, while standardization is carried out in the font area.

There is a general requirement to include environmental information-such as font metrics, aspect ratio, and predefined bundles-with graphical information stored in a metafile. It is not clear whether this information should be included within or alongside a metafile. If the information is stored within the CGM it could be done using APPLICATION DATA or ESCAPEs. This use however, is contrary to the stated purpose of the APPLICATION DATA element.

ODA solves this problem by transporting environmental information with the document. The concepts developed for ODA may be applicable to the search for a solution.

4 Metafile Descriptor

Much of this discussion related to the current draft MAP/TOP Application Profile which uses the METAFILE DESCRIPTOR to store information which tells the interpreter that the metafile conforms to the profile. The METAFILE DESCRIPTOR should not affect the behaviour of the interpreter of the CGM. Other elements, such as METAFILE VERSION and METAFILE ELEMENT LIST are provided for this purpose. The descriptor is designed for general information, such as the user identifier and time.

SC24 extended metafile work defines a metafile category which is more appropriate for this use than the METAFILE DESCRIPTOR. Category is an indicator to the interpreter of the contents of the metafile. In the near term it might be appropriate to use an ESCAPE for metafile category. In the future, a category relating to profiles could be registered.

5 VDC Extent

The concept of VDC EXTENT is often misinterpreted. VDC EXTENT is the region of interest and not simply the addressable range.

6 File Formats

The MAP/TOP profile specifies that metafiles be exchanged as fixed length records. Such a specification is technically incorrect in the MAP/TOP environment where OSI FTAM services provide transparent data transfer to applications. In other environments-for example, transfer of metafiles on tape or by non-OSI file transfer protocols-a fixed length record transfer may be appropriate. In these cases, where an application program directly controls reading and writing a communicated metafile, portability may be enhanced by fixed length transfers.

7 Image Data

Image data transfer is difficult in the present CGM. Further data compression methods than those in the CGM are required. This has been proposed for the CALS environment by Carson. The extended metafile work is likely to include new concepts for image data transfer.

8 Using CGM With GKS

Item type values returned to a GKS program are not standardized. This is necessary for GKS program portability. Item types might be those defined in GKS Annex E (with a suitable mapping) or could be related in some way to CGM elements.

Using the CGM Within Application Profiles

1 Introduction

An application profile (AP) is a specification appropriate to a given application environment. An AP can tailor a standard toward the needs of a specific user group. CGM Application Profiles clarify the CGM standard where ambiguities exist, provide extensions to the standard, and define additional conformance requirements. This discussion group examined three aspects of CGM AP's : the purpose and content of AP's; inclusion of proposed registered items in AP's; and the choice of CGM encoding.

2 Purpose and Content of AP's

The first issue concerned the purpose and content of AP's. All AP's should have the same format and structure. This format and structure is driven by the goals and purposes of an AP. Different AP's would have different values representing unique requirements, but the areas addressed across all AP's would be the same.

An AP's primary purpose is to define conformance of an implementation to the AP. Thus, an AP should define conformance in terms of interpreters and generators. In general, a conforming interpreter is defined as an interpreter that correctly interprets any conforming basic metafile and may have more capability as well. A conforming generator produces only conforming basic metafiles. Thus, an AP would serve as a "ceiling" for generators and a "floor" for interpreters.

The semantic specification of the CGM is purposely not complete. Some finer details of geometric primitive elements, such as the precise appearance of joins and endpoints in lines, are unspecified. This intentional underspecification allows a wider range of existing systems to be accommodated and makes CGM more adaptable. However, it means that extensions to the semantics of the standard, in the form of ESCAPEs and GDPs must be defined. Such definitions are another function of an AP.

The CGM standard contains another area of underspecification. It specifically excludes standardization of the behavior of metafile generators and metafile interpreters. Unless such behavior is specified in an AP, it leads to unpredictable results when viewing a graphics image on different graphics devices.

Lastly, an AP could provide clarifications of the semantics of the CGM standard where appropriate.

3 Inclusion of Proposed Registered Items in AP's

It was previously noted that extensions to the CGM in the form of GDP's and ESCAPES should be included in AP's. Proposed GDP's and ESCAPES may go through a process called registration in order to be accepted by standards developers. A Register for Graphical Items, maintained by the National Bureau of Standards, will eventually contain all registered GDP's and ESCAPES. This register will also contain other unspecified graphical items from the CGM standard such as additional line types, hatch styles and marker types. However, there is usually about a two year delay between the time when these items are proposed for registration and their official inclusion into the register. This discussion group examined the alternatives of including proposed registration items (but those which have not yet been officially approved and thus are not yet a part of the register) in the AP or excluding them from the AP.

If the proposed items are included in an AP, the danger exists that the items will be modified during the registration approval process. Thus, the AP will contain different specifications for these GDP's and ESCAPES. On the other hand, excluding them from an AP means that implementors may not include these features which have been deemed to be useful for a given application environment. Moreover, if implementors choose to include these features, they may all provide them in a different way since no written specifications will exist for them. The compromise solution reached by the discussion group was to suggest that AP developers include line types, hatch styles and marker types in the AP since they were not apt to change, but exclude GDP's and ESCAPES since they were much more controversial and more likely to change.

4 CGM Encodings

An AP must also choose among different alternatives when the CGM standard allows a choice. One example of this is the choice within the AP of encoding. The standard gives guidelines as to when it is appropriate to use each encoding. The character encoding is intended to provide an encoding of minimum size and to facilitate simple file transfer. The binary encoding requires minimum effort to generate and interpret on many systems. The clear text encoding can be created, viewed and edited with standard text editors. The group concluded that, although these guidelines can be of general use, the assertions made have not been proven. Furthermore, even if the assertions are correct, most application systems have requirements for both minimum size and minimum effort.

Another question is whether an AP should specify the "best" encoding or whether it should require that two or even all three of the encodings be supported?

The discussion group noted that a binary encoding may not be transported across all communication links and that a binary to character translator can easily be developed. The group noted that the way conformance is defined in the existing AP's, the inclusion of more than one encoding means that vendors must support all encodings. This puts a large burden on the vendor in terms of administrative support. All in all this is not an easy issue to resolve and more thought is needed concerning the ramifications of requiring more than one encoding and which encoding(s) to require.

User Requirements

1 Introduction

The workshop looked at necessary CGM extensions to meet user requirements in a number of specific application areas. The scope was limited to describing those CGM extensions necessary to transfer documents whose content was intended for presentation to a human user. Such presentation might involve softcopy imaging on graphics display devices or hardcopy printing/graphing of document contents for subsequent use by humans. So that there is no misunderstanding of this scope, the following paragraph includes definitions of several key terms, such as user requirement, presentation, application, and document.

The workshop's conclusions are depicted in Table 7.1. This table lists user requirements requiring CGM extensions in specific applications areas. The workshop also discussed a number of general requirements not fitting into specific application areas.

2 Definitions

User Requirement - In defining user requirements, the perspective we take is that of a human user working in an application area. One method by which such users communicate is through the creation and exchange of documents.

Presentation - Construction of an image on a hard or soft copy device for viewing by a human user of the system.

Application - An organized area of human endeavor in which graphical images created on hard or soft copy devices are used to transfer information among human users.

Document - A hard or soft copy collection of information whose content may be text, graphics, imagery, sound or other media intended for presentation to human users.

Table 7.1 CGM User Requirements

USER RQMT	REQUIRED EXTENSIONS	APPLICATION CALS ENG. DRWG.	CALS TECH. MAN.	BUS'N GRAPH	OFFICE SYST.	PUBLISH-ING
Advanced 2D Graphics						
	CURVE/BEZIER	X	X	X	X	X
	PATH	X	X	X	-	X
	PEN	-	?	-	-	-
	CLOSED FIGURES	X	X	X	X	X
	ARBITRARY CLIPPING	X	X	-	-	X
	SPLINES (COMPLEX/B-)	X	-	-	-	-
	USER DEFINED: LINE TYPES	X	X	X	X	X
	LINE CAP,JOIN, MITRE	X	X	X	X	X
Text/Fonts						
	IMPLEMENT ISO FONT MODEL	-	X	X	X	X
	COMPATIBLE GRAPHICS AND TEXT	-	X	X	X	X
	FONT MODELS	-	X	X	X	X
	ARBITRARY PATH	-	X	X	-	X

Table 1 continued

USER RQMT	REQUIRED EXTENSIONS	APPLICATION CALS ENG. DRWG.	CALS TECH. MAN.	BUS'N GRAPH	OFFICE SYST.	PUBLISH-ING
Compound Document						
	ARBITRARY CLIPPING	X	X	-	-	X
	ALIGNMENT	X	X	-	X	X
	SHIELDING	X	X	X	-	X
Color						
	INTERPOLATED FILL	-	X	X	-	X
	CYMX COLOR MODEL	-	-	-	-	X
	NAMED COLS	-	-	-	-	X
CIE COLOR MODEL		-	-	X	-	X
Compactness (1)						
	STORAGE	X	X	-	X	-
	TRANSFER	X	X	X	X	-
Editability						
	APPLICATION STRUCTURE	X	X	X	X	X
	SEGMENTS	X	X	X	X	-
	RANDOM ACCESS	X	X	X	-	X
	MACRO	X	X	X	X	X

Table 1 continued

USER RQMT	REQUIRED EXTENSIONS	APPLICATION CALS ENG. DRWG.	CALS TECH. MAN.	BUS'N GRAPH	OFFICE SYST.	PUBLISH-ING
Image						
	RASTER ATTRIBUTES	X	X	X	X	X
	DEVICE INDP RASTER DATA	X	X	X	X	X
Symbols (Library)						
	EXTERNAL INTERFACE	X	X	X	X	X
	USER-DEFINED	X	X	X	X	X
Patterns/Hatches						
	USER-DEFINED	X	X	X	X	X
	APPLICATION AREA SPECIFIC (2)	X	X	X	X	X

Notes:

1. Compactness was recognized as a general need for all application areas, not necessarily falling under the scope of future additions to CGM.

2. Carson, George S., "Extending the CGM for Publishing and Technical Drawing Exchange," GSC Associates, Inc., 7 August 1987.

3 Results

Table 1 presents the workshop results in graphical form. Requirements listed on the vertical axis divide into these areas: advanced 2-D graphics, text and fonts, compound documents, color, compactness, editability, image related, symbol libraries, and patterns/hatch styles. Within each area, a number of needs were identified. For example, in the advanced 2-D graphics area, the needs considered were curves, path constructs, pen characteristics, (caligraphic drawing models), arbitrary closed figures, clipping to arbitrary boundaries, user defined line types, spline curves, and controls over the ends and joining of lines (such as line cap styles, line join styles, and line mitre limits).

The applications considered divide into four areas: business graphics, office systems, publishing, and the CALS (Computer-Aided Acquisition and Logistics Support Program of the US Department of Defense. Each of these areas is further defined below.

One additional area not described in the table was also considered. This is a Computer Center user requirements area where general purpose tools are required to support a wide variety of graphical devices within computing systems in the same organization. In addition to specific CGM extensions, this area requires a variety of "tools." These include:

- graphical exchange format generators;
- graphical format translators;
- graphical format exchange interpreters;
- generic editors;
- application specific editors.

Examples of the types of translators required are:

- CGM to CGM Translators (changing the CGM encoding);
- CGM to Postscript Translators;
- IGES to CGM Translators;

3.1 Business Graphics

This application area includes generation and presentation of materials, reports, and other office documents in written form or as viewgraph transparencies, 35 mm slides, microfiche or other media. It includes production of hardcopy products such as bar charts, pie charts and other types of graphics that are commonly included in business reports and interactive displays and to aid the comprehension of information by human users.

3.2 Office Systems

This area is broader in scope than business graphics and includes the generation, presentation, and transfer of office documents. Such documents today often contain both text and graphical content and in the future may contain other media such as photographic images or sound.

3.3 Publishing

This application area encompasses systems ranging from simple desktop publishing systems consisting of a single computer and a laser printer to graphics arts quality publishing performed using special purpose workstations and photo typesetting equipment. It is the most demanding of the application areas considered in terms of the quality of graphical output needed to meet user requirements and the degree of control over presentation of information that the generator of a document must have.

3.4 CALS

CALS is a major initiative of the US Department of Defense (DoD) which seeks to apply existing and emerging communications and computer systems technologies to the DoD and US industry in general. Its goals are:

- Integrate and improve design, manufacturing and logistics functions thereby bridging existing "islands of automation."
- Actively influence the design process to produce defense systems that are more reliable and easier to support and maintain.
- Shift from the current paper intensive defense system support processes to highly automated mode of operation based on a unified DoD interface with industry for exchange of logistic technical information in digital form.

One of the standards to be utilized by the CALS program is the Computer Graphics Metafile. There are two types of document transfer with special importance to the CALS project. These are engineering drawings and technical manuals. Therefore, when considering user requirements, we subdivided CALS requirements into those two areas.

4 General Requirements

Several other user requirements are of a general nature, affecting most application areas. Principal among these are the need for high quality, public domain fonts, the need for presentation consistency among graphics devices, and the need for general purpose application data exchange mechanisms.

4.1 High Quality Fonts

The most widely used fonts in computer graphics applications today are the Hershey Fonts, developed in the 1960s by Dr. A. V. Hershey for the National Bureau of Standards. These fonts are in the public domain and are available for a nominal fee from the National Technical Information Service in the United States. Although the Hershey Fonts are reasonably high quality stroke-precision fonts (especially considering the era in which they were developed), they are not suitable for many applications. First, they are not typographic quality fonts and do not adhere to the font model and sizing conventions followed by the publishing industry. Second, many modern graphical output devices require raster rather than stroke fonts.

Although a relatively small set of fonts is adequate for all but the most specialized office and publishing applications, it is common practice today for each graphical output device to contain proprietary descriptions of these fonts licensed from firms (such as ITC, Bitstream and Adobe Systems) that specialize in developing high quality fonts. Not only can differences among versions of these fonts cause compatibility problems as images are transferred between different systems, but large amounts of money are expended each year to license proprietary fonts for applications where equivalent public domain font--were they available--would suffice.

Recommendation:

> In large organizations such as the US Government, great cost savings could be realized by paying the cost once to develop a family of fonts adequate for most applications rather than paying a separate license fee for similar fonts embedded in each high quality graphical output device (e.g. laser printer, photo typesetter, bit-mapped display). The availability of low cost, high quality graphics systems would be increased and compatible presentation of graphical and textual information on different graphical devices enhanced if a set of typographic quality fonts were developed by the US Government and placed in the public domain in the same manner the Hershey fonts were developed twenty years ago. These fonts could then be registered as graphical items and be available for use with the CGM and other graphics standards.

4.2 Presentation Consistency

In many application areas--notably engineering documentation and publishing--there are precise and demanding requirements on the presentation of graphical information to a human user. Precisely positioned graphical symbols and text are used to convey domain-specific information to the user and create effects that are artistically pleasing. Thus, the exchange of information is enhanced if the creator of a document can precisely define the manner in which it should be presented to a user.

Obviously, the requirement to precisely define how a document is rendered conflicts with the philosophy of device-independent transfer of graphical information. This desire for device independence across a family of graphic standards (implementable using a wide range of graphical output device technologies) has led to standards that value the distinguishability of various aspects of graphical primitives within a document--using whatever features the device has available to best advantage--and device-dependent "transformation" of graphical primitives--in a manner suited to the device technology--over allowing the creator of a document to specify exactly how it is to be rendered. This is especially evident in the degree of control given a user over the characteristics and placement of text. As a result, the CGM in its present form is ill-suited for the definition and exchange of documents in application areas such as presentation graphics, engineering drawing, and publishing where the creator must be able to control the presentation of a document to communicate effectively.

If computer graphics standards--including the CGM--are to be accepted in such application areas, then suitable extensions must be defined. Further, minimum sets of capabilities for graphical devices must be developed for specific application areas. This might be done through the use of Internationally Standardized Profiles (ISPs) developed by user groups or trade organizations in specific application areas and standardized through the ISO/IEC JTC 1 (formerly 1S0 TC97) registration mechanism for such profiles.

4.3 General Purpose Exchange Mechanisms

In most application areas, documents can be exchanged among systems at several points in the creation process. Exchanges of documents in Processible form transfer application-specific semantic information regarding the structure and meaning of the document's contents, along with the content itself. Examples of such content are the paragraph structure of a text document and the association of a filled rectangle on a bar chart with the textual data representing its meaning. Exchanges of documents in formatted form transfer only enough information to create and present images of a document. The CGM was intended as an exchange mechanism for formatted form graphical pictures.

There are two different approaches to "extending" the CGM for transfer of processible form documents. In the first, the CGM becomes one part of the content of a higher level exchange format which carries additional application specific semantic information. This extension approach was used in ODA/ODIF where the CGM defines Part 8, the Graphics Content Architecture, of ISO 8613. In the second extension approach, the CGM itself is used as the exchange mechanism. The additional semantic information is carried within the CGM by incorporating it in EXTERNAL DATA or APPLICATION DATA CGM elements. Such elements can be used to build a structure relating graphical primitives where necessary. This second extension approach appears to be worth further investigation, especially in the areas of business graphics and "spreadsheet" data transfer.

Testing

1 Introduction

Workshop discussions showed the value of the CGM in a variety of environments. In some application areas it is desirable to restrict the contents of a CGM via application profiles to ensure interworking of systems. In other environments, the CGM is insufficient for all picture storage and transfer requirements and needs to be extended to meet these requirements. Whether a CGM is restricted by an application profile or its contents are unrestricted, there is a need to test for conformance to ensure that systems can exchange metafiles. The discussions described in this section concern requirements for testing and the mechanics of test procedures.

2 Testing and Evaluation

The CGM standard contains only limited conformance requirements. The only requirement is that a specific metafile conform "syntactically" to the standard. This may be either conformance to the functional specification or to both the functional specification and one of the standard encodings. In this way the standard does not define conformance of metafile generators or interpreters. Thus, there is no guarantee that a picture transferred as a CGM will be drawn in the same way on different devices. This requirement is important in some environments as Reed noted in his paper on the use of metafiles at Los Alamos National Laboratory and Carson noted in his paper on CALS metafile requirements.

The importance of applications profiles was discussed at the workshop. The use of restricted CGMs defined via application profiles, such as the MAP/TOP and CALS Profiles, will be an important way of exchanging metafiles in the future. Since development of test software is expensive, such software needs to reflect commercial requirements of industry. There must be a way to test metafiles for conformance to the CGM standard and also for conformance to an application profile which specifies a subset of the CGM. There are requirements in some environments for testing interpreters. This is true for applications in the CALS environment where accurate reproduction of pictures is important.

3 The Test Model

The ideas presented by Carr and Pink at the workshop are a useful model for testing. ODA testing is similar to CGM testing, so any ODA test strategies are directly applicable to CGM testing. ODA includes the concept of application profiles. This might be a useful concept for the CGM.

Automated testing is difficult but necessary if a test service is economic. The test centre must have a reference implementation of the CGM which is capable of producing any legal and illegal metafiles. The reference implementation must be capable of checking that a metafile conforms to the standard or to an application profile.

The CGM is not exceptional amongst graphics standards in requiring some testing by manual picture comparisons. This method is used for GKS testing and has proved successful, although labour intensive. Use of picture-comparison tests is necessary when testing an interpreter during on-site testing. Any use of test pictures and comparison work should be based on the GKS test pictures and accompanying scripts developed for GKS operator testing. Although these form a starting point, additional tests are needed to test the limits of metafile contents.

The test centre should be able to specify any restrictions in an application profile to the reference implementation. The tests should be configured as a result. A database of metafile fragments should be available at the test site for inclusion in test files depending on the profile of the system under test. All metafiles generated by the test centre must be generated in an automatic way and conform to the restrictions of the profile for the system under test. For this method to work, the profile specification must be complete and unambiguous. Descriptive information given by the implementor of the CGM interpreter or generator under test must be automatically interpretable by the test centre in a straightforward way.

Options for specifying test metafiles as described in Pink's paper were considered. Some form of formal specification seems to be needed. A clear text encoding gives a useful, readable representation of a metafile. It could be used to describe to the metafile generator under test the metafiles that it must produce. This concept may need to be extended in some areas, such as inclusion of encoding dependent parameters, but it is a useful starting point. Within ISO/IEC JTC1 SC24 there is consideration of a Fortran language binding for CGI and some support for extending it to the CGM. While there is not full support for this idea philosophically, the practical advantages of having a standard programming interface for test routines are very clear.

Testing of private encodings is not economic. However, any test system should not preclude the addition of a further encoding.

4 Document testing

ODA includes the CGM as its Geometric Content Architecture. Test methodologies for ODA and CGM should be similar where feasible. This would enable testing facilities for both standards to be the same in concept and the same in fact where the two overlap. The use of CGM in documents is an important application.

5 Conformance requirements for Graphics Standards

The concept of application profiles has wide relevance for graphics standards. GKS uses a similar concept via its definition of levels which define conformance requirements. This concept is applicable to any implementation which does not use all the standard but only a subset. Some profiles will be widely used, such as the MAP/TOP and CALS Application Profiles. The way application profiles are defined must be clearly specified. Such specifications have direct relevance to CGI application profiles and to the concept of metafile categories being developed as part of the extended CGM work in SC24.

Errors in the CGM Standard

1 Introduction

This chapter concerns errors in the CGM (ISO and ANSI) text as printed in 1987. The errors presented here have no official status and are simply a list of errors which the editors of this volume believe to exist. It is hoped that the information is useful to implementors wishing to use the standard.

2. Part One - Functional Description

2.1 Clause 4.7.6 Figure 10

The last example in Figure 10 should read:

TEXT ALIGNMENT = (continuous horizontal,top,-2.0,0)

2.2 Clause 5.3.14 Character Set List

In the fifth paragraph from the end of the clause (paragraph beginning 'CHARACTER SETS INTENDED...') the fourth sentence should read:

'The complete code escape..' instead of 'The compete..'.

2.3 Clause 5.7.15 Character Orientation

In the first sentence of the Note add the word 'itself' after the second 'metafile generator'.

2.4 Clause 6: Metafile Defaults

The default for AUXILIARY COLOUR should read:

'if Colour SELECTION MODE is 'indexed', 0; if COLOUR SELECTION MODE is 'direct', device dependent background colour.'

2.5 Annex A: Formal Grammar

A.3.1 Metafile Structure

The grammar for <metafile contents> should read:

```
<metafile contents>        ::=    <extra element> *
                                  <picture>
                                  <extra element> *
```

A.3.2 Metafile Descriptor

The grammar for <characteristics> should read:

```
<characteristics>  ::=   <optional descr element> *
                         <element list>
                         <optional descr element> *
```

Under the production for <element default>, <attribute element> should read <primitive attribute element>.

3. Part Two Character Encoding

3.1 Clause 8.2.6 Index Precision

The last sentence should read:

'parameter would be 10.'

3.2 Clause 8.5.8 Polygon Set

In the description of the point list replace the word 'incremental' by 'displacement'.

3.3 Clause 8.7.2 Domain Ring

Replace 'ring size' by 'radius' as in 6.6.2.

3.4 Clause 9 Defaults

Replace 'ring size' by 'radius' as in 6.6.2.

3.5 Annex A Formal Grammar

The <data record> is written as a string to the metafile as noted in the description in the body of Part 2.

4. Part Three Binary Encoding

Clause 7.7 Table 8

The parameter range symbol ER has not been defined. This should be replaced by:

'0..4'

with an indication of negative values for private use.

5. Part Four Clear Text Encoding

5.1 Clause 6.3 Metafile Descriptor Elements

The production for REAL PRECISION should define MINREAL and MAXREAL to be of type R.

The CHARACTER SET LIST production should read:

```
CHARACTER SET LIST      ::=   CHARSETLIST
                                <SOFTSEP>
                                <CHARSETDESIGNATOR>
                                <<SEP><CHARSETDESIGNATOR>>*
                                <TERM>

CHARSETDESIGNATOR       ::=   <STD94>|
                              STD96|
                              STD94MULTIBYTE|
                              STD96MULTIBYTE|
                              COMPLETECODE>
                              <<OPTSEP>|<HARDSEP>>
                              <S:TAIL>
```

CHARACTER CODING ANNOUNCER should read:

```
CHARACTER CODING ANNOUNCER    ::=   CHARCODING
                                      <SOFTSEP>
                                      <BASIC7BIT|
                                      BASIC8BIT|
                                      EXTD7BIT|
                                      EXTD8BIT>
                                    <TERM>
```

5.2 Clause 6.4 Picture Descriptor Specification Modes

The LINE WIDTH, MARKER SIZE and EDGE WIDTH SPECIFICATION MODEs include the following in the production:

```
<ABSTRACT|SCALED>
```

this should read:

<ABSOLUTE|SCALED>

5.3 Clause 6.5 Control Elements

The production for VDC REAL PRECISION should define MINREAL and MAXREAL to be of type R.

5.4 Clause 6.7 Attribute Elements

Replace 'CHAREXP' by 'CHAREXPAN' in ASFNAME and ALLTEXT.

5.5 Annex B Example

BEGDEFAULTS and ENDDEFAULTS should read BEGMFDEFAULTS and ENDMFDEFAULTS.

In line 4 of the example drawingplus should be surrounded in quotation marks because the argument of mfelemlist is a string.

Acknowledgment

We would like to thank Neil Bowers, Ken Brodlie, Richard Horton, Alasdair Liddell and Eckhard Moeller for assistance in compiling this part.

Contact Addresses

Peter Bono	Peter R. Bono Associates Inc, PO Box 648, Gales Ferry, CT 06335, USA
Richard Carr	National Computing Centre Ltd, Oxford Road, Manchester, M1 7ED, UK
Steve Carson	GSC Associates, 13663 Prairie Avenue, Suite B, PO Box 2286, Hawthorne, CA 90251, USA
Glenn Davison	Digital Equipment Corporation, 110 Spit Brook Road, ZK02-3/R56, Nashua, NH 03062, USA
Kern Hardman	Boeing Computer Services, PO Box 24346, MS 7R-50, Seattle, WA 98124-0346, USA
Lofton Henderson	Henderson Software, PO Box 4036, Boulder, CO 80306, USA
Sharon Kemmerer	National Bureau of Standards, Room A266, Technology Building, Gaithersburg, MD 20899, USA
Steven Jepsen	Boeing Computer Service, Engineering Tech. Applications Div., PO Box 24346, Mailstop 7L-22, Seattle, WA 98124-0346, USA
Anne Mumford	Computer Centre, University of Technology, Loughborough, LE11 3TU, UK
Chris Osland	Rutherford Appleton Laboratory, Computing Division, Chilton, Didcot, Oxon OX11 0QX, UK
Jane Pink	National Computing Centre Ltd, Oxford Road, Manchester, M1 7ED, UK
Ted Reed	Los Alamos National Laboratory, C6, MS B272, Los Alamos, NM 87545, USA

Brian Rossin	Wang Labs, One Industrial Avenue, Lowell, MA 01851, USA
Gary Silverman	MAGICorp, 50 Executive Blvd., Elmsford, NY 10523
Mark Skall	National Bureau of Standards, Room A266, Technology Building, Gaithersburg, MD 20899, USA
John Stoll	McDonnell Douglas Corporation, W315/101/C5/198, PO Box 516, St. Louis, MO 63166
Charles Tucker	Nova Graphics International, 1515 Capital of Texas Hwy, Austin, TX 78746, USA

MIX
Papier aus verantwortungsvollen Quellen
Paper from responsible sources
FSC® C105338

If you have any concerns about our products,
you can contact us on
ProductSafety@springernature.com

In case Publisher is established outside the EU,
the EU authorized representative is:
Springer Nature Customer Service Center GmbH
Europaplatz 3, 69115 Heidelberg, Germany

Printed by Libri Plureos GmbH
in Hamburg, Germany